A SURREAL LIFE:

EDWARD JAMES

1907–1984

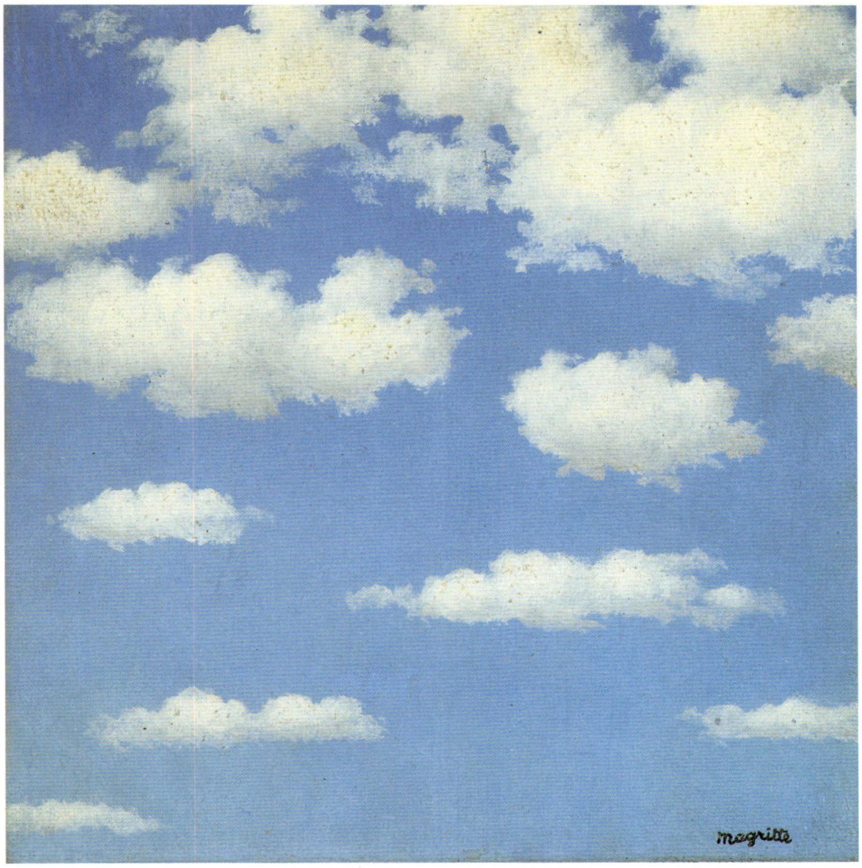

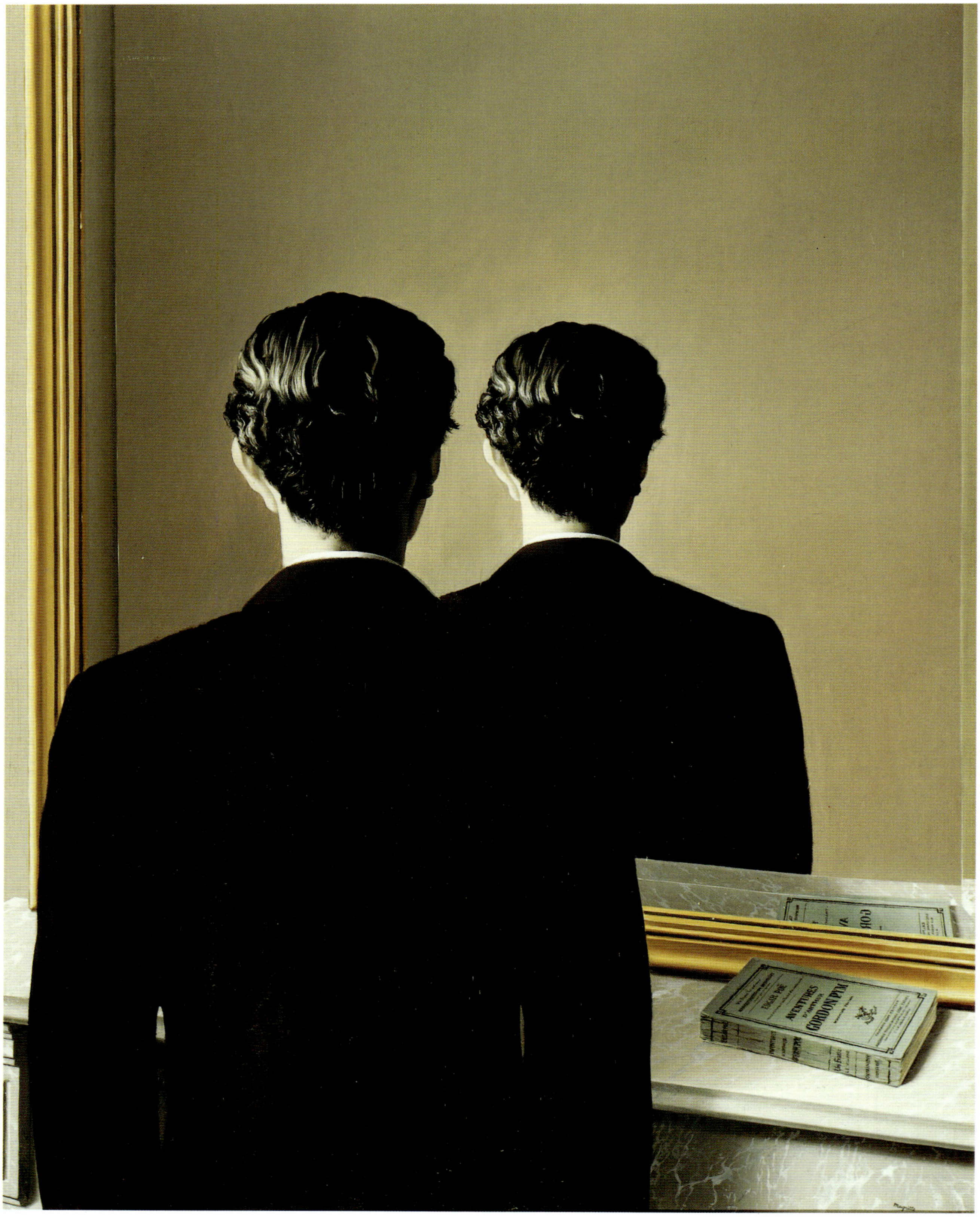
AVENTURES
GORDON PYM

A SURREAL LIFE:
EDWARD JAMES
1907–1984

EDITED BY NICOLA COLEBY

PUBLISHED BY THE ROYAL PAVILION,
LIBRARIES & MUSEUMS, BRIGHTON & HOVE
IN ASSOCIATION WITH
PHILIP WILSON PUBLISHERS

SUPPORTED BY THE FRIENDS OF THE
ROYAL PAVILION, ART GALLERY & MUSEUMS,
BRIGHTON AND THE TRUSTEES OF
THE EDWARD JAMES FOUNDATION

ALL THE WORKS ILLUSTRATED IN THIS BOOK, UNLESS OTHERWISE INDICATED, FORMERLY BELONGED TO EDWARD JAMES.

First published in 1998 by the Royal Pavilion,
Libraries & Museums, Brighton & Hove
in association with
Philip Wilson Publishers,
143–149 Great Portland Street
London W1N 5FB

on the occasion of the exhibition
A Surreal Life: Edward James 1907–1984
held at Brighton Museum & Art Gallery, 25 April–26 July 1998

Supported by The Friends of the Royal Pavilion, Art Gallery & Museums, Brighton, The Trustees of The Edward James Foundation, Foundation for Sport & the Arts and the Esmée Fairbairn Charitable Trust

Exhibition curated by Sharon-Michi Kusunoki
Exhibition organised by Nicola Coleby, Senior Exhibitions Officer and Helen Grundy, Exhibitions Officer, Royal Pavilion, Libraries & Museums, Brighton & Hove

The publication of this catalogue is supported by The Friends of the Royal Pavilion, Art Gallery & Museums, Brighton and The Trustees of The Edward James Foundation

Editor, Royal Pavilion, Libraries & Museums: Nicola Coleby
Editor, Philip Wilson Publishing: Melissa Larner
Designed by Peter Ling/Sara Robin
Catalogue picture research by Helen Grundy

ISBN 0-85667-493-1 (hardback edition)
ISBN 0948723 38 6 (paperback edition)

Distributed in the USA and Canada by
Antique Collectors' Club Limited
Market Street Industrial Park
Wappingers' Falls
NY 12590
USA

Colour origination by Saxon Photolitho, Norwich, UK
Printed and bound by Snoeck, Ducaju & Zoon, NV, Ghent, Belgium

Front cover photograph: *Lobster Telephone* designed by Salvador Dalí for Edward James, shown on the edge of *Mae West Lips Sofa*.
Back cover photograph: René Magritte: Letter to Edward James with sketch for *Le printemps éternel* (18 May, 1937). Museum Boijmans Van Beuningen, Rotterdam.
Half-title page photograph: René Magritte: *Le malédiction*. Edward James Foundation.
Title page photograph: René Magritte: *La reproduction interdite*, 1937.

Brighton & Hove

Foundation for sport and the arts

THE EDWARD JAMES FOUNDATION

CONTENTS

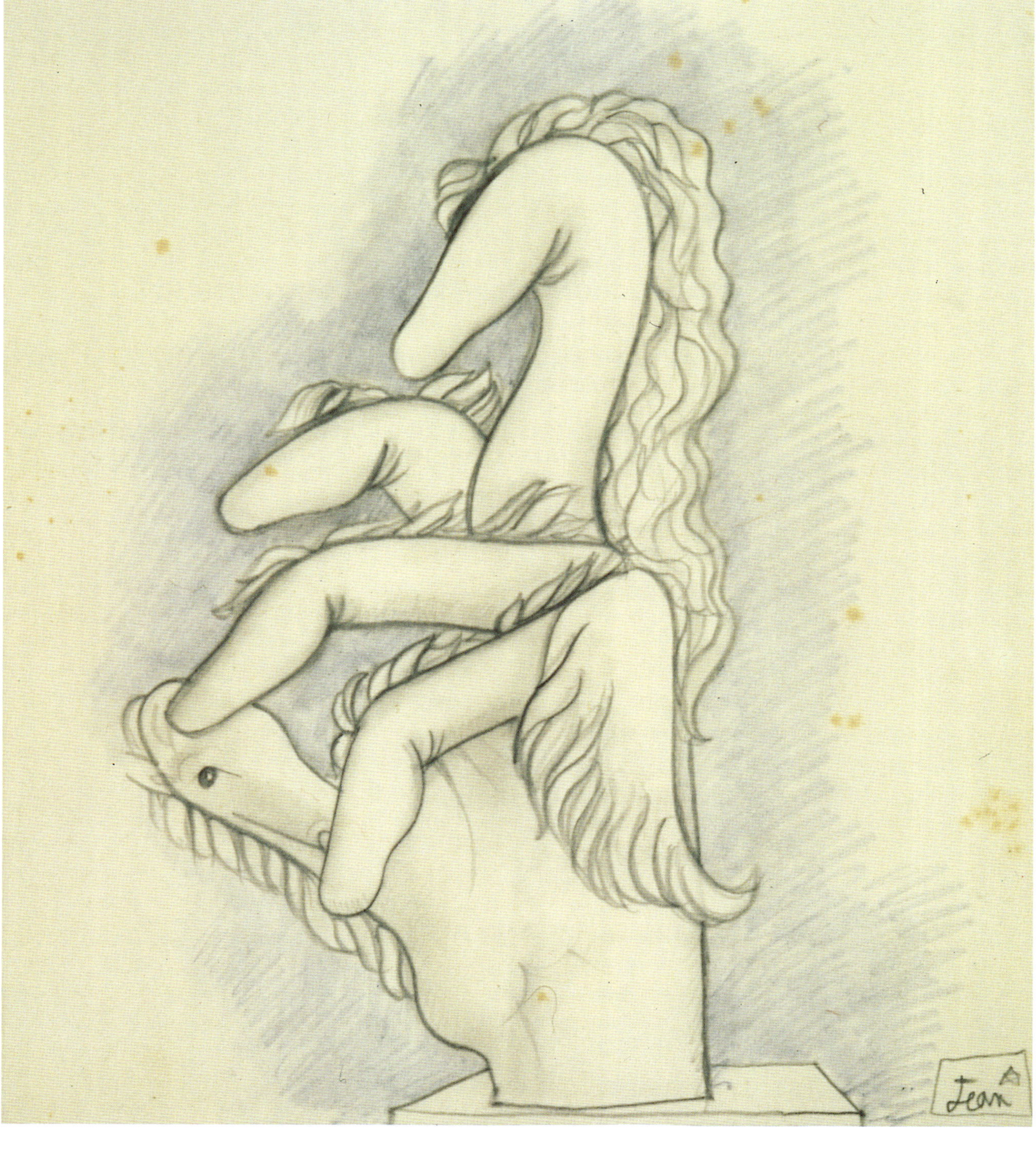

JEAN COCTEAU
Horse Hand
1936 (one drawing from a series of eight).
EJF. Catalogue no. 172.

LENDERS

Museum Boijmans Van Beuningen, Rotterdam

The Trustees of the Edward James Foundation

Freud Museum, London

Christopher Gibbs

The Mercury Gallery

National Portrait Gallery, London

The Tate Gallery, London

Mr Hugo Vickers

The Board of Trustees of The Victoria & Albert Museum

Private Collection

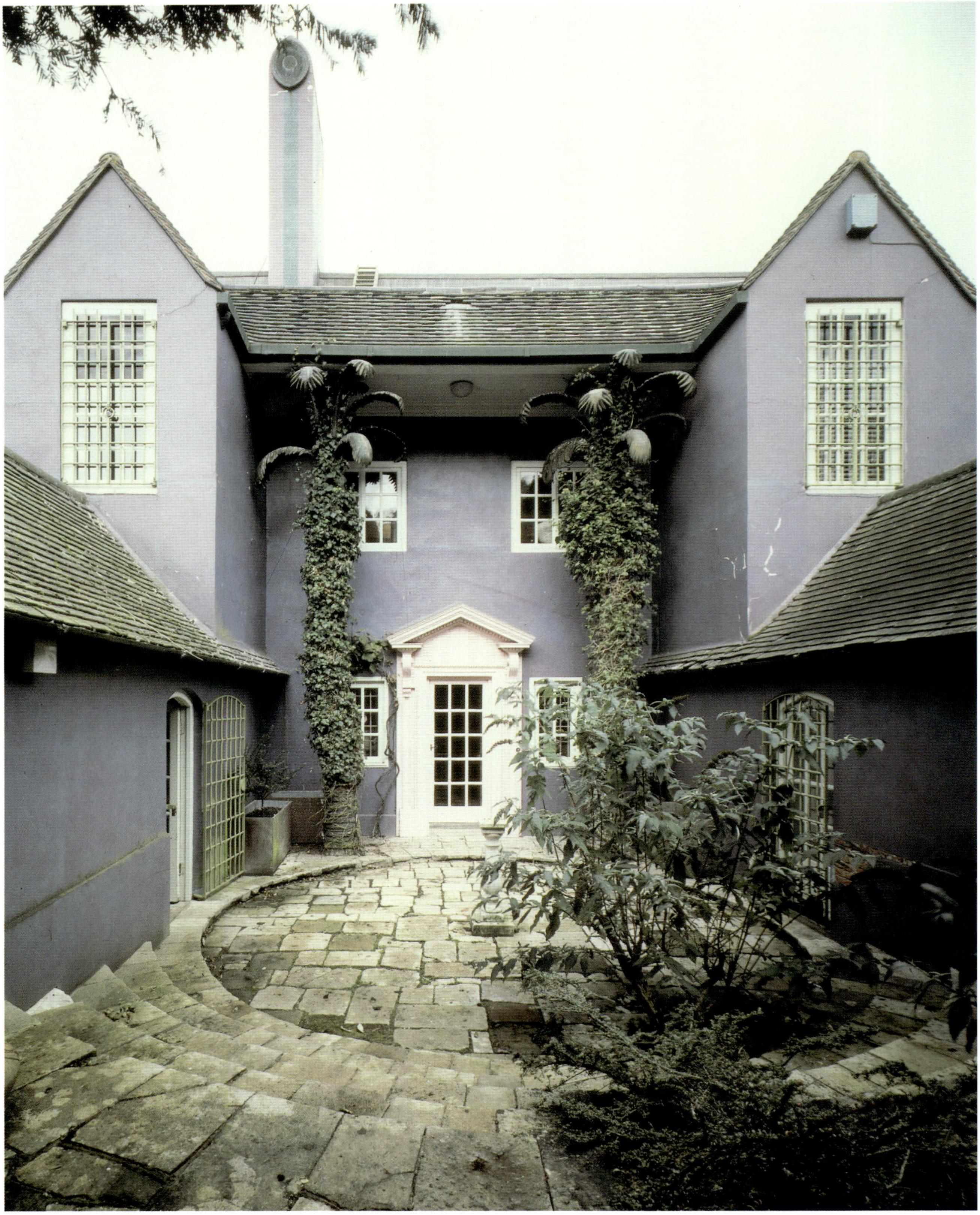

FOREWORD

JESSICA RUTHERFORD
Head of Libraries and Museums, Director of the Royal Pavilion

EDWARD JAMES'S association with Brighton began nearly 35 years ago when he first met Clifford Musgrave (then Director of the Museum and Art Gallery), whom James subsequently described as 'a kindred spirit'. From 1964 onwards, consignments of James's collections poured into the Museum: French and English furniture of the 18th Century, Aubusson carpets, Chelsea, Bow and Derby 18th-Century porcelain, Surrealist and neo-romantic paintings, furniture and artefacts.

Most significant was a selection of some 70 works by de Chirico, Dalí, Bérard, Ernst, Magritte, Picasso, Carrington, Spencer and Tchelitchew, lent in 1966 and at the time valued at a mere £45,000. By the end of the decade these works, combined with loans from the artist, collector and author Martin Battersby and the Museum's own emerging 20th-Century collection, had transformed the impressive central gallery in the Museum. This new direction, enthusiastically driven by Musgrave's successor, John Morley, marked the most radical change to the Museum's image since its creation in 1873. It was not, however, received with universal approval: in 1971 a leading Councillor demanded that the Director be called to account for these appalling and unauthorised changes, complaining that the main central gallery had become like 'a modern cinema foyer' and lamenting the loss of its old 'charm and dignity'.

The following year I made my first visit to the Museum and Art Gallery as part of a course I was teaching on Art Nouveau and Art Deco. I remember peering closely at Magritte's *Boot Feet on the Beach* (as it was then called; now it is known as *Le modèle rouge*), wondering if this picture (as well as the paintings by Dalí, Tchelitchew, de Chirico, Spencer etc.) was real or a reproduction, so staggering was the assemblage of Surrealist paintings. In the subsequent years I met James only a couple of times but was electrified by his stream of anecdotes ranging from Coco Chanel's activities as a collaborator in the war to James's desire to design a trapezium-shaped car park at West Dean to defeat the tidy-minded owners of motorised vehicles. In the mid-1970s, further 20th-Century objects by Giacometti and Dalí from both The Edward James Foundation and James's personal collection came to the Museum, as well as the gift of the

An exterior view of Monkton House.

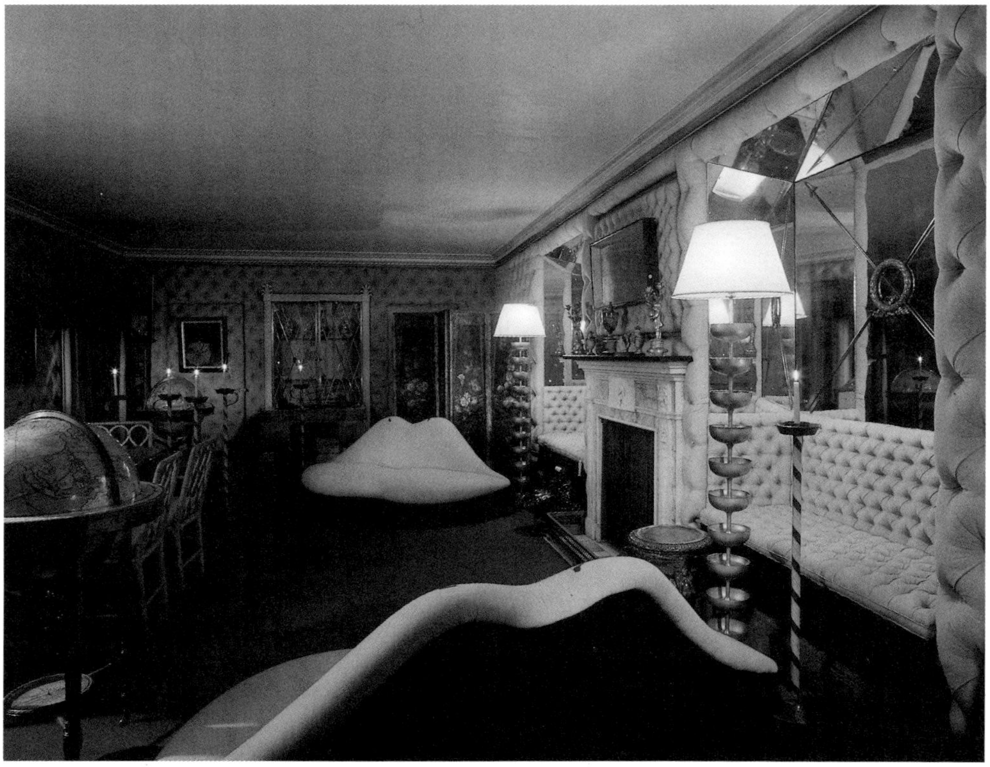

Dining Room, Monkton House, 1986.

surviving sets, costumes and backdrops from Les Ballets 1933, retrieved from garages at West Dean.

The 1930s, the era of Surrealism, Art Deco, Modernism, Vogue Regency and Victorian revivalism, marked the Royal Pavilion's emergence from over a century of denigration and ridicule, finally appreciated for its romance and exuberance by such literary figures as the Sitwells. In James's Monkton House, on the estate of West Dean, all these styles combined to reflect the unique and extraordinary vision of its owner, made concrete by his designer Norris Wakefield working in a manner not dissimilar to the Prince Regent and his architects and designers. It might be fanciful to draw parallels between James and the Prince Regent but both men, separated by a century and by the sober reign of Queen Victoria, were driven by a consuming passion for the arts and a determination to achieve the realisation of their dreams regardless of social convention, accepted taste and financial constraints. Both were patrons and collectors of international significance and fortunately for successive generations, examples of their patronage have survived in the form of the Royal Pavilion and Monkton. I suspect the architectural establishment in the 1930s would have regarded Monkton with the same disdain it applied to the Royal Pavilion: 'a curiosity which arouses only a vague, transient wonder in the visitor ... simply a minor historical monument' to quote Sir John Summerson writing in 1935.

During the 1970s a few small exhibitions held in Sussex and Edinburgh drew on aspects of James's collection. None did justice to his artistic vision or to the richness of his patronage of all aspects of the visual, literary and performing arts. For many years I have wanted to hold an exhibition on Edward James, and Brighton seemed the most appropriate location. Such a task is perhaps almost impossible to realise, but hopefully the exhibition and accompanying publication will provide further insight into the life of this extraordinary man and will finally establish him as one of the great patrons of this Century, a figure of truly international importance.

The exhibition and accompanying publication would not have been possible without the generosity and support of The Edward James Foundation at West Dean. We would particularly like to thank Sharon-Michi Kusunoki, Curator of the Exhibition, Archivist and Special Administrator to The Trustees of The Edward James Foundation; David Leigh, Principal of West Dean College; The Trustees of The Edward James Foundation, in particular Robert L. Farmer, Chairman, and Christopher Gibbs.

Generous support and funding for the exhibition and this publication has been received from The Friends of the Royal Pavilion, Art Gallery & Museums; The Trustees of The Edward James Foundation; the Esmée Fairbairn Charitable Trust; and the Foundation for Sport and the Arts.

The help and advice of a large number of individuals has been invaluable throughout the project. Louise Tythacott, Curator of Ethnology at Liverpool Museum, enthusiastically carried out much of the initial planning for the exhibition in her former position at Brighton Museum & Art Gallery. Professor Dawn Ades and Professor Christopher Green deserve particular thanks for their advice throughout the development of the project. Chris Dercon, Director of the Museum Boijmans Van Beuningen, Rotterdam and Piet de Jonge, Senior Curator, Modern Art, Museum Boijmans Van Beuningen, Rotterdam have generously supported the exhibition.

Generous help in a wide variety of areas has been forthcoming from the following individuals: I. M. Bickerton, Chris Barron, Sally Brown, Christopher Clarkson, David Dorning, Simon Draper, Emilie d'Estresse de Lanzac, David Gill, Dr Didier Girard, Professor Bram Hammacher and Mrs Renilde Hammacher, Amy de la Haye, Jackie Herrington, John Trevor Howick, Anne Jackson, Kate Garmeson and Anna Swinbourne in the Impressionist and Modern Art Department, Sotheby's, London, Emma Kennedy, Juno Leigh, Rosemary Marley, Valerie Mendes, Laurence Mynott, Ian Jean Odin, Terence Pepper, Terry Pickering, Philip Purser, Peter Sarginson, Dennis Sharp, Pat Taylor, John Warren, Jill Wilkinson, Gareth Williams, and staff of The Edward James Foundation.

We are extremely grateful for the generosity of all the lenders to the exhibition, who are listed separately, and to all the authors who have written for this publication.

The dedication of a large number of staff and helpers at Brighton Museum and Art Gallery and the Royal Pavilion has enabled this exhibition to come to fruition. The exhibition has been organised by Nicola Coleby with the assistance of Helen Grundy. We would like to thank in particular Stella Beddoe, who researched and curated the Les Ballets 33 section, Mike Jones, who has been responsible for creating the design of the exhibition and David Beevers, who helped research the content of the exhibition. Much credit is also due to the following: Robin Abbott, Sharon Bacon, Janita Bagshawe, Pam Barber, Christine Barlow, Cara Bowen, Janet Brough, Louise Brown, Anne Burrill, Camay Chapman-Cameron, Birthe Christensen, Nigel Cunningham, Charlotte Drew, Jonathon Fell, Roy Flint, Alex Hawkey, Gerry Hawkey, John Powell, Maureen Simmonds, Felicity Tanous, Heather Wood and Linda Wood.

Finally, I would like to thank all those individuals who have expressed enthusiasm for the project and helped in numerous ways throughout its development.

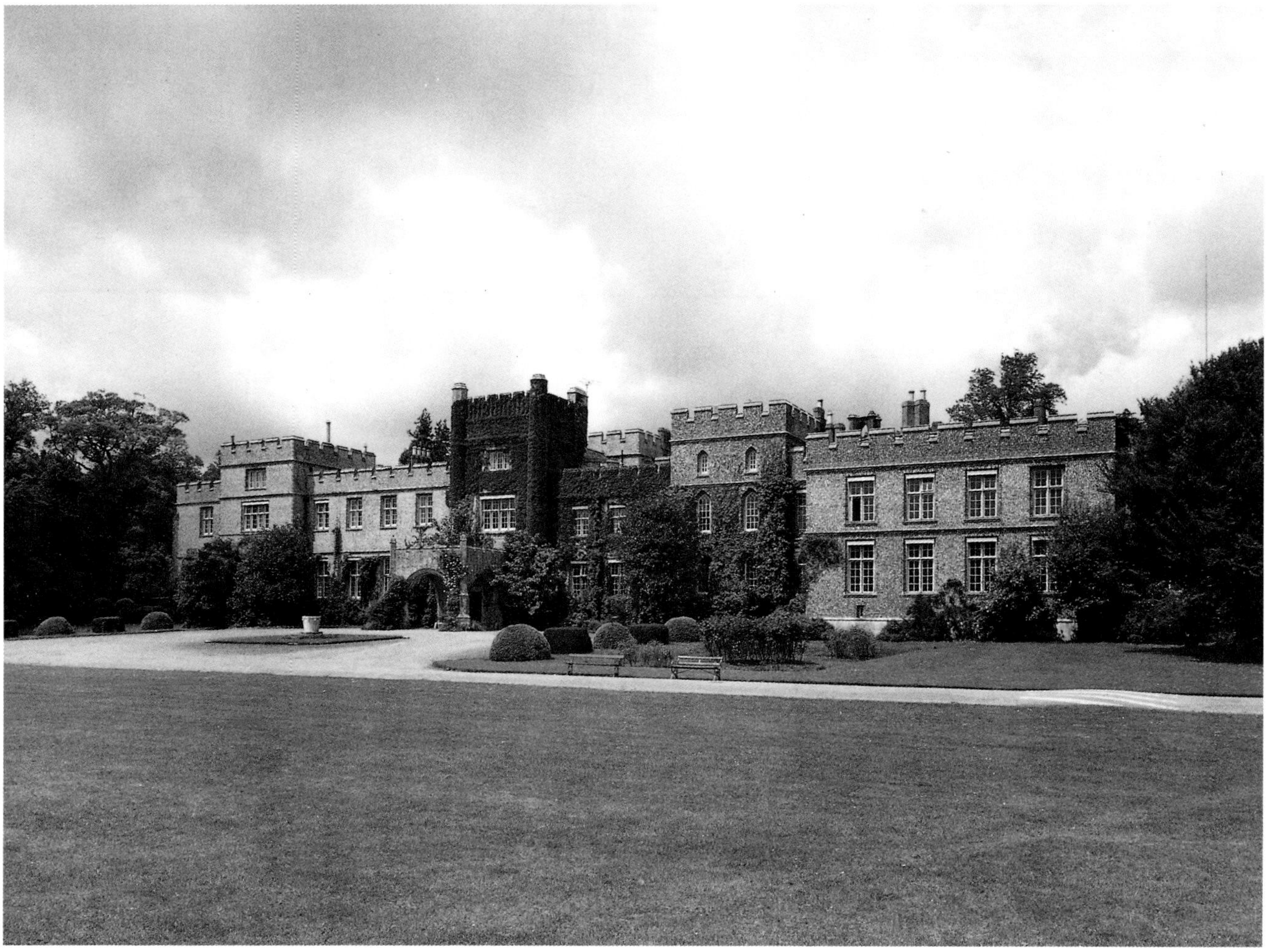

West Dean House, 1980s.

PREFACE
West Dean Today

DR DAVID LEIGH
Principal, West Dean College

EDWARD JAMES's constant desire throughout his life was to keep his father's West Dean Estate intact. He tried donating it at various times to the Boy Scouts, the Vedanta Movement, even to a Chinese university, but no one was interested in what they considered to be a white elephant: a large estate without any monetary endowment. Then in the 1950s Edward James met a young Californian tax lawyer by the name of Robert Farmer who devised a vehicle for achieving what he desired: a charitable educational trust.

The main educational purpose of The Edward James Foundation, eventually established in 1964, is served by West Dean College, which occupies a large, flint-faced mansion designed by James Wyatt in the early 19th Century, set in extensive grounds near the southern extremity of the 6,000-acre West Dean Estate. The Foundation is formally guided in its endeavours by its Trust Instrument, and informally by glimpses of the founder's mind in a letter he wrote to Aldous Huxley in 1939 inspired by the latter's *Ends and Means*:

> *... agricultural life is not dead in England yet and industrial techniques are not lost: but at the end of a very destructive war some of them may be. What is more likely is that certain arts will be completely lost, and artists will need protection. I feel that the West Dean community should therefore concentrate, to begin with, on helping young artists and young craftsmen; and in teaching others to be craftsmen.*
>
> *... The community could also be a refuge for composers as well as for painters and writers; and one might have a branch for musical students, and the community could have its own orchestra.*

In 1964 James made over the house, its contents and the Estate to his new Foundation but it is not clear whether his vision of over two decades earlier had consciously survived. Robert Farmer recalls that the overriding motive was the retention of the Estate as a whole, in perpetuity, for general educational purposes. The Foundation was not established as a fixed community of artists or musicians, and it was built on no particular philosophical base. Yet, whether consciously or perhaps by surreal influence, significant parts of the vision did materialise, notably an organisation in which arts and crafts could be nurtured and preserved in the privileged, secluded milieu of West Dean House and its grounds.

The College itself eventually emerged in 1971, under the leadership of Major-General Cyril Lloyd, formerly Director General of the City & Guilds of London. James was present intermittently throughout its formative years when he was not in America or Mexico or elsewhere; by then a tax exile, he could never stay for more than three months at a time. The way in which the College developed owed most to the commitment of the Trustees, chaired since James's death by Robert Farmer, and to the direction given by successive Principals, especially Peter Sarginson, incumbent from 1978 to 1995. Over sometimes turbulent and sometimes lean years – for there was at first little cash other than income from the Estate – they took the germ of the idea and created an organisation that respects the vision for preserving crafts and for housing art and music, using the building as an inspiration for students.

More than a quarter of a century later, Edward James's College still influences and transforms lives, subtly contributing to national and international culture and its preservation. About 50 people a year – mainly young – spend from one to three years learning to make early stringed musical instruments, or to conserve and restore artefacts: ceramics, clocks, furniture, fine metalwork and books and manuscripts. They also learn to weave tapestry, in association with the commercial West Dean Tapestry Studio, which has created some of the most important tapestries of this century, including works by Henry Moore and John Piper.

Full- and part-time tutors, all of them craftspeople or conservators in their own right, run these courses to the highest standard in studios and workshops that have been converted from former out-buildings of the main house. Most of the students live on site; they relax in the former Steward's Room and attend lectures in the old house, sometimes in its Edwardian furnished state rooms. Their library is the old smoking and billiards room where James's father once entertained Edward VII – a family friend and James's godfather.

The other main strand of studies at West Dean consists of the Short Courses. About 400 such courses run each year, lasting from one weekend to ten days. Around 190 external tutors offer as many topics, and teach in newly converted, well-equipped studios. Purpose-designed facilities include a silversmithing workshop, a potters' studio, and a blacksmithing forge. All manner of practical arts and crafts are taught and there are also music classes and lecture courses on varied subjects such as opera and art history.

James's love of gardens influenced the development of the West Dean grounds. In 1991 the Trustees established a fresh approach, focusing on the restoration of the Victorian and Edwardian walled kitchen gardens, complete with 13 original glass houses. In 1996 a new Visitor Centre was created, designed in association with the Prince of Wales Institute of Architecture. Thousands of visitors each year and the College's pro-

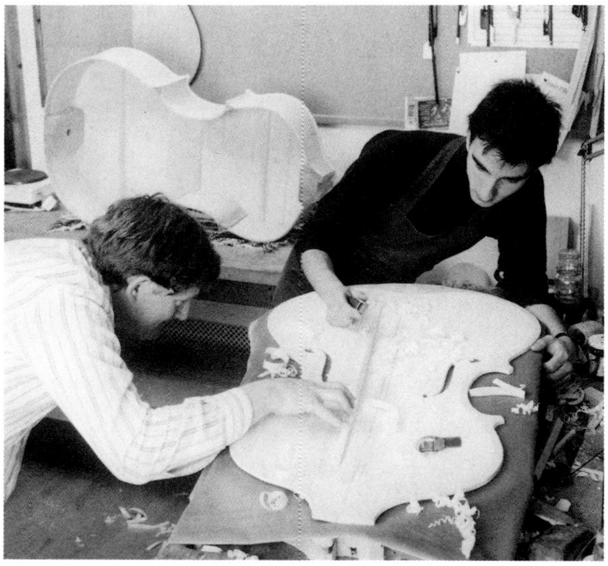

Students on the Apprenticeship Scheme in the Making of Early Stringed Musical Instruments, West Dean College.

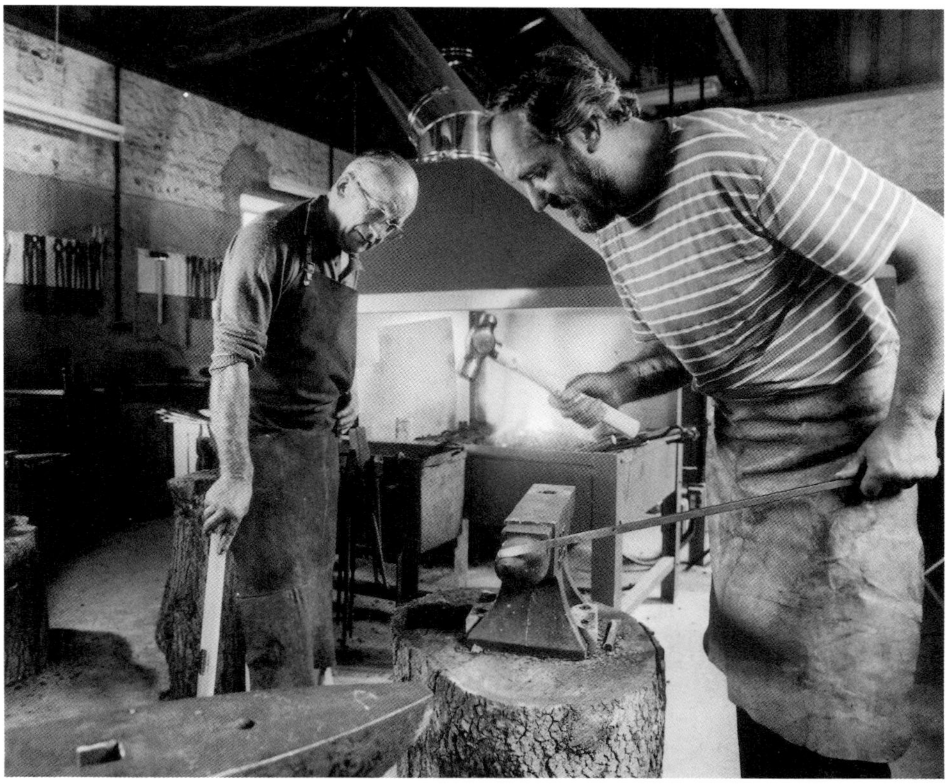

Short Course Students in the blacksmithing workshop, West Dean College.

gramme of short courses in gardening ensure that the educational purpose of the gardens is fulfilled.

The musical strand of James's life is reflected not only in the various short courses in music and performance but by masterclasses and summer schools in early and 20th-Century music for flute, classical guitar and string quartet. The House is also a centre for debate and for education beyond formal programmes, functioning as a training or meeting venue for other like-minded organisations: conservation bodies, heritage or training organisations, antiquarian and arts groups.

The Edward James Foundation rigorously pursues its primary formal educational purpose, and in support of this, retains the Estate intact. Perhaps it is too fanciful to suggest that the College continues to be driven by Edward James from his grave in the arboretum, for the growth and success of the college owes most to those staff and trustees who laboured and continue to labour with insight, drive and inspiration. Yet there is no doubting the sense of James's creative, imaginative and rebellious spirit, made palpable in his influence, handed down to new generations through his archive, which continues to reveal his thoughts and to fuel our imagination. There can be little better explanation for what makes West Dean a unique phenomenon.

It is hoped that this exhibition will foster a wider appreciation of James's life and works, and a greater understanding of the important part he played in the cultural life of the earlier part of this Century, as well as extending awareness of his Foundation and of the work of the College. It is certain that no more appropriate curator could be found for this exhibition than Sharon-Michi Kusunoki who has dedicated many years to setting in order and making sense of the amazing inheritance of letters and other documents that bear evidence to James's extraordinary surreal life.

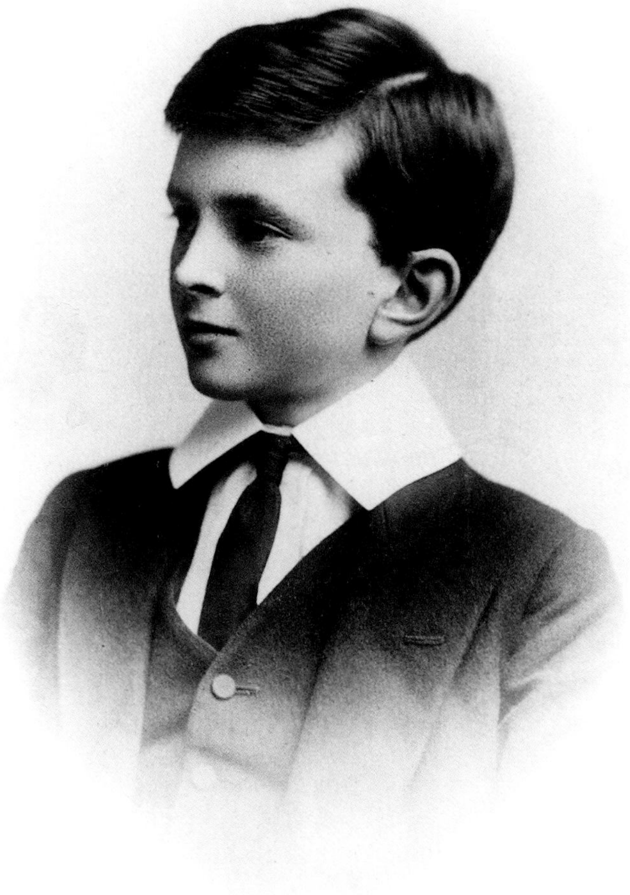

Edward James at Eton, c.1920.
EJF. Catalogue no. 13.

INTRODUCTION
Edward James: An insight

CHRISTOPHER GIBBS
Trustee of the Edward James Foundation

I FIRST heard of Edward James when I was a boy at Eton. I had a friend, worldly, glamorous and louche, and his Godfather and cousin, Edward, sent him from Mexico a bolt of vicuna to make the smartest suit I had ever seen. Clothes to me were battered tweeds handed down from brothers, and this seemed the acme of chic – exotic, delicious and decadent. Ten years later I made friends with Edward's handsome nephew Angus, learned a lot more of the legend, met his sister, Audrey. Later still, mysterious Monkton became the focus of fascination and on a memorable afternoon in the company of two Rolling Stones, and two lamented friends, Robert Fraser and Michael Cooper, I drove there from West Wittering, past the violet- and yellow-striped tree guards and the Dawyck beeches, only to be repelled at the last fence by Edward's redoubtable housekeepers, Arthur and Joyce Sawyer. Eventually I met Edward at a party given for him by Norman Rosenthal, about to embark on a stint as his secretary. We jabbered about mazes and labyrinths, exchanged rainbow letters, books and photographs, and were quickly friends. Later still, thanks to Desmond and Penny Guinness, in whose Irish castle the bearded wanderer was stopping, he asked me to be a Trustee of his Foundation.

My first meeting took place in a newly built Dublin hotel. The Trustees had pressing business to sort out but Edward had other things on his mind – in particular the question of where in due course he might (or might not) be buried. There were options: as near as possible to Keats in the shade of the pyramid of Cestius in the Protestant cemetery in Rome, or beneath the Norwegian hut in the heart of the arboretum at West Dean, but the real issue was much more complicated and might involve international agreements, diplomatic intervention and certainly much useful work for clever lawyers. Deyrolle, the long established Parisian stuffer and pickler of Natural History specimens (installed in the ravishing Louis XV palace of the financier Samuel Bernard in the rue du Bac) was now working in Lucite. They would freeze Edward's naked body in their plastic aspic and we could arrange to have it taken to Mexico and suspended on chains in one of the waterfalls at Las Posas, his jungle kingdom ... Edward's incantatory vein was hard to stem. The meeting went on till night fell.

The American Jameses had scaled the social heights swiftly and surely. The transition from plush Merseyside suburbia to West Dean must have been hastened by the dashing James's brothers' Harrovian

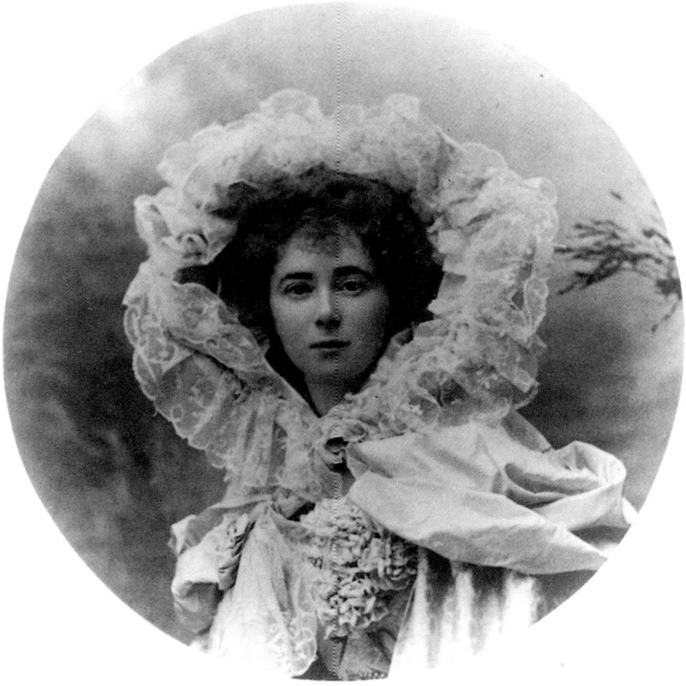

Portrait of Evelyn James, late 1800s.
EJF. Catalogue no. 20.

There was much of the child in Edward all of his life, a charming, brilliant, rich, spoilt, chaotic, mercurial child, imaginative, manipulative, inventive, repetitive, a thoroughly exhausting child, continually testing the tolerance of companions, picked as playmates for a mix of penury, looks and capacity for caprice. Whilst venerating the memory of his father and his works at West Dean, he deplored his lovely but conventional and rather silly mother, and early rejected her stifling view of the public life she thought he ought to aspire to.

But the full-throttle West Dean backdrop with King Edward and the huge parties for shooting and Goodwood died with Willie James in 1912. Edward was four and his minority began with the house let and Evie soon married to her lover Dosie Brinton. The war came and it was time for Eton, a school where gifts and skills can be nurtured or at worst outed. He read volu-

friendships, and Willie James's marriage to the beautiful Evie Forbes propelled them to the very pinnacle of society – the slightly raffish entourage of the Prince of Wales. Edward's grandmother, Lady Forbes of Newe (to rhyme with 'miaou', as Edward used to say) was one of the famously lovely daughters of Sir Thomas Moncrieff, along with Lady Dudley and the Duchess of Atholl. Good, hard-earned American money and Scottish lineage and beauty allied, bred four little girls and finally and most preciously Edward, who arrived by torchlight, cheered by linen-smocked tenantry, to a West Dean luxuriously rebuilt and furnished as a setting for a sparkling new dynasty.

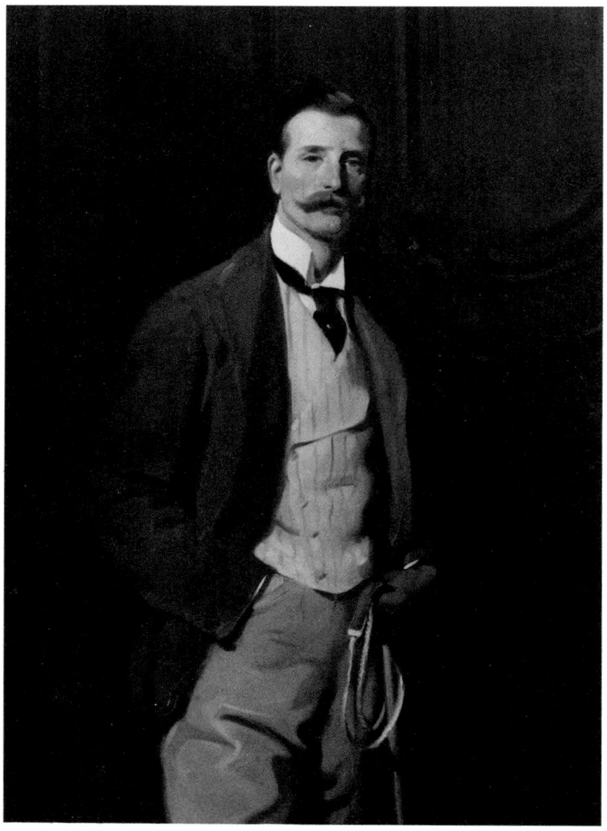

Portrait of William James,
print after portrait by
R. Brough, 1905.
EJF. Catalogue no. 4.

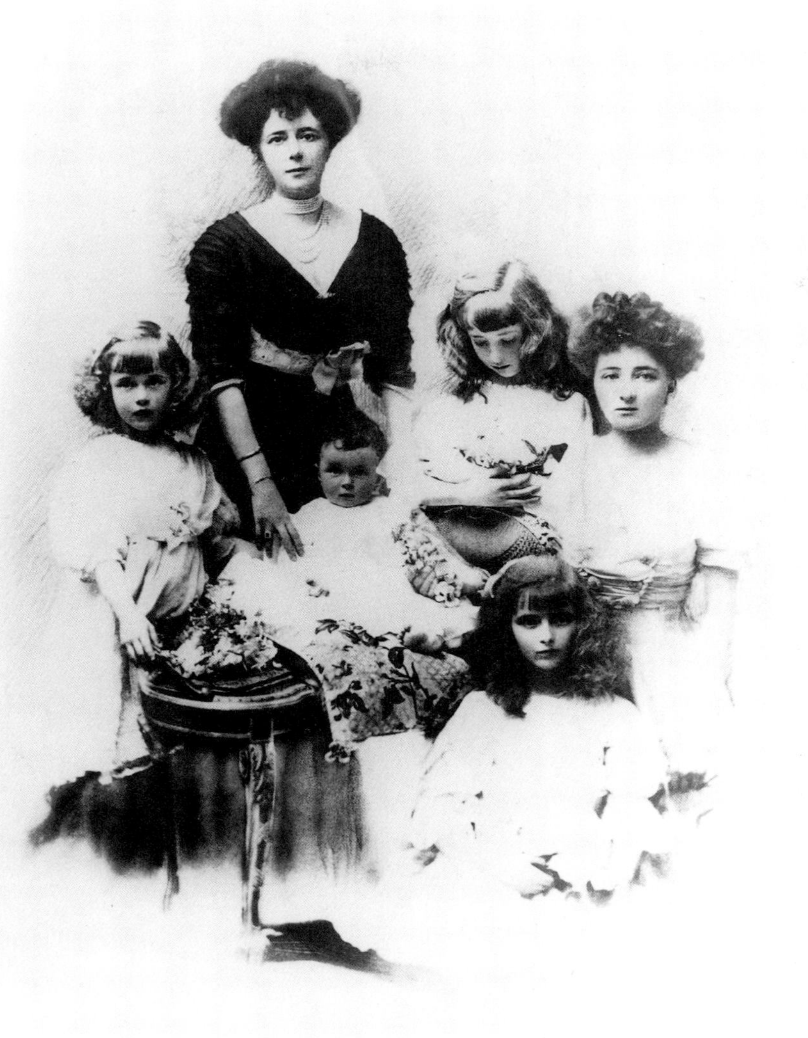

Evelyn James with Edward, Millicent, Xandra, Audrey and Silvia, c.1908. EJF. Catalogue no. 6.

minously, wrote poetry, learned to draw and paint, forged friendships with the bloods as well as with the aesthetes. His mother was horrified. The arts were not in her catalogue of the manly virtues.

When Roger Fry gave Edward the Drawing Prize at Eton, his bent towards the creative life was confirmed. To discover what manner of an artist he was to become took longer, perhaps a lifetime. He put what money came to him to work swiftly. At Oxford he cultivated an image of defiant aestheticism, which was tolerated, because he was rich, rumoured to be the son (or grandson) of King Edward (a rumour that he did little to refute), good looking, in his neat little way, sophisticated and witty. Surrealism, that licence to derangement in art, was about to get him off the hook, to release the troubled, sexually confused, poor-little-rich-boy to the freedom of an artist's life.

His inheritance allowed the pursuit of artists and their patronage. Perceptive and probing, with a nose for what was more interesting than fashion decreed, in music, in literature, in painting and dance, he could decorate his always temporary perches lavishly and arrestingly. The fashionable world knew him and his antics were influential. His disastrous and doomed

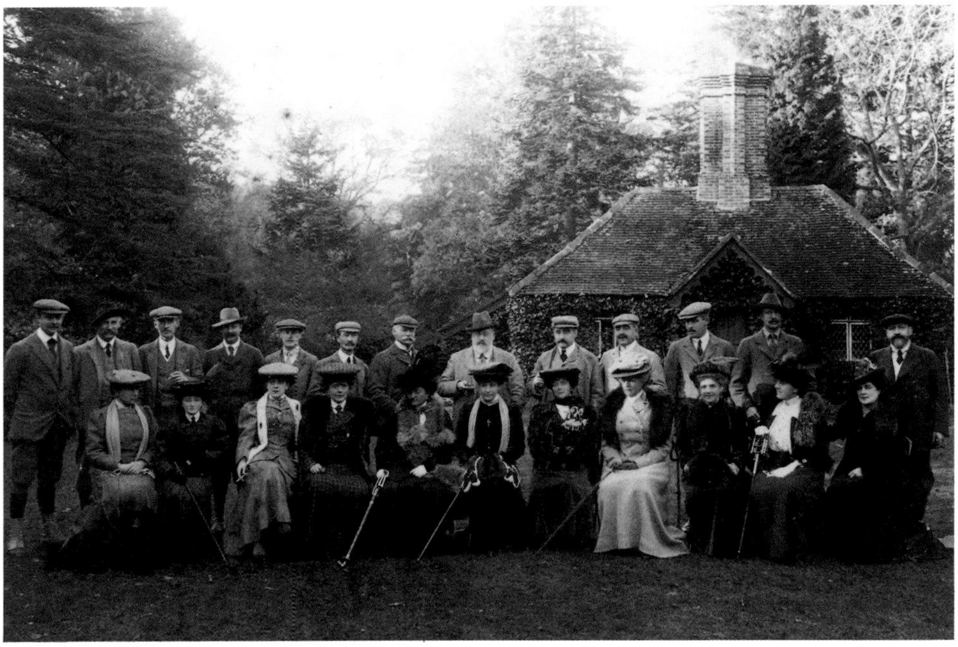

Shooting Party at West Dean, 19–24 November, 1906. First row: 7th from left, Evelyn James; 2nd from right, Alice Keppel. Second row: 6th from left, William James; 8th from left, Edward VII.
EJF. Catalogue no. 38.

marriage to Tilly Losch and the divorce that followed plunged him into the world of artists and thrust him from England to explore a wider, freer, more exciting theatre.

He was first of all an artist. He painted. He wrote poetry all his life. And published some of it in elegantly produced editions. He was an incorrigible, dazzling, sometimes bemusing raconteur, and created at Xilitla in Mexico, on his estate of Las Posas, a truly extraordinary, beautiful and surprising garden, now, as he knew it would be, being reclaimed by the throttling jungle. There, perhaps, he tasted love and happiness. He nurtured the talents of fellow artists, continually throwing out lifelines of patronage to a huge circle. Finally, by creating, with the guidance of his lawyer Bob Farmer, The Edward James Foundation, he preserved the Estate of West Dean, a noble act of filial piety which renewed and expanded its function as fountain of patronage and creativity.

It is proper that the world should know more about him. Brighton Museum and Art Gallery, Jessica Rutherford, Nicola Coleby and our own indefatigable Sharon Kusunoki have summoned him up in all his wonderful diversity, and if the plangent stream of anecdote, the darting eyes, the wild cackle above the parrot's screeching are now extinguished, his generosity and deep-dyed, passionate concern that the skills of artists and craftsmen should survive, flourish and blossom, live on at West Dean College and in the works of his Foundation. What drove him, what moved him, what possessed and ruled him, at what altars he worshipped, no man knows, but this exhibition asks all of these questions and begins to answer some of them.

BREAKING CANONS
Edward James: His Life and Work

SHARON-MICHI KUSUNOKI

'... Aldous Huxley tells me that once a week the Bishop Devour of this diocese visits all the beds in the hospital ... and that the one thing not to do when he, the bishop, talks to you, is to mention God. It shakes him terribly. In fact, it turns him green. It is very bad taste to talk shop to the bishop. This is one of the canons of Twentieth Century convention. I am so longing to break it. Breaking canons always had the same appeal for me as pulling crackers, in fact makes quite a momentary Christmas just for me!'

Edward James, letter to the artist Esteban Frances, written while James was in hospital in Los Angeles, California, 6 June, 1949 (The Edward James Archive)

EDWARD JAMES's life was art, in its broadest sense, and his contribution to Surrealism lay not in the amount of works he collected, but rather in the way he came to surrealise his life. By 1939, at the age of 32, he had amassed what is now being recognised as one of the finest collections of Surrealist art in the world. Yet both in continental Europe and in his native England he remains a relatively unknown figure, his contributions marginalised by the labels, myths and realities that dogged his life. More a patron than a collector, James engaged in a unique form of avant-gardism, a form that embraces not only the patron and collector but also the artist. At the centre of all his activities was the stimulation of creative energy, not, as with many other collectors, civic responsibility, investment, social status or possession.

Emerging from a background that was, on the one hand, hedonistic, yet on the other, imbued with the sense of duty of a country squire, James struggled to resolve the contradictions of his upbringing. The pastimes of the social élite did not interest him, nor did the traditional system of titles, honours and the quest for political power. Instead, he moved into the world of the imagination, the world, it could be argued, of a Surrealist, where bourgeois values were subverted and where spontaneity, irrationality and the unconventional were legitimised. However, James's transition into this world was not without contradictions: his Surrealism was a luxury he could afford. By employing professional agents and trustees to handle rational matters, James was free to indulge his imagination without constraint.

Interestingly, James began seriously to patronise Surrealist art at a time when the English art critic Herbert Read was speaking out against English society and its aspirations to 'normality'. To Read, the English were an insular society with codified modes of behaviour so ingrained that a 'well-dressed gentleman' was described as 'a man whose clothes you do not remember; a man who in every detail, from the colour of the cloth to the number of buttons on his sleeve is so normal that he is unnoticeable, unseen'.[1] James responded to these constraints by revolting against them. Although he could not change the power structures of society, he attempted to change people's values by the way he lived and behaved.

Initially, James's life appears to be easily broken down into eight distinct pieces of a very complex puzzle: an Edwardian Child; the Twenties Aesthete; the Squire of West Dean; the Patron of the Ballet; the English Surrealist; the Californian; the Nomad; the

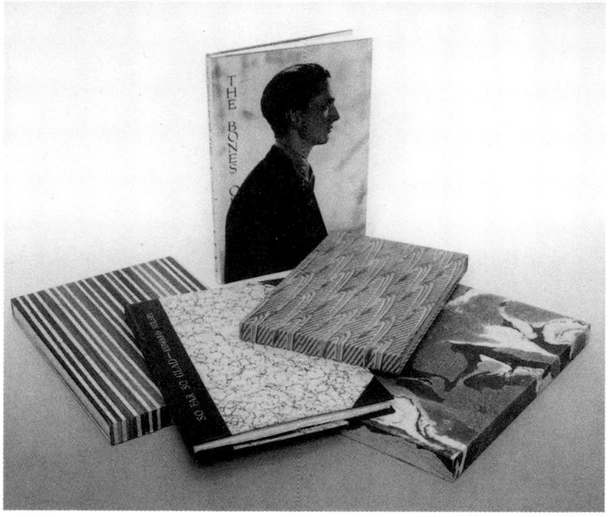

Selection of publications by Edward James: *Carmina Amico*, 1932, The James Press; *The Bones of My Hand*, 1938, Oxford University Press; *So Far So Glad*, c.1937/8, under the pseudonym Edward Selsey, Duckworth. EJF.

Architect of the Surreal. Yet the removal of any element of this puzzle results in the whole losing its significance, which lies in the very complexity of the interlocking pieces. The phases of his life were distinct and at the same time overlapping, with a continuous dialectical tension between the rational and the irrational. Any serious study of Edward James must therefore examine his life in the light of this tension as well as in the context of contemporary notions of social status and acceptability, which served to highlight such contradictions.

Born in 1907 in Gullane, Scotland, Edward Frank Willis James was the son of William James, a wealthy landowner,[2] and his wife, Evelyn, the daughter of Sir Charles Forbes, a Scottish aristocrat. Edward was the last of five children, a long awaited boy. The fact that King Edward VII, then Prince of Wales, was Edward James's godfather, is of particular significance.

At the time of James's birth, aristocratic society in Britain was fragmenting. The Industrial Revolution and agricultural depression, the advent of travel and, to a degree, of democracy meant that the aristocratic class no longer enjoyed the status of a social and political élite and their country estates were being broken up. A different class of landowner was emerging, with new-found wealth derived from sources other than agriculture. From the beginning it was apparent that this emergent class, to which William James belonged, was attracted by the recreational aspects of landownership rather than by the responsibilities that went with traditional land management.[3]

As the power of the old élite declined, the new one increasingly set the tone of high society, now centred on Edward VII. The terms of social acceptability were irrevocably changed by the new class structure – something that the ousted élite bitterly resented – and James was forced to confront the dichotomy that would be fundamental to his later outlook on life. Whilst his mother had had an aristocratic upbringing, his father, although educated at Harrow and a country gentleman, was not only a member of the *nouveau riche*, but also possessed a fortune made in America, representing all that was perceived to be loud and vulgar.

After William James's death in 1912, the house parties at West Dean ceased and Evelyn James was faced with the task of ensuring that Edward would develop into the perfect country squire. She attempted to instill in him the values of the exclusive society with which she mixed, and sought to bring him up with a patrician's sovereign sense of duty. Edward thus spent most of his childhood in boarding schools, including Eton, where his correspondence reveals that he felt constrained by the conventions of his privileged position, especially as he was prevented from pursuing his creative interests.[4]

At the age of 15, James was awarded the Gunther Memorial Prize in art by the critic and painter Roger

Fry. In his speech to the boys at Eton, Fry highlighted an early affinity between James's work and Dalí's later concept of Surrealism, referring to an art where ideas and a 'clarity of vision' were considered more important than the medium. While James took pride in his award, his mother never acknowledged his accomplishment and instead continued to squash James's attempts at creativity and to indoctrinate him with what she believed was to be his duty: to live a public life.[5] In a letter to James's agent, Evelyn James writes that James should 'CUT OUT MUSIC AND WRITING POETRY, and concentrate on his university degree and his future at West Dean and in Parliament'.[6] By the age of 17, however, James was already hinting at the attitude that came to epitomise the way he lived and behaved. In a letter dated May 1925, James writes to his mother:

> *... I would not have left you to believe that I anything but admired Mr. Bridgeman*[7] *and men of his type. I was only trying to say that I could not be like him, because I am not like him. If I am to be great it cannot be in such a gentle and steadily successful way ...*
>
> *But that does not mean that I am less 'public spirited' than Mr. Bridgeman or any less capable of doing good in another way ... there are more ways than one of living a good and noble life and one cannot change one's stamp completely ...*
>
> *P.S. To be a poet is not my aim at all, I am far more public spirited – although a great poet benefits the world more than most people.*[8]

But James's interest in literature and poetry began well before he received his mother's reprimand and throughout the rest of his life, his one great desire was to be known as a poet. His first serious attempts at writing poetry commenced at the age of 15; he continued without respite until his death in 1984.

In 1926, when he was 19, James published his first book of verse through the Shakespeare Head Press, and then in 1931 founded his own publishing company, the James Press, in order to produce John Betjeman's first book of poetry, *Mount Zion*. He took the clenched fist as the company crest, 'before it had become the Communist salute internationally',[9] because it represented to him the German word for fist: 'Faust', his favourite literary figure. In later years, the motif became a recurrent image in his life and work.[10]

The James Press operated until c.1938–39, publishing no less than 11 volumes of James's own work; when acknowledged, these were more often admired for the typography and luxuriousness of the hand-printed slip-cases than for the quality of the verse within. The early poetry received very little critical acclaim, but its sense of releasing repressed feeling anticipates his later attempts at Surrealist writing. This became more evident in his publication *So Far So Glad* (c.1937–38), a Surrealist text in prose set around the world of a circus on the planet Venus.

In 1937, James's only novel, *The Gardener Who Saw God*, was published in England and New York to favourable reviews. Although the story is not written in a Surrealist vein, it explores Surrealism through its subject matter and was based on a vision that James claims to have had while eating dinner at West Dean. Suddenly the dining room started to spin and on the ceiling he saw what he 'knew' to be a projection of his own unconscious. A circle of all creation span faster and faster around a central light to the last movement of Beethoven's *Eroica* Symphony until it exploded in the sky.

James's book of poetry, *The Bones of My Hand*, was published in 1938 through Oxford University Press. Although it received some favourable notices it elicited a harsh review from Stephen Spender in *The New Statesman and Nation*.[11] James was deeply hurt, certain that Spender was dismissive of his work simply because of his reputation as a man of wealth. As a result, with the exception of the few syndicated articles he wrote for Lord Beaverbrook in *The London Evening Standard* between 1938 and 1939, James never published under his own name again. He continued to write, almost obsessively, on scraps of paper, old matchbook covers, or even on the walls of his home, yet his only published volumes of verse were issued privately among his friends under pseudonyms such as Edward Selsey, Edward Silence or, later, Edward Vayarta.

While reading History and Modern Languages as an undergraduate at Christ Church, Oxford, James had been encouraged by Betjeman to finance and edit the student publication *Cherwell*, resigning only after numerous protests from his mother. However, James's interest in the arts did not stop with literary matters. In 1926, through his designs for the interior of his Christ Church rooms in Canterbury Quad, he indulged in his first attempt to create a reality that was no longer dictated by the 'majority'. For James, Oxford was a watershed, providing him with freedom from maternal supervision and a ready audience for his creative ideas and exotic tastes. While not outwardly Surrealist, James's designs and juxtapositions, which included speakers wired into the classical busts of Roman emperors so that from their mouths 'belched the latest in American and French music',[12] questioned conventional reality and created a disjunction between object and function, and the organic and the inorganic, which in effect encouraged a form of participatory free association that can easily be linked with Surrealist practice.

James's activities at Oxford clarify his later attraction to the theory first postulated by Dalí in his article published in 1930 for the periodical *Le Surréalisme au Service de la Révolution* (Paris, No.1): the 'paranoiac-critical method'. This was a system enabling many different things to be read into a common arrangement of form, as when one looks at the shapes of clouds, or as in Dalí's *Paranoiac Face* of 1935 (oil on panel, Paris, private collection), where an African village can be read as a face when turned through 90 degrees. The taste that James shared with Dalí for the transformation of images and objects and for a dualism that embraced the old and new, tradition and rupture, would become a constant factor in his life. It both confronted and provoked new ways of seeing and, as such, supplied the energy for his battle against the canons of convention.

James's rupture with the world of his parents came in 1929 following the death of his mother and the receipt of his inheritance. From the 1920s onward, James supported artists and composers, and dedicated himself to the imagination, both in his writing and in his life. His attraction to the French Surrealists was a natural progression. Like them, James sought imaginatively to reconstruct the real and to challenge the values of society.

James left Oxford before graduating and in 1929 fell in love with an Austrian ballet dancer, Ottilie (Tilly) Losch, after seeing her perform in C.B. Cochran's *This Year of Grace*. Overwhelmed by Losch's mesmeric charm, James responded with extravagance and affection. They corresponded briefly when James was appointed Honorary Attaché at the British Embassy in Rome in 1930, and then married in 1931, James having resigned from the diplomatic service after only seven months of duty. As he began remodelling the interior of his homes in Wimpole and Culross Streets in London, Losch served as James's muse. Nevertheless, their marriage was a disaster and by December of that year they were living apart.

In 1933, in an effort to save his failing marriage, James funded the ballet company Les Ballets 1933, founded by George Balanchine and Diaghilev's former secretary, Boris Kochno. Two ballets were created for Losch: *L'Errante* (*The Wanderer*), and *Les Sept Péchés*

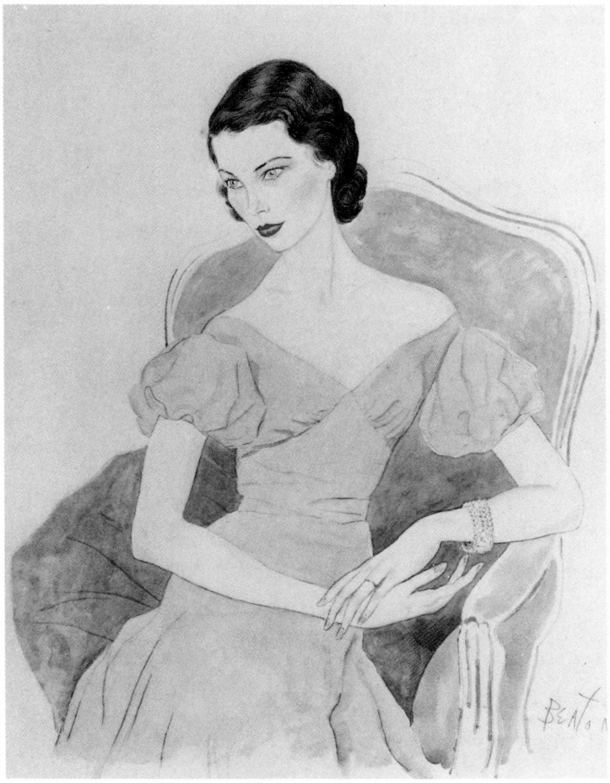

CECIL BEATON
Portrait of Tilly Losch
58 x 44.5cm.
EJF. Catalogue no. 82.

Capitaux (*The Seven Deadly Sins*). James always claimed that the main outline for *Les Sept Péchés Capitaux* was based on his conviction that the conventions of a capitalist-bourgeois world destroyed the opportunities for personal fulfilment. A collaboration with Kurt Weill and Bertolt Brecht, it demonstrates vividly the participatory aspect of James's patronage.

Despite James's efforts to save his marriage, Tilly Losch brought a motion for judicial separation the following year. In a most unusual action for the time, James scandalised society by filing a countersuit based on Tilly's adultery with Prince Serge Obolensky. Although the *decree nisi* was declared in James's favour, he was shunned by English society, and his only truly sympathetic and supportive friend appears to have been Edith Sitwell, who alone encouraged James to rebuild his life.

Emerging from this devastating divorce and ostracisation with a desperate energy, James travelled extensively throughout Europe, spending a great deal of time in France. Although his style of patronage and collecting was new in England, particularly in contrast to the conventional collection of his father, it was less so across the Channel. By the late 1920s, among his acquaintances, the Comte and Comtesse de Beaumont and the Vicomte and Vicomtesse de Noailles were well established as patrons of modern art, following, to some degree, a tradition of aristocratic patronage that dated back to the Renaissance.[13] In a pattern established by the de Beaumonts before him, James broadened his activities to include not only the purchasing of works of art and the financing of ballets, but also the sponsoring of concerts promoting the work of contemporary artists and composers, many of whom were probably introduced to him by the Vicomtesse de Noailles with whom he is believed to have had an affair. He became a member of La Sérénade, a committee of patrons who sought to assist young, talented composers who had not yet achieved recognition, and began commissioning work from composers such as Hans Fleischer, Nicolas Nabakov, Darius Milhaud, Henri Sauguet, Igor Markevitch and Francis Poulenc.

James always asserted that he purchased his first piece of art at the age of 18. By the time of his death, his holdings had grown to include pieces by the School of Arcimboldo, Arp, Bérard, Berman, Bosch, de Chirico, Cornell, Delvaux, Duchamp, Ernst, Fini, Giacometti, Grosz, Klee, Man Ray, Mesens, Miró, Nash, Noguchi, Picasso, Tanguy, Whistler, and particularly extensive collections of Leonora Carrington, René Magritte, Pavel Tchelitchew and Salvador Dalí, the first Surrealist whom James supported on a grand scale. Among the early Surrealists he admired was Max Ernst, whose painting *Aux Antipodes du paysage* (1936, oil on canvas, Christie's, West Dean, 5 June 1986) he purchased, and whom he championed for his use of figures in dream sequences of collages. Another favourite was Magritte, who was his guest in 1937 at 35 Wimpole Street, where he executed *Le modèle rouge* (Museum Boijmans Van Beuningen, Rotterdam), *La jeunesse illustreé* (Museum Boijmans Van Beuningen, Rotterdam) and *Au Seuil de la liberté* (The Art Institute of Chicago, Gift of Mary and Leigh Block) for the ballroom.

Although Surrealism did not officially reach England until 1936, James discovered it much earlier. In the late 1920s and early 1930s, the de Noailles's villa at Hyères had become known among the Parisian avant-garde as a centre for everything modern.[14] Artists and potential patrons met there in an atmosphere carefully designed to stimulate the imagination. While it is not known exactly when James first became attracted to Surrealist art, it is certain that at the end of 1932 or the beginning of 1933 he went to Hyères as a guest of the de Noailles,[15] where he was entranced by a portrait of the Vicomtesse painted by Dalí. From that time on, James kept in touch with Dalí's activities through his friendship with the Vicomtesse and became one of his most important patrons.

During one of James's visits to Hyères, and before his formal introduction to Dalí sometime in 1934 or 1935, the Vicomtesse told James of a discussion she had had with Dalí in which he commented on Hitler's popularity in Germany: 'Hitler's shirt was brown, and his torso looked as if it had been made of gingerbread. The subconscious of the German people thought that the Nazis were made of gingerbread'.[16] James was fascinated by this image and a few months later, when he saw Dalí at a concert in the gardens of the Princesse de Polignac, accompanied by Bettina Bergery,[17] it is said that he walked up behind the artist and asked in a loud voice: 'Bettina, do you know that Hitler's back is made of gingerbread?' Overhearing the remark Dalí swung round saying: 'How do you know that? What you say is right. Who are you?'

From 1934 to 1939 James rented the Villa Cimbrone in Ravello, Italy from Lord and Lady Grimthorpe, which he encouraged his friends to visit, especially if they were creative artists. In 1935, James and Gala and Salvador Dalí were guests at a house party hosted by the Spanish painter José María Sert. During the party, one of the guests, Prince Alec Mdivani, was tragically killed in a car accident leaving Dalí shaken and depressed. Hoping to lift Dalí out of his depression and to give him new inspiration, James persuaded the Dalís to visit him in Italy, enticing them there with surrealistic images describing the baroque statue of the Madonna of Melba-Murillo as 'fishing the cup of seven sadnesses, soft Neapolitan ice cream, girded with plaster clouds, crowned with stars of golden pewter, a little chipped, a little tarnished'.[18] He arranged for the Dalís to arrive in Italy by sea and was disappointed when the repairs on his yacht made it impossible for such an arrival to take place:

> *It would have been a superlatively poetic way of bringing my guests to the Castello, to have had my cutter ready in Naples to meet us and sailed on her round Cape Pipparreggia (that is my name for the Capo di Sorrento) to Amalfi: then to have landed them beneath the arches in the boat-filled piazza of the tiny port of Trani at the foot of the hill to Ravello, where the sea washes against the steps of the houses and where beneath the viaduct which is formed by the high-road the surf sighs in the shadows of the vaulted*

masonry and the fish-nets hang drying between the rusted balconies.[19]

Nevertheless the Dalí's trip to Italy was a success. In a letter written to the Catalan poet J.V. Foix after their arrival in Rome, Dalí stated that he found Italy to be 'more surrealist than the Pope'.[20] In a letter to James after his return to Cadaqués, he wrote: 'Tomorrow, Monday, I'm starting work with all my soul, and I'm not going out any more except in the evening from time to time – I've never had so many ideas as I have now ...'[21]

In May 1936, James and Dalí initiated an especially significant collaboration: the exploration of interior and exterior design as a new and creative means of surrealising everyday life. From this exploration came paranoiac-critical interiors, furniture and Surrealist assemblages such as Dalí's *Lobster Telephone*. In this connection, Dalí has been credited with 'single-handedly bringing a new dimension, a new lift, to an ageing Surrealism'.[22] In fact, the correspondence in The Edward James Archive tells a very different story. It establishes that the inspiration for the schemes often came from James, whose imagination enabled him to visualise in three dimensions what the Surrealist artists realised on canvas. Following James's initial idea, Dalí was commissioned to produce the basic drawing, with James retaining control over the working design and its final execution.[23]

The experimentation James began at Oxford with incongruous juxtapositions of dissimilar objects resurfaced in the further transformations he was attempting in his homes at 35 Wimpole Street in London and at Monkton, a small cottage originally built by Lutyens on his West Dean Estate. In 1986, when Monkton was put on the market after James's death, it was publicly acknowledged to be Britain's most remarkable example of a three-dimensional Surrealist creation.[24]

Where Dalí often replicated aspects of his environment in his Surrealist paintings, James wanted to take the environment and transform it, thereby creating a new reality. In 1936, James planned to recreate in three dimensions the rocks of Cap Creus on the walls of his drawing room at Wimpole Street. Dalí, however, discouraged James from this idea saying that it might not only be technically impossible but, even worse, an odious pastiche. Nevertheless, Dalí's hungry imagination was stimulated and together, he and James began proposing the most ambitious Surrealist schemes for interiors, each feeding off the ideas of the other. Dalí suggested a room with pulsating walls designed to resemble the inside of a sick dog's stomach. James wanted it coated with dog's hair.[25] James suggested a chair in which the back was made of carved hands playing cat's cradle. Dalí amended James's initial design and James supervised and financed its production. He saw Dalí's picture entitled *The Face of Mae West (Usable as a Surrealist Apartment)*, 1934–35 (gouache on paper, The Art Institute of Chicago) and suggested that the lips be manufactured as a sofa, again supervising its production.[26] Together they combined and reconfigured fragments of the world to challenge reality.

Although James was never actively involved with the leaders of the Surrealist movement in England, the friendships he maintained and the work he stimulated helped to disseminate Surrealism in England. By the time of the first International Surrealist Exhibition in June of 1936, James had acquired at least four paintings by Dalí: *Tête Paranoiaque* (1935, Paris, G.E.D. Nahmed), *Car of Death* (location unknown), *White Calm* (1936, Geneva, private collection) and *Suburb of the Paranoiac-critical Town; Afternoon on the Outskirts of European History* (1936, Christie's, London, 31 March 1981). Dalí wrote to James asking him to lend *Tête Paranoiaque* for the London show,[27] which was followed by a letter from Roland Penrose requesting a painting by Picasso for the same exhibition.[28] In the end, James lent both the Dalí and his recently acquired *Head of a Woman* by Picasso (1934, oil on canvas, sold 9 January 1981).

The 1936 exhibition showed the works of over 50 artists and was attended by at least 20,000 people. The 23 British artists selected by Herbert Read and Roland Penrose found themselves labelled Surrealist overnight, without a real understanding of, or commitment to, Surrealist principles.[29] Despite the fact that David Gascoyne published his survey of Surrealism in 1935, the British encounter with the movement, up to this point, was relatively minimal, and even in 1945 when Maurice Nadeau published *History of Surrealism*, there was no mention of an English group. While not a member of, and not necessarily in complete sympathy with, Surrealism as a movement, James nevertheless helped to publish the next two issues of the Surrealist review *Minotaure* with Albert Skira in Paris.

James did not take an active part in this exhibition, but Dalí chose him to translate his speech for the lecture he was to give in connection with it. James's extemporaneous translation came off without a hitch and he was described in the press as 'a charming chairman'. Intending to show that he was 'plunging down deeply into the human mind',[30] Dalí donned a diving suit in which he found himself unable to breathe and it was James who had to prise him out.[31] One newspaper described it thus:

> *The diver's helmet had a motor car radiator cap on top. Plasticine hands were stuck on the*

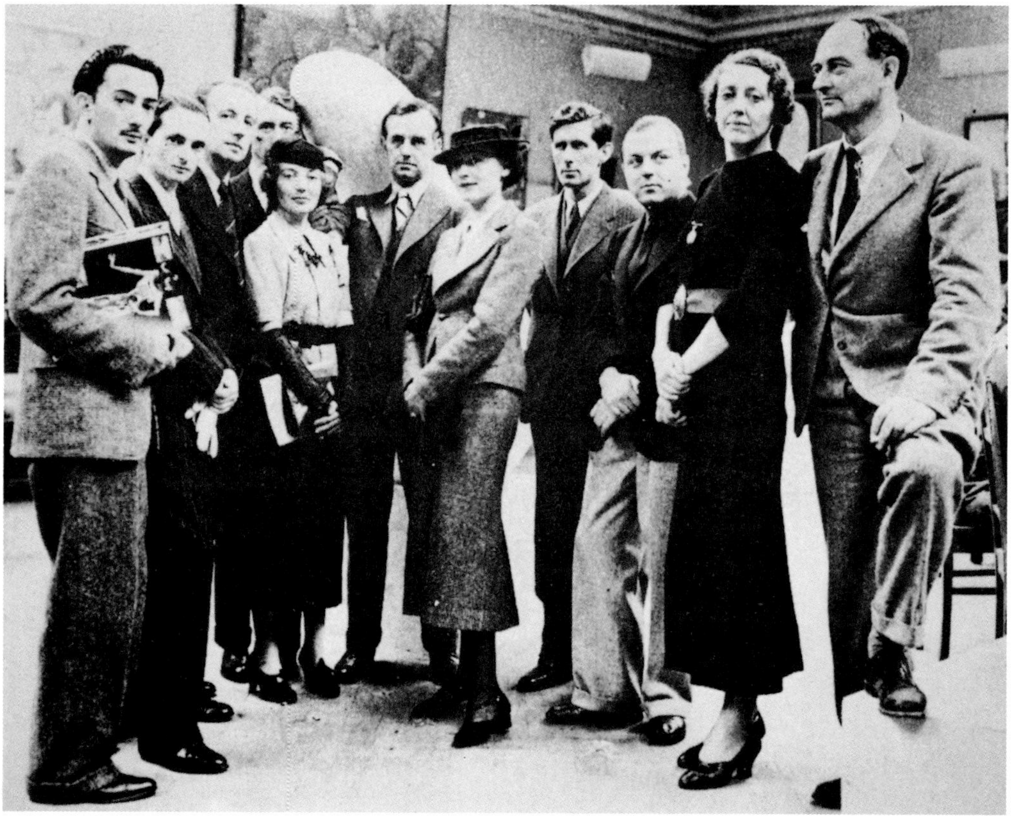

First International Surrealist Exhibition, London, 1936, right to left: Rupert Lee (Chairman), Diana Brinton Lee (Secretary), E.L.T. Mesens, Roland Penrose (Hon Treasurer), Nusch Eluard, Stellan Mörner, Herbert Read behind Eileen Agar, Paul Eluard, Edward James, Salvador Dalí.

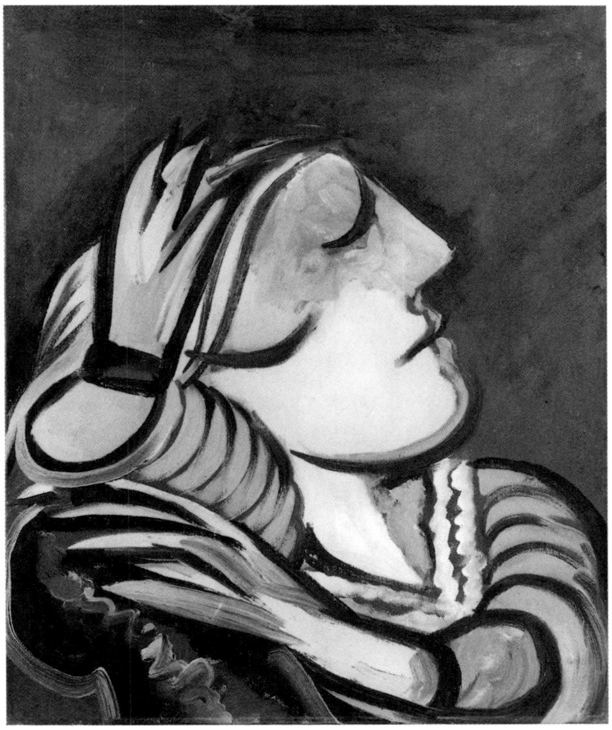

PABLO PICASSO
Head of a Woman
1934, oil on canvas
53.5 x 46.5cm.
Sold 9 January 1981.

bodice. Round his waist was a belt with a dagger. He carried a billiard cue, and was escorted by two big dogs. To make the performance more mystifying he spoke in French through loudspeakers. Half-way through his patter he began to get warm and asked somebody to take his helmet off. It had stuck and a spanner was no use, but the billiard cue came in handy as a can opener. Now and again the lanternist put the slides in sideways or upside down, but nobody knew or minded. "Surrealism is like that ..." [32]

The International Surrealist Exhibition coincided with Dalí's one-man show at the Reid and Lefevre Gallery, launched in an effort to exhibit more progressive art. For this exhibition, James lent two paintings, *White Calm* and *Suburb of the Paranoiac-critical Town* (now subtitled *Afternoon on the Outskirts of European History*), both of 1936. He also purchased from the Gallery six oil paintings and two untitled drawings by Dalí: *Sun Table* (1936, Museum Boijmans Van Beuningen, Rotterdam), *Anthropomorphism* (1936, location unknown), *The Anthropomorphic Cabinet* (1936, Düsseldorf, Kunstsammlung Nordrhein-Westfalen), *Primal Melancholy* (1936, location unknown), *Fossil Automobile of Cap Creus* (now known as *The Fossilised Automobile of Cap Creus*, 1936, Geneva, G.E.D. Nahmed), and the silhouettes of

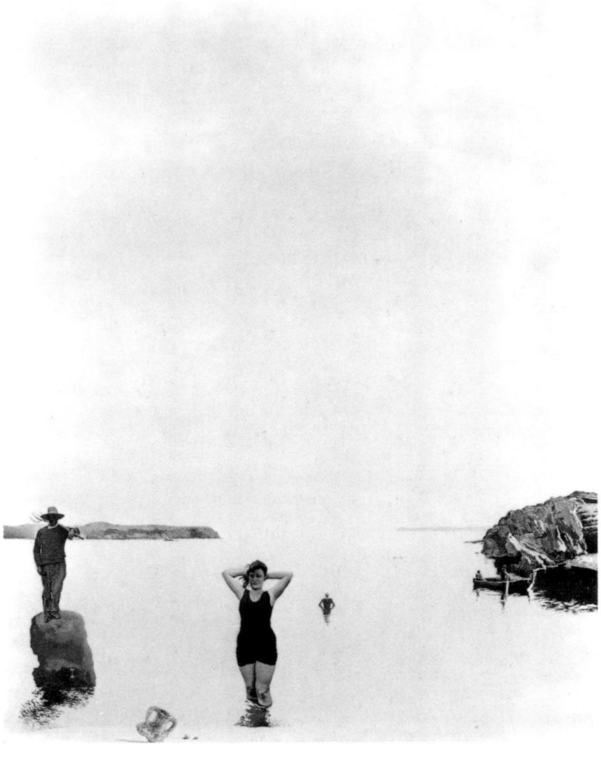

SALVADOR DALÍ
White Calm
1936, oil on panel
41.5 x 33cm.
Geneva, G.E.D. Nahmed.

A Couple with their Heads in the Clouds (1936, Museum Boijmans Van Beuningen, Rotterdam).

In 1939, James left for the United States and, together with Dalí, embarked on what would be their last creative collaboration, the *Dream of Venus* pavilion for the New York World's Fair. Perhaps inspired, to some degree, by James's Surrealist creations for Monkton, Dalí's pavilion was to be a monumental installation of a complete Surrealist environment largely financed by James. James, in turn, had a hand in some of the designs and was left to make decisions on suitable alternatives when Dalí left for Europe after becoming enraged that his original ideas were prohibited by the organising committee.

In May 1940, James moved to Taos, New Mexico and lived among a community of artists in the colony where D.H. Lawrence, Frieda Lawrence, Dorothy Brett and the heiress Mabel Luhan Dodge had settled. In September 1940, he moved again, this time to California, where he purchased a home in the Hollywood hills. Although he travelled extensively, James remained a resident in Southern California for a period of at least 30 years, living in a succession of homes and hotel suites, and writing longer and longer letters to his friends. While in California, James met a number of people, including Igor Stravinsky, whose friendships had a profound influence on his life. He also found a new outlet for his energy in the Vedanta movement of Hindu meditation, then fashionable in Hollywood. But perhaps one of the deepest relationships he established in California was with his lawyer, Robert Farmer, now Chairman of The Edward James Foundation, who not only oversaw his finances, but devised the vehicle by which James could keep his English estate intact. In later years, James would state: 'Bob Farmer, like my own father, saved me from myself. Without him, I would be bankrupt.'[33] James's friendships frequently ended acrimoniously with James feeling victimised, but his relationship with Bob Farmer was one of the few that endured relatively unscathed. Perhaps this is because, as James himself would admit, he needed Farmer whereas Farmer did not need him.

In 1944, James travelled to Mexico to visit the home of Geoffrey Gilmore, a friend from his Oxford days. During this time with Gilmore, James met Plutarco Gastelum, a man of 29 who was part Yaki Indian, and who worked in the telegraph office in Cuernavaca. He would become James's closest friend and most regular companion.

The following year James travelled to Xilitla, in Mexico, in search of orchids and was so entranced he purchased a property there in 1948. He grew over 20,000 orchids, but when they were destroyed by a frost, he decided to bring in materials that would not be affected by the weather and began to give form, using concrete, to his imagination. 'Houses shaped like whales, concrete pistols sprouting forth into brightly coloured flowers, and buildings that grew slowly but prodigiously and tall'[34] took shape, integrating, almost naturally, with the foliage. However, in order to build this Surrealist environment, James needed ready cash, and began to liquidate his Surrealist collection. After all, it was not the possession of precious objects that mattered to James, but rather the life of the imagination.

After James's death, the maintenance of his structures in Xilitla was to prove problematic: in danger of being overtaken by the jungle, their preservation would cost money, which usually involves commercial exploitation, something that James always fought to avoid. To commercialise Xilitla would mean to lose some of its magic, and it is important to note that although James amended his will several times after he first began building in Xilitla, he never made provision for the preservation of these structures. During his lifetime, James described art as a magic box capable of taking one back through time far beyond the past.

Might it be then, that this is why he did not provide for the preservation of his structures, that this is what he would have preferred: a magical box filled with chance and surprise, swallowed up by the jungle, waiting to be opened? After all, to James, the discovery of ruins, such as the Mayan remains in Chichén Itzá, needed to occur as if without warning, framed by coppice with grey flights of stone steps glittering under the secrets of their past:

> *Instead of entering La Zona Archeólogica through the main public entrance, I slipped (rather typically) in a back way, through a thick covert of brush and underwood, under a barbed wire fence – not to avoid paying my 2 pesos entrance fee, but to take Chichén Itzá by surprise, which I did.*[35]

The last years of James's life were divided between his two most ambitious works – Xilitla and the establishment of an educational Foundation, which bears his name. Although James was seemingly irresponsible, he had always ensured that his estate and affairs were well managed. In 1964, he conveyed his family mansion and 6,000-acre Estate to The Edward James Foundation, a charitable trust established on the twin pillars of Estate preservation and his life-long love of the arts. In 1971 the Foundation established West Dean College.

Born to privilege, James was expected to play a conventional role in society. Instead, he chose a distinctly provocative way of life, investing in creativity for its own sake and confronting the norms of society with alternative perspectives on reality. Patrick Waldberg states that 'The Surrealists had two passwords: "To change life" (Rimbaud) and "To transform the world" (Marx).'[36] In 1941, James wrote to his friend, the American actress Ruth Ford:

> *So I sum up my point of view in relation to that inherited fortune by saying that money seemed to me to have been given to spend ... But I was not going simply to give it away to some uncreative institution called a charity. I felt that I could do more to alter the face of the world, more to usher in that new world, by spending it in my own way – in particular, by fostering any and all creative spirits I could meet with, who had something individually to contribute to the building of that more vivid and more living future ... Moreover, I could see hardly anyone who supported the sort of stairways to imagination which seemed to me to be so vital and necessary to the spiritual potency of this future ...*[37]

Where other Surrealist collectors such as Breton, Eluard and Aragon often exchanged and sold the works in their collections,[38] James's were most often lent to friends, anonymously wrapped in tissue paper and packed in trunks. These actions, described by one of James's biographers as 'undisciplined', 'wayward' and 'eccentric',[39] demonstrate that for James, even more than for Breton, the action of the imagination took precedence over the product.

James's name and his place in cultural history continue to be plagued by a widespread belief that he was simply an eccentric and not creative in any profound sense. In reality, it is perhaps more accurate to say that the adjectives used to describe him – 'millionaire', 'collector', 'eccentric' – do not define him but merely identify some of the roles he chose to play. As early as 1910, Roger Fry spoke out against British insularity and its associated conventional attitudes towards art,[40] and this was echoed by Herbert Read when he questioned a society in which individuality was discouraged, where the only criterion for good taste was the conventional, and where anyone deviating from the

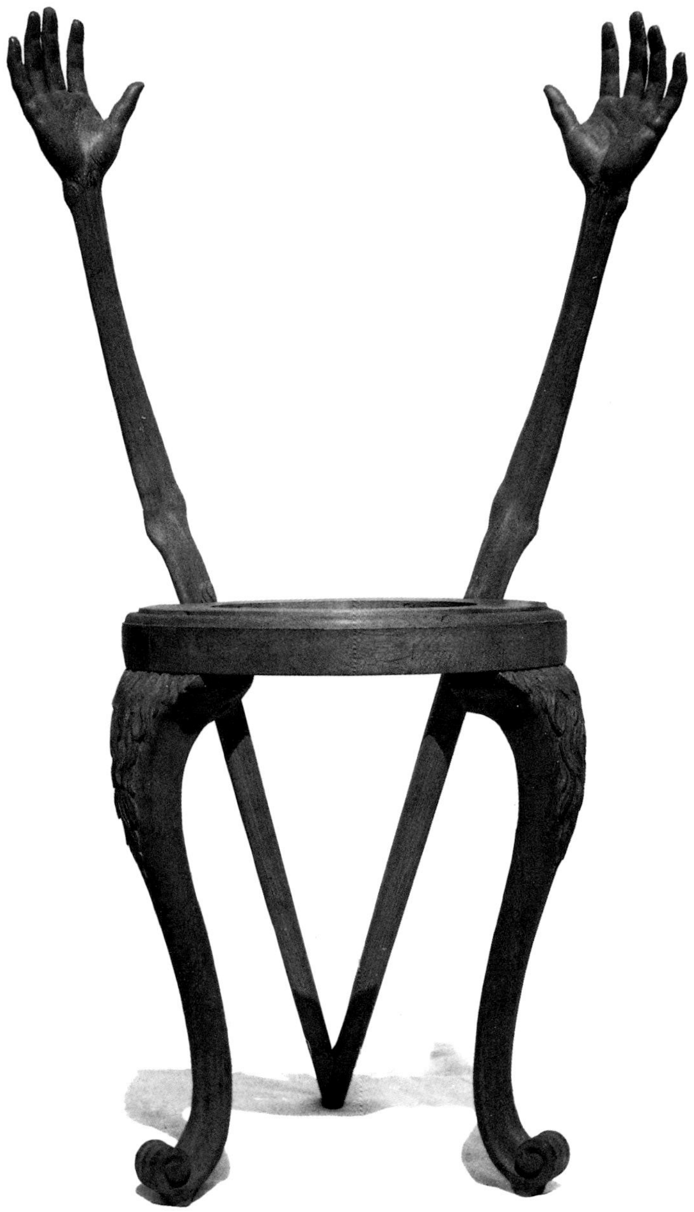

Chair, c.1936, designed by
Salvador Dalí.
EJF. Catalogue no. 193.

Edward James also has remarkable, less orthodox ideas of interior decoration ... 40-feet-tall damask curtains decorated with human eyes made of felt ... Sofa made of two gigantic bronze hands playing cat's-cradle ... In a secluded glade he is having built a grand piano of white marble. From a fissure in its 'keyboard' will spout a fountain.

Indulgence of such fantasies is at any rate an amusing change from most rich people's way of spending money[42]

If the article had been written about Dalí, its emphasis would have been very different. It is too clear cut, too simple to identify Dalí as the artist and James the eccentric. Visual, literary and musical, James's life, when viewed as a whole, was far more than the lifestyle of an eccentric dilettante. His overwhelming need to be at the centre of creative activity ensured that whether he inspired passion, pleasure, hatred, contempt, frustration or envy, contact with Edward James changed people.

norm was disempowered through the use of reductive labels invented solely to preserve that normality.[41]

Being wealthy afforded James the opportunity to transform his own reality. On the other hand, it also meant that he would be judged by a different value system which, according to social conventions, restricted his role in culture to that judged fit for the aristocracy and for the exceptionally wealthy, as the following extract from the *Daily Express*, London, June 26 1936, makes clear:

MAKING THE ILLOGICAL LOGICAL:

The Organisation of The Edward James Archive

SHARON-MICHI KUSUNOKI

LEADING ARCHIVIST T.R. Schellenberg writes of the two basic principles of archival management:

> *The first, which is known as the principle of provenance, is that records should be kept according to their source. The second, which is known as the principle of original order, is that records should be kept in the order originally imposed on them.*[1]

What Schellenberg does not tell us, however, is how to apply these laws to an archive whose contents appear to have been either systematically disorganised, or arranged following the 'laws of chance'. The extraordinary way in which Edward James left his archival material gives interesting insight into the man himself and results in a meaning that is often ambiguous and open to multiple interpretations.

The contents of the Edward James Archive were collected, and are still being collected, from various parts of the world. Its major holdings came primarily from James's Estate and houses in England, and from Hollywood, Xilitla, and Italy, where they were either left with friends, sent to store, or packed within James's luggage and carried around the world. For the last 30 years of his life, James spent as much on excess baggage duty as he did on the price of the ticket. In Xilitla his luggage was referred to as 'las culpas del pobre inglés', 'the sins of the poor Englishman'.

The material found within his bags has revealed that he was a prodigious letter writer. His correspondence with his friends spanned over four decades and he saved not only every letter he received, but carbon copies of his replies. Just prior to his death, James describes his attempts to 'arrange' some of this material:

> *And bewildered I … run, like a child playing rounders or musical chairs, from letter to letter, adding a sentence here and an asterisk there, as I scurry by, dragged on by cries and whimpers from the next gaping letter. When I am too out of breath, I merely pepper them with occasional commas as I pass. For, from the adjacent room, are heard – louder and longer than any letters – the howls and sobs of my uncorrected proofs, thirsty and shivering for attention. You see, I try to divide my energies equally between satisfying the demands of my contemporaries and those of posterity – with the result that neither are satisfied. I have had some bitter complaints from posterity lately.*[2]

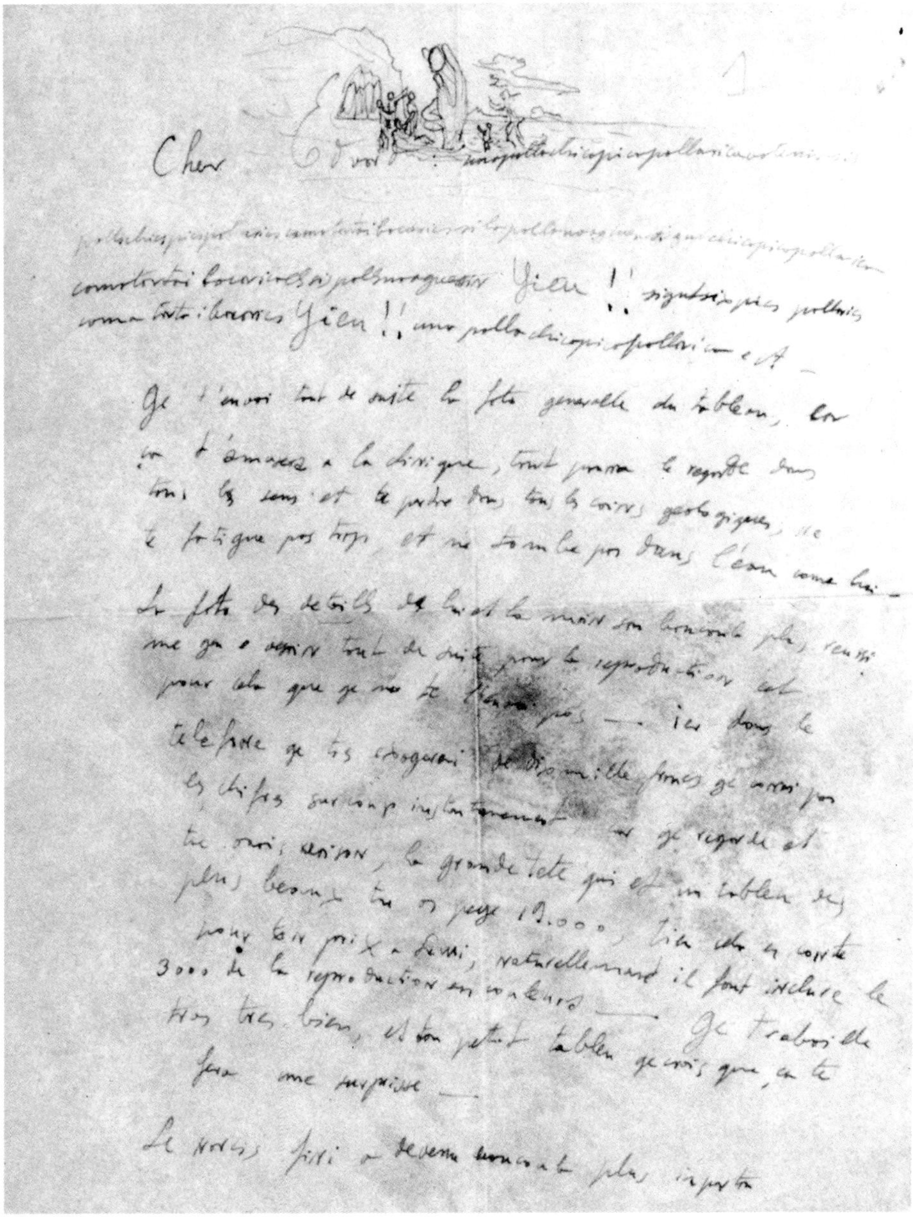

Letter to Edward James from Salvador Dalí, 15 June 1937, with sketch for *Metamorphosis of Narcissus* (1937). EJF. Catalogue no. 169.

The bulk of the archive was uncovered in a warehouse in Hollywood where James's American lawyer had been paying rent for the storage of his personal belongings for a period of approximately 20 years. There, a collection of tattered leather suitcases, battered steamer trunks, aged wooden packing crates and rows of old filing cabinets were stacked floor to ceiling, their contents known only to James. Inside these containers, which numbered well over 1,000, were found dirty socks, old underwear, unopened packets of sugar and a desiccated piece of chocolate cake, jumbled together in anarchic disorder and wrapped in tissue paper, together with paintings and drawings by many of the most eminent artists of the Surrealist movement, their letters to James, and copies of his to them.

From their tissue paper shrouds came Salvador Dalí's *Paranoiac Face* (1935, oil on panel, Paris, private collection), his *Tristan and Isolde* (1941, oil on canvas, Geneva, G.E.D. Nahmed) and his 1936 preparatory study for a portrait of James found lodged between the pages of an old, completely blank notebook in a warehouse in Los Angeles. Also discovered were George

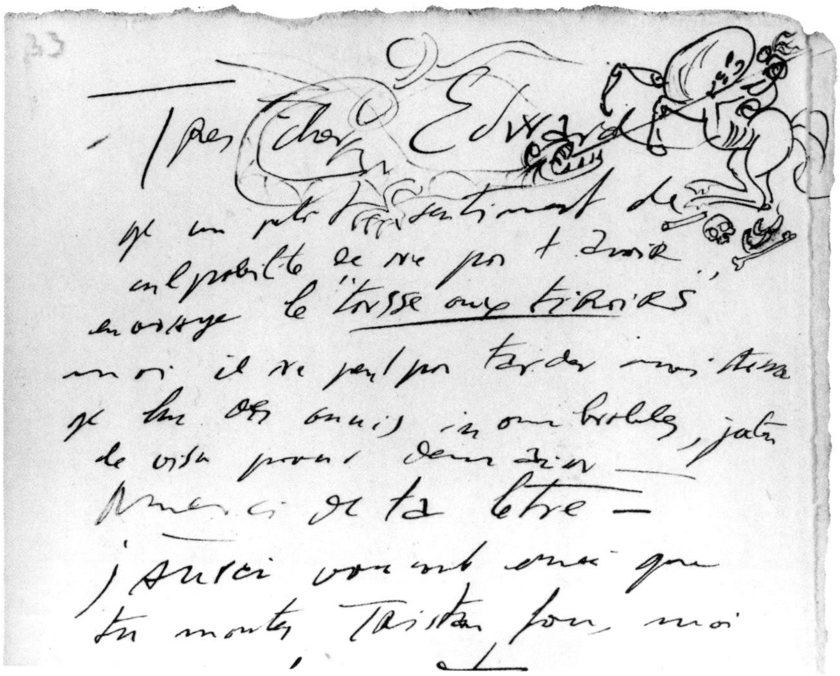
Très cher Edward

Detail from letter to Edward James from Salvador Dalí, undated, EJF. The sketch of a man on horseback incorporates the names of Edward James, Dalí and Gala. Catalogue no. 246.

Grosz's *Street Fighting* (c.1934, watercolour on paper, Christie's, West Dean, 5 June 1986); an illustrated booklet by René Magritte and Belgian Surrealist poets, presented to James in 1937 (The Trustees of The Edward James Foundation); Joseph Cornell's *Cabinet of Natural History* (1936–40, glass vials in mahogany box, Christie's, New York, 6 May 1986); an untitled gouache by Yves Tanguy, and works by Marcel Duchamp, Jean Cocteau, Leonora Carrington, Leonor Fini, Eugène Berman and Gio Pomodoro.

In one parcel alone, one could find correspondence and fragments of letters belonging to James and his family covering a period of over 100 years. These filled hundreds of the suitcases and shipping crates, and looked as if they had been shuffled together, thrown up into the air, and then picked up by the handful, just as Dadaist artists, such as Jean Arp, tore up their drawings and pasted the fragments onto larger sheets exactly as they fell. Each random batch was then meticulously cocooned in tissue-paper[3] and packed in James's trunks and cases and scattered throughout the world.

> *It is a disorder through which only I could pick my way; and since it is a madness with method, if anyone were to move these things in my absence the method would be lost and only the madness would remain.*[4]

Fragments of writings made in a selection of coloured pens and pencils on napkins, envelopes, matchbooks and scraps of brightly coloured paper of various sizes, were placed by James in envelopes, one inside another, arranged without order, address, date, or even addressee. As a consequence, the organisation of his archive was much like piecing together a jigsaw puzzle containing over 300,000 colourful pieces constructed from a variety of materials:

> *I rather enjoy making my letters like Chinese boxes or old Bohemian toys, one envelope inside another envelope inside another envelope. I suppose that primitive people, such as the Bohemian peasants of what is now Czechoslovakia, and the*

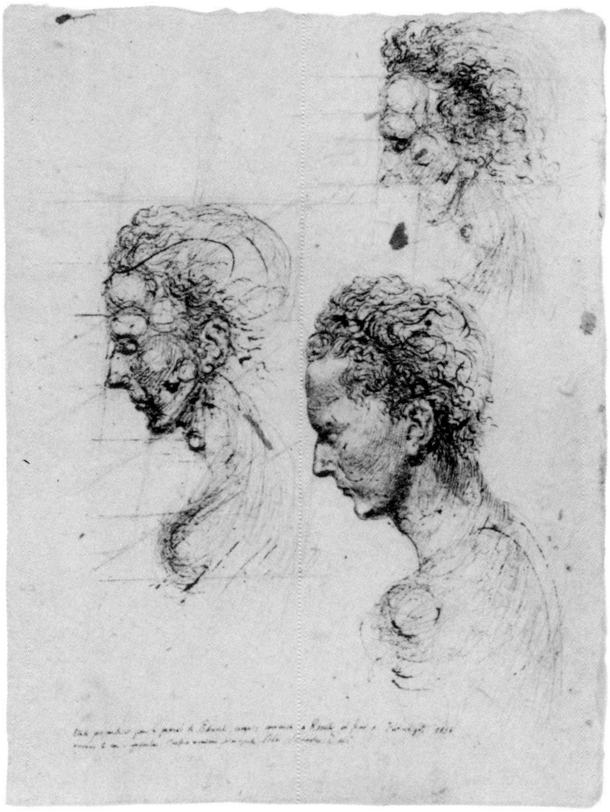

SALVADOR DALÍ
Study for a portrait of Edward James, 1936, begun in Ravello, Italy, and finished in Port Lligat, Spain.
EJF. Catalogue no. 78.

Right:
JOSEPH CORNELL
Cabinet of Natural History, 1936–40, glass vials in a mahogany box, 19 x 14 x 8cm.
Christie's, New York, 6 May 1986.

> *traditional Chinese village craftsmen, who used to make lacquered boxes to fit one inside another, all have retained a certain infantilism. Thus in my second childhood I like hiding things inside other things and wrapping things inside other wrapped up things. But then … I cannot with any justification call it my 'Second Childhood', never have I really grown out of my first.*[5]

James left the reconstruction of his material to others, but its false trails and unprecedentedly overt defiance of any conventional rules of organisation was at odds with traditional methodological techniques. Attempts to date letters by comparing stationery often proved fruitless since James would carry around writing paper that he had taken from various hotels over a period of more than 50 years and often intermixed it within the same letter. Dating was also inaccurate because James sometimes took years to write his letters and even then did not always send them, or purposely dated them inaccurately. Text alone was also deceptive for he sometimes copied paragraphs of one letter into others and kept numerous drafts of the same letter. At first sight, page numbering appeared to be consistent, but this also turned out to be misleading, for just as one felt assured that a letter was complete, one would uncover a parcel containing pages 3AAA or 102YYYZZZ, often created as footnotes to unidentified correspondence.

In a letter to the philosopher Gerald Heard, James writes:

> *It is useless to act as though anything were permanent; and yet, so great are the pressures by which every day we are surrounded, to make us conform to these insane criteria of greed, of hoarding (for what?) – of planning for an indefinite future which takes no account of death, that one finds oneself constantly acting as though one could arrest the passage of time.*
>
> *Even little tricks like my numbering pages '2A' and '2B' in my letters and other typescripts … and so on – these I believe are in part tricks of my subconscious to make me feel that the march*

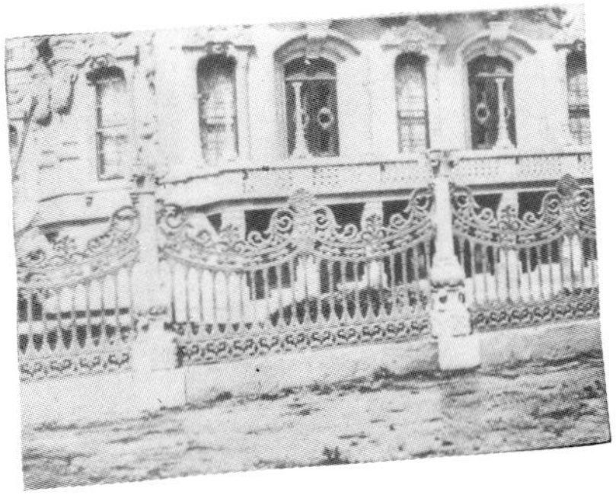

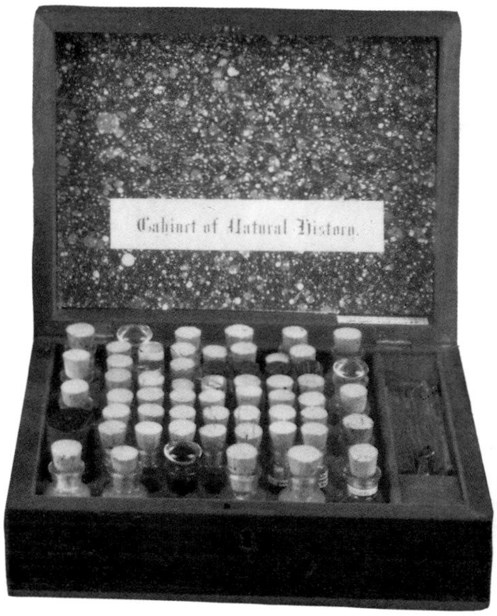

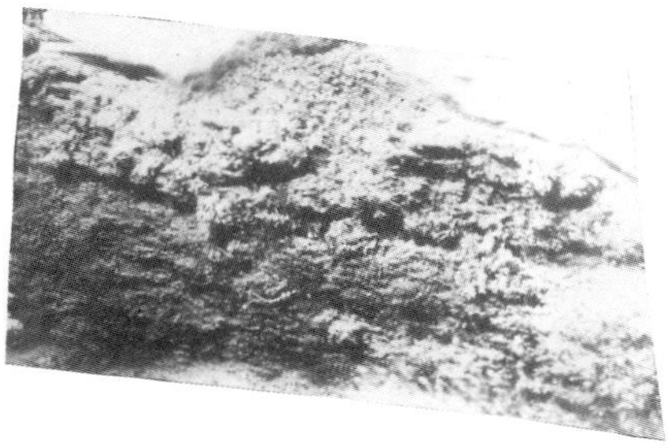

of numbers has stopped ... to delude myself into thinking that so much water has not really flowed under the bridge, this bridge upon which we stand seems so secure, but is itself not permanent.[6]

If a Freudian view of James's explanation for his unique method of numbering is taken, one might conclude that his rationalism parallels the thought patterns of a child in the narcissistic stage of development who believes that the power of his or her thoughts can affect the external world. Such propensities were not only evident in the idiosyncrasies of James's life, but also in his own understanding of the motivations behind his patronage of the arts. Further affinities can be drawn with André Breton's ideal that the 'mind' of the Surrealist painter should recapture that of the 'primitive', and with the structure of 'primitive thought' as postulated by the French anthropologist, Lévi-Strauss in *The Savage Mind*, where he states that the 'primitive' artist believes he can intervene and modify the course of events, by 'inserting supplementary links in the natural chain of causes and effects'.

This idea, as expressed by James himself, both overtly and through the anarchy of his archive, cannot be divorced either from the context of Surrealism and psychoanalysis, or from that of developmental psychology, whence its principles may have derived. Not only does it highlight one of the common denominators of Surrealism – the desire to use the interior world of the mind to shape the exterior world of reality – it also brings into play the apparent contradictions between Surrealism and psychoanalysis, to which it claimed an affinity. In psychoanalysis, it is the associations that can be drawn from the dream or unconscious mind that are important. For the Surrealists, the dream itself is the field, the canvas so to speak, which encourages the alternate and hallucinatory perspectives to which the Surrealists were so attracted.

James's archive is the archive of a Surrealist, and what is important to our understanding of Edward James the man is not only looking at the content of the material but, perhaps more importantly, trying to understand the manner in which he left it. Archival organisation is empiricism in its most extreme form: a post-Cartesian logic that assembles, assimilates, identifies, elucidates, and preserves that reality for posterity. Surrealist thinking, however, is suspicious of everything that organises and is especially suspicious of taxonomies, or iconographies of signs that label and define. The disorder is a Surrealist disorder; disorder as

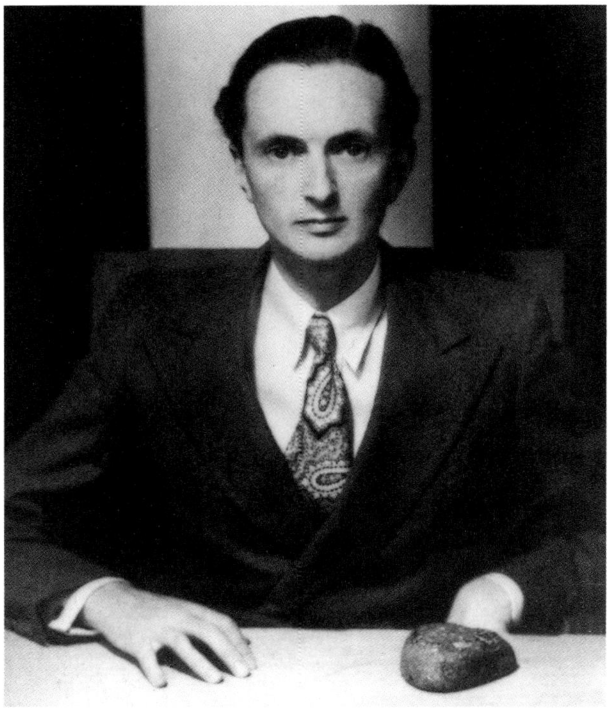

MAN RAY
Photograph of Edward James,
1937.
EJF. Catalogue no. 167.

Below:
Letter to Edward James from René Magritte, 18 May 1937, with sketch for *Pleasure Principle* (1937) and instructions for Man Ray photograph.
EJF. Catalogue no. 168.

the means of exploration, and as the negation of organisation. Its deconstruction can be read in several ways.

By one reading, the deconstruction or disorganisation of James's material can be seen as a catalyst for psychological regression, where understanding and organisation is achieved only by first regressing to an earlier stage. The archivist, presented with a chaos of

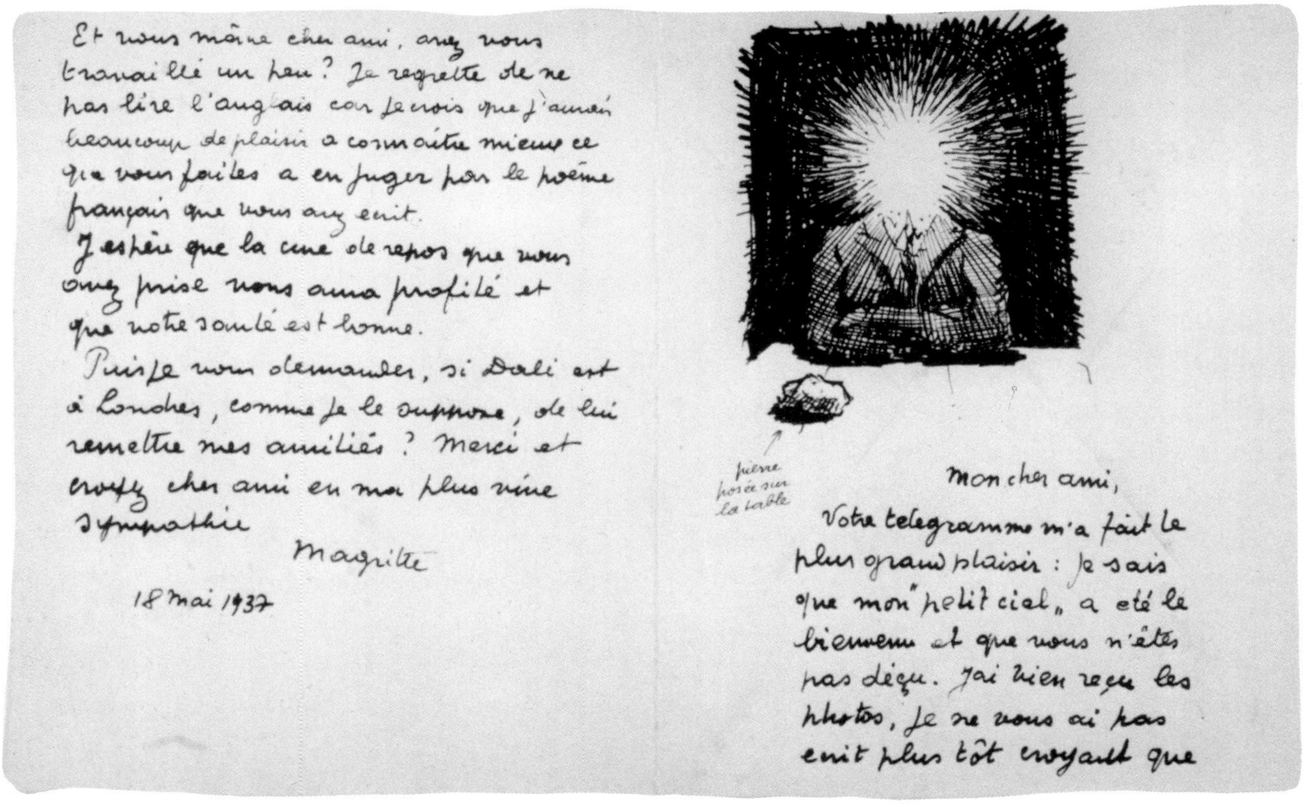

Et vous même cher ami, avez vous travaillé un peu? Je regrette de ne pas lire l'anglais car je crois que j'aurais beaucoup de plaisir à connaître mieux ce que vous faites à en juger par le poème français que vous avez écrit.
J'espère que la cure de repos que vous avez prise vous aura profité et que votre santé est bonne.
Puis-je vous demander, si Dali est à Londres, comme je le suppose, de lui remettre mes amitiés? Merci et croyez cher ami en ma plus vive sympathie

Magritte

18 mai 1937

pierre posée sur la table

Mon cher ami,
Votre telegramme m'a fait le plus grand plaisir : je sais que mon "petit ciel" a été le bienvenu et que vous n'êtes pas déçu. J'ai bien reçu les photos, je ne vous ai pas écrit plus tôt croyant que

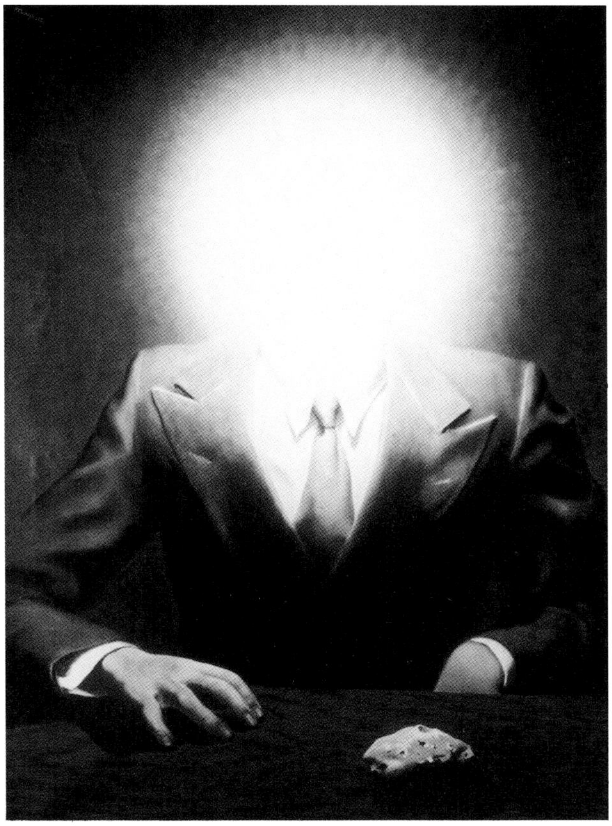

RENÉ MAGRITTE
Pleasure Principle
1937, oil on canvas
73 x 54cm.
Sotheby's, 28 June 1978.

dislocated signs, explores the nature of signification itself by going through various stages of development in the pursuit of elucidation; a process, in a sense, of development towards 'adult' understanding. By another reading, James's archive is suggestive of a process of reduction, which is at once innocent and at the same time shows signs of sadistic, violent and self-mutilating behaviour. The tearing apart and scattering of his life through the fragmentation of the Archive, can be read as a ritual sacrifice to society, an act of self-mutilation with James as both sacrificer and victim.

But perhaps the strongest reading of James's behaviour, is one that brings out its ludic character: his desire to use games in order to stimulate the unconscious mind. In a letter to Leonora Carrington, James describes a game he wanted to devise which, in its orientation, confronts the issues common to the Surrealists: chance, reduction, process, imagination and reconstruction:

> *My poem ... is an incantation written for my godson, Plutarcito [Gastelum] ... to go with a piñata* [7] *which I intend to have made for his next Christmas ... The idea of the piñata is to teach him and his sisters to read – the words will tumble out of the piñata when it is struck as though they were sweets, toffee, candy, dulces. I shall have a hundred words cut out and pasted on small blocks of wood. The verbs will be printed in scarlet, the nouns in green (no the other way round is preferable – for verbs grow and should therefore be green: nouns are more static, but more dominant). The pronouns shall be printed in blue: the adjectives in yellow and the conjunctions in mauve. I will start by including all of the words of my poem translated into Spanish, the other words, to complete the one hundred shall be all essential Spanish words. Don't you think that this is a good gimmick to give small children a taste for learning to read? Each word will thus be a small treasure for them.*[8]

To some degree, the piecing together of James's archive can be seen as a similar sort of game: a game whose rules are undisclosed, in which the hundreds of suitcases, trunks and boxes become the gameboard and the fragments of correspondence are the pieces – small treasures cast at random in an act of play. This forces the archivist, robbed of the formal language of conventional

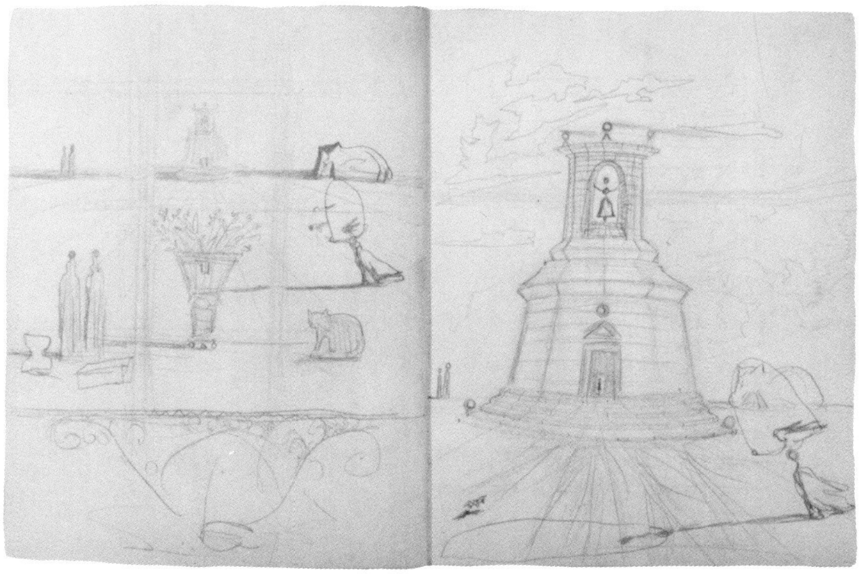

SALVADOR DALÍ
Sketchbook with pencil sketch for *Girl Skipping Rope*, c.1936.
EJF. Catalogue no. 173.

taxonomy, to move from the condition of observer to that of active participant in order to complete what has now become a creative process aimed at the restructuring of meaning; the archivist must devise a set of rules framed by his or her own view of reality. Chance is a factor, as is surprise, for as the archivist carefully unwraps each layer of tissue paper, packets of sugar, or sometimes drawings by Dalí or Magritte, tumble at random from their shrouds.

In his archive James forces a reordering of the visible world through a revision of objective form, an affinity he shared with both Dalí and Magritte. Although it cannot be proved conclusively that the disorder was intentional, it is interesting that James left provision in his will for the organisation of the material, which he proclaimed would 'burst forth upon an astonished world'[9]. By its very nature, James's archive encourages active participation and endless interpretation and, on the face of it, appears to be a meticulously and purposefully constructed psychosis.

Whilst the French Surrealists, led by André Breton, sought to bring together the worlds of dream and reality, James shared more of an affinity with Dalí and his paranoiac-critical method, which sought actively to change the world and society through a form of confrontation and deconstruction. With James, as with Dalí, reality is reconstructed by taking the given, the apparently logical, and reconstructing it in terms of an imposed, paranoiac order. Whether intentionally disordered or not, his archive remains one on which the imagination can act. In this very concrete sense, James surrealised not only his life, but the traces of it that he left behind, and even the empirical arena of the archive became Surreal.

> *... If I'm a Surrealist, it's not because I got linked with a movement ... You see, long before the Surrealist movement, there were people, like Lewis Carroll, who were Surrealists. A great number of people are Surrealists without ever having heard of the movement, but it is people who are close to their subconscious. The world is not completely logical all the time. They make the illogical logical, and they make it more vivid than life, in the way that dreams can sometimes be more vivid than actuality.*[10]

EDWARD JAMES AND LES BALLETS 1933

STELLA BEDDOE

In February 1933, Edward James attended a rehearsal in Paris of the newly formed dance company, Les Ballets 1933, and was captivated by what he saw. So inspired was he that he needed little persuasion to agree to sponsor a short season of performances in Paris and London. Thus, he embarked on what was arguably one of his most important acts of artistic patronage and certainly his most ambitious.

The group had gathered around Boris Kochno, secretary and scenarist to Sergei Diaghilev (who had died in 1929), and George Balanchine, the choreographer, both late of the Ballets Russes. Their ideas had proved too progressive for Colonel de Basil who had formed the Ballets Russes de Monte Carlo, and who preferred to stage the popular, early Diaghilev ballets by Fokine and Massine. Fortunately the gifted young principals, Tamara Toumanova, Roman Jasinski and Lucienne Kylberg, declined to renew their contracts with de Basil in order to be free to work with Balanchine, who plucked more dancers from Olga Preobrajenskaya's studio. Artists of the calibre of Christian Bérard and André Derain were cultivated by Kochno to design productions for which leading composers Darius Milhaud and Henri Sauguet would create music. However, as yet there were no funds to realise these ambitions.[1]

James had been interested in commissioning a ballet since 1931 when he produced a scenario in the form of a play called *Laengselia*, based on Hans Christian Andersen's story, *The Little Mermaid*.[2] His inclusion of a chorus and mezzo-soprano soloist looked forward to the use of voices in *Mozartiana* and *The Seven Deadly Sins*, two of the works staged by Les Ballets in 1933. He asked his friend, the artist José María Sert to design *Laengselia* and intended to invite Ravel or Stravinsky to compose the music but Sert persuaded him to approach the French composer Georges Auric instead. James paid an advance to each of them but neither designs nor music emerged and the commission foundered.

James's interest led to a meeting with Charles and Marie-Laure, Vicomte and Vicomtesse de Noailles. Leading patrons of the arts in Paris, they had bought paintings from Braque and Picasso before Cubism became fashionable and in 1932, they commissioned Salvador Dalí to paint a portrait of Marie-Laure, which impressed James when he visited them. They were early supporters of Jean Cocteau and helped fund Buñuel's seminal Surrealist films, *Un Chien Andalou* and *L'Age d'Or*. They also championed avant-garde musicians and composers and were understandably intrigued by Kochno and Balanchine's new ballet project, particularly since Christian Bérard already belonged to their circle of artists.[3]

Marie-Laure and the couturière Coco Chanel accompanied James to the rehearsal of *Mozartiana* (designed by Bérard and danced to arrangements of Mozart by Tchaikovsky) and *Les Songes*, written by Darius Milhaud. André Derain had already undertaken to design *Les Songes* and *Fastes*, with music by Sauguet. There was a notional plan that the cost of creating the ballets and presenting them for one season would be borne by four potential patrons, but although the Vicomtesse contributed her share, Chanel and Lady Juliet Duff backed out when James agreed to fund the production costs, a bill that would amount to some £100,000. His motivations have been debated: whether he embraced the project simply to win back the affections of his estranged wife, Tilly Losch, by using the company as a showcase for her dancing talents, or whether, as a contemporary reviewer noted, he saw himself as an English Diaghilev, is uncertain. In any event, John Lowe regards his financial backing as the wisest investment he ever made, providing the dance genius George Balanchine with the means to develop his talents and those of the next generation of world-class dancers.[4] Les Ballets 1933 marked a turning point in ballet history.

It was agreed that two new ballets would be created for Tilly, for whom Balanchine had already choreographed a dance number in C.B. Cochran's 1929 revue, *Wake Up and Dream*. He was aware that she lacked classical training but she was an expressive dancer with a magnetic stage presence. The problems resulting from her joining a company that already had, in the 14-year-old Tamara Toumanova, a prima 'baby' ballerina, were only some of the many that beset the new company. In order to stage a season in London as well as Paris, James had to satisfy the stage union Equity's conditions by engaging British dancers. Four young women were selected from Marie Rambert's Ballet Club including Diana Gould, now Lady Menuhin, who later recalled how James had forgotten to secure work permits for them to dance in Paris, and how they christened their rehearsal room the 'Black Hole of Calcutta'. The fledgling impresario obviously had much to learn but threw himself wholeheartedly into the project. In Lady Menuhin's words: 'He would dart up and down the

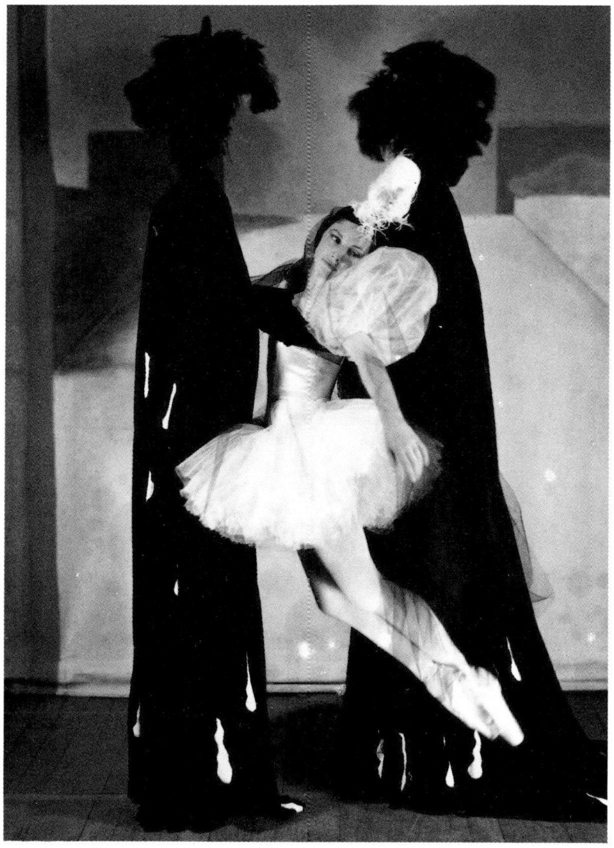

Pearl Argyle in 'The Preghiera' from *Mozartiana*, Savoy Theatre, London, 1933. EJF. Catalogue no. 89.

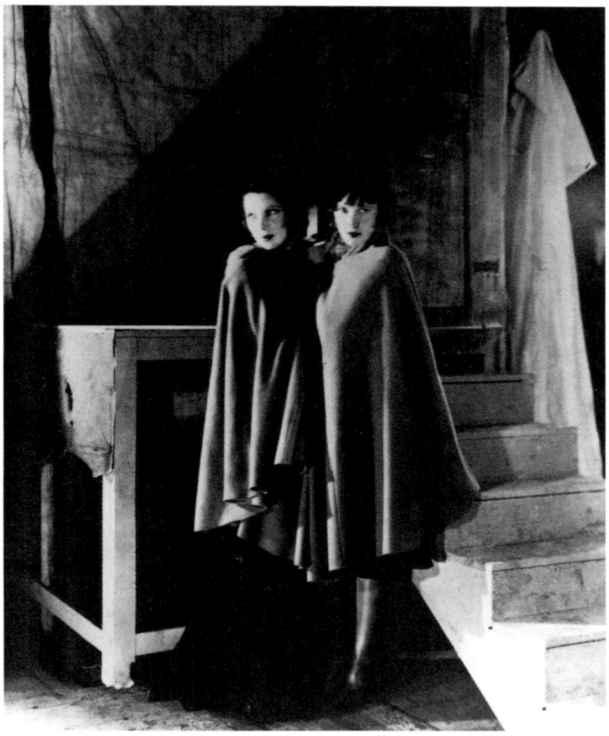

Tilly Losch and Lotte Lenya as Anna/Anna in *The Seven Deadly Sins*, 1933.
The Kurt Weill Foundation for Music, New York.

stalls to see the stage from different angles. Or if he was sitting in his seat he'd jump up and clap his hands with enthusiasm. He was in love with it all!' She believed, however, that he was ruthlessly exploited: 'Those Russians were just running away with his money!'[5] He certainly paid generous salaries to everyone, even the *corps de ballet*.

Although he had not been involved in creating *Mozartiana*, a ballet without specific narrative, composed of technically demanding solos and ensembles, James persuaded Balanchine to agree to the addition of some original Mozart songs at the beginning since it lacked an overture. He was hoping to promote a gifted baritone called Fernando Gusso whom he had discovered, but when the conductor, Maurice de Abravanel heard of the scheme he insisted that his own wife sing instead, to disastrous effect.[6]

Voice and movement were combined in the split personality of *Anna-Anna*, as *Les Sept Péchés Capitaux* was called in London. (It was conceived as *Die Sieben Todsünden* but is better known as *The Seven Deadly Sins*.) This was a daring commission, realised from one of James's ideas by Bertolt Brecht, with designs provided by his friend, Caspar Neher. The music and cabaret songs were written by Kurt Weill who, together with his wife, Lotte Lenya, had recently fled the Nazis and was attempting to establish a career in Paris. In addition to temperamental difficulties between individuals in the company, splits emerged amongst different groups: notably objections made by the Russian contingent that *The Seven Deadly Sins* was essentially a music-drama and contained too little ballet. Balanchine attempted to redress the balance. The piece was a morality tale concerning two American sisters, danced by Losch and sung by Lenya, first spied wearing a double cloak, who encounter or commit each of the sins while visiting seven cities in the United States, on their quest for work. The set comprised seven huge banners painted with Neher's cartoons, which hung from the roof above a semicircular arcade with seven paper archways, each labelled in French with the name of a sin, through which the dancers burst.

Of all the ballets, *The Seven Deadly Sins* has enjoyed the longest and most varied life and has been regularly performed ever since. At the time it met with hostility on the part of many of the dancers: Lady Menuhin recalled that 'We all hated the Brecht number ... because of the awful costumes we had to wear', and its drabness was also remarked upon by the press. Other critics were intrigued by the coexistent morality/immorality of the piece. Jean Genêt noted archly that 'Herr Weill, who is always reported an intellectual Communist, was ... a house guest of the Vicomte de Noailles and his wife, [and] took his bow and his boos for the premiere while standing in the door marked "Luxure"'.[7]

The songs were performed in German, translated into French in the programme. James collaborated with Kochno on an English translation of the libretto for the London performances but found Brecht totally intransigent as far as modifications were concerned. They clashed later when James, who had paid a generous sum for the rights to the piece, attempted to stage it in Copenhagen in 1936 and Brecht had it stopped in mid-performance.

André Derain's sketches for *Les Songes* (now in the Bibliothèque Litteraire Jacques Doucet in Paris) suggest knowledge of such Bauhaus experiments as Oskar Schlemmer's *Triadic Ballet* and his *Figural Cabinet*, both of 1922, or even Schawinsky's *The Circus*, staged in 1924.[8] His designs for the strange creatures that trouble the dreams of a famous ballerina (danced by the youthful Toumanova) show a similar interest in disguising the performers' bodies in oversized costumes, many based on geometrical structures: three women encased within a sphere, figures with schematic, cubic heads. While the more extreme designs for *Les Songes* were abandoned for practical reasons, Jasinski's Acrobat costume, covered in hoops and circular motifs suggesting springs, was realised to spectacular effect. Balanchine retained the rights to the ballet and took the costumes with him to the United States in 1934.

The designs for *Fastes*, Derain's other commission, show a change of direction for the artist. The scenario concerns the celebration of the Lupercalian festival in an ancient Etruscan town. Jane Pritchard has observed that many of the costumes derive directly from mural decorations in the Etruscan tomb of the Triclinium, reconstructed in the Louvre. The ballet itself was performed to give the impression of an animated frieze, perhaps continuing the exploration of *movement all'antica* , inspired by Greek and Roman sculpture, vase paintings and frescoes, which Nijinksy had initiated in *L'Après-midi d'un faune* in 1912. The critic of the Daily Telegraph noted that 'There is very little opportunity for dancing, although the company certainly exhibited the hectic excitement of [Sauguet's] music'.[9] The ballet was never revived after the London performances.

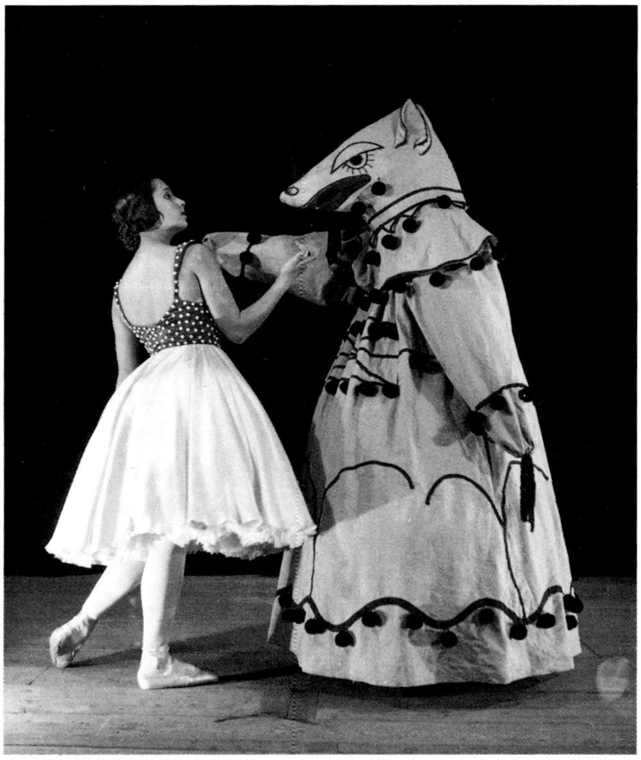

Tamara Toumanova as the Ballerina and Roman Jasinski as the Rat/Acrobat in *Les Songes*, 1933.

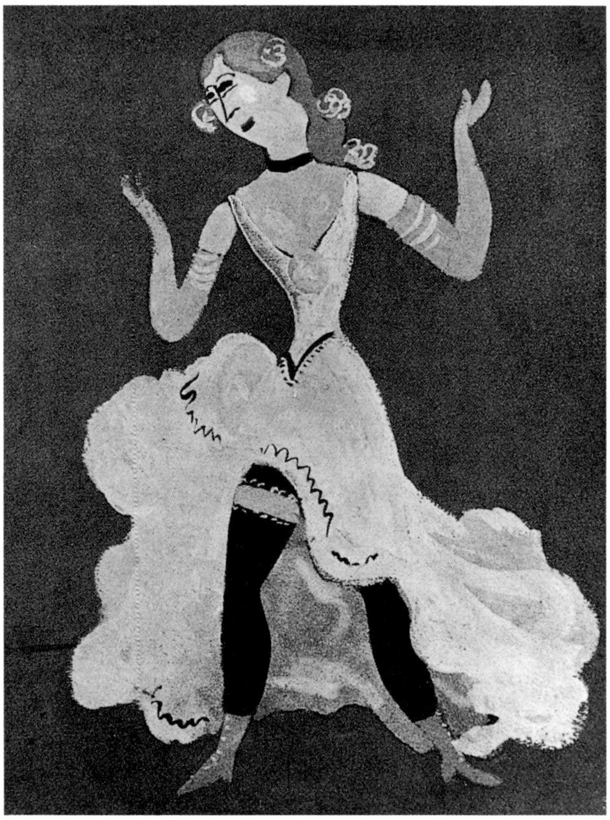

ANDRÉ DERAIN
Costume sketch for the 'Demi-Monde' from *Les Songes*, 1933, taken from the original programme, Royal Pavilion, Libraries & Museums, Brighton & Hove.

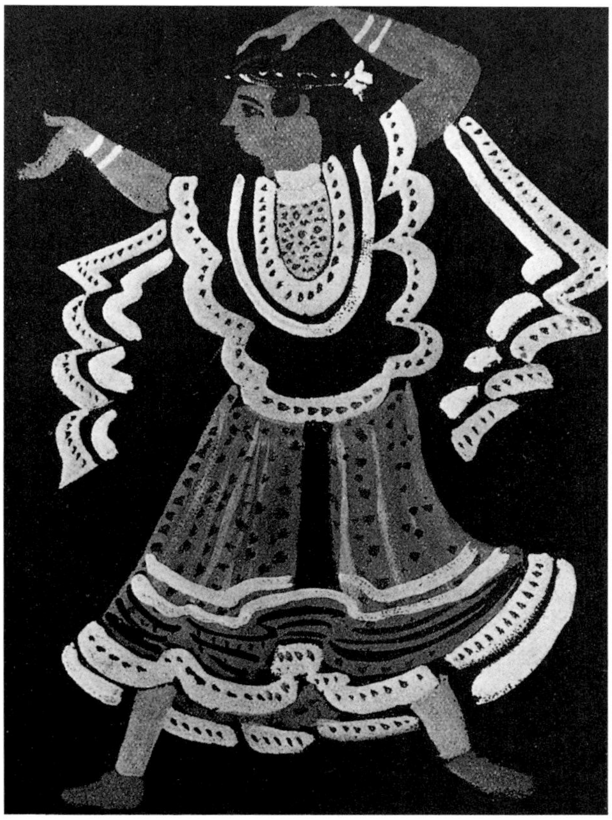

ANDRÉ DERAIN
Costume sketch for an Etruscan matron for *Fastes*, 1933, taken from the original programme, Royal Pavilion, Libraries & Museums, Brighton & Hove.

L'Errante, subtitled 'A Choreographic Fantasy', was conceived as a vehicle for Tilly Losch, and was probably the most ambitious, certainly the most abstract, but also the most successful of the six productions. Using Liszt's transcription of Schubert's 'Wanderer' sonata, orchestrated by Charles Koechlin, the ballet described the psychological wanderings of its heroine through a world of shadows, which sometimes took the form of androgynous angels, mottled phantoms of the storm, or red-clad revolutionaries. The artist Pavel Tchelitchew, who had been taken up by James after Edith Sitwell had introduced them in 1929, was responsible for the total concept, the scenario and designs, in close collaboration with Balanchine. There was no painted set; effects were created by lights and back-projection on to white muslin, and at the climax a huge cloud of damp, white silk fell from the flies, obliterating the action.

Tilly's spectacular dress (now lost) was variously described as 'a masterpiece'[10], and 'a gown of nightmare length and intractability'.[11] Made by the couturier Edward Molyneux, it was bias-cut and clinging, in deep 'salamander' green, with a fifteen foot train, which Tilly managed deftly to manoeuvre as she ran about the stage. Donald Windham declared that 'the lacquered green silk ripples behind her like waves of the sea'[12] while Edith Sitwell saw in it, 'the green of forests, the green of water'.[13]

The last of the six ballets, the least prepared and least satisfactory was *Les Valses de Beethoven*, in which the composer's little-known waltzes were orchestrated by Nicolas Nabokov. Loosely based on the mythological story of Apollo and Daphne, it featured personifications of the elements in a 'moderno-baroc' cavern or grotto, designed by another gifted member of the de Noailles circle, Emilio Terry. However, the costumes were made to a very tight schedule and appear crudely finished, falling way below the standard of the legendary Mme Karinska who had executed the majority of costumes for the other ballets. Lady Menuhin played Earth, 'in a deplorable sort of chiton in Bovril-coloured chiffon (Old Mother Manure, I called myself)'. At the last moment she was excused from having to wear a head-dress formed like a 'monstrous sort of cairn at least two-foot high and made of plaster and mud'.[14] Although advertised for the London run, the ballet was vetoed by Terry following more complaints from the dancers concerning their apparel.

The Paris season opened on 7 June at the Théâtre de Champs-Elysées. *Mozartiana*, *Les Songes* and *Les Sept Péchés Capitaux* were followed two days later by *L'Errante* and *Fastes*. The Company aimed to attract the élite of Parisian audiences who seem to have applauded the new ballets, which extended the boundaries defined by Diaghilev's Ballets Russes. So successful were they that two further performances were staged to include the only showing of *Les Valses de Beethoven* and Nicolas Nabokov's oratorio, *Job*, characteristically rescued by James when the Princesse de Polignac's soiree, at which it should have been performed, was cancelled.

Les Ballets 1933 opened at the Savoy Theatre in

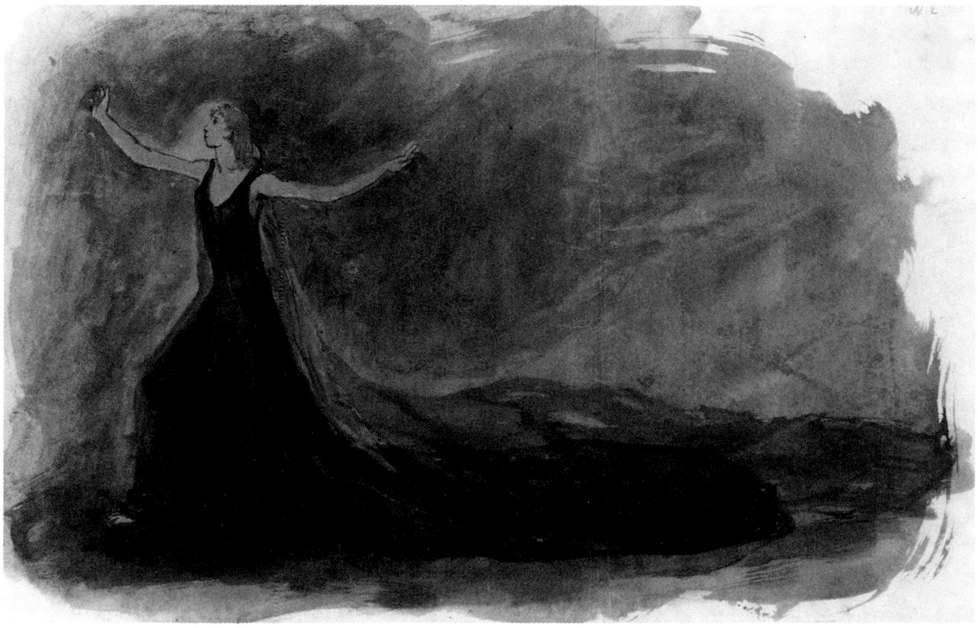

PAVEL TCHELITCHEW
Study for Tilly Losch
for *L'Errante*
1933. Mercury Gallery, London.
Catalogue no. 118.

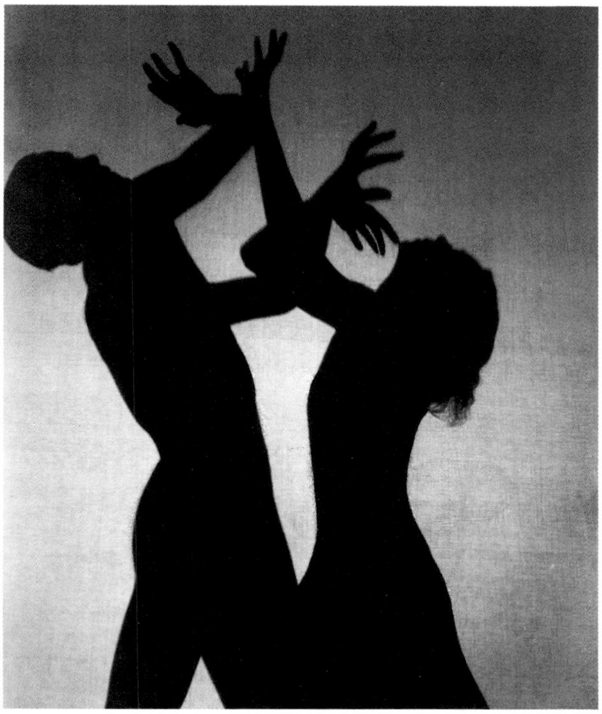

London on 28 June. Unfortunately, the British capital, which had been starved of ballet performances for many years, was overwhelmed by them in 1933. Moreover, the Ballets Russes de Monte Carlo, who had coincided with Les Ballets in Paris, were also booked for a London season at the Alhambra Theatre. In Paris their repertoire was already familiar from their previous season and they had performed on different nights from Les Ballets, but in London they posed a much more serious threat. In addition Serge Lifar was booked into the Aldwych Theatre with a small group of Russian dancers.

James worked feverishly to ensure that Les Ballets would open ahead of its rivals and bribed Lifar to break his contract with the Aldwych to perform alternately with Les Ballets at the Savoy in the final week of their season. Despite his best efforts, the project was beset

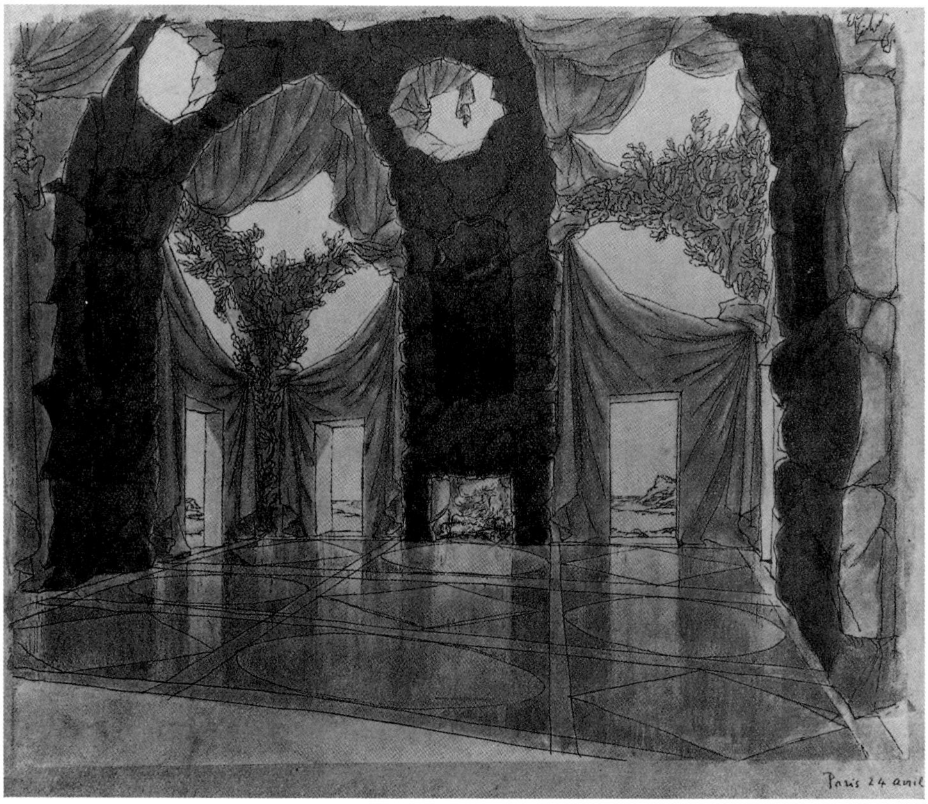

Above:
SACHA (Alexander Stuart)
Publicity photograph for *L'Errante* showing Roman Jasinski and Tilly Losch in silhouette, 1933.
EJF.

EMILIO TERRY
Set design for *Les Valses de Beethoven*, 1933, taken from the original programme, Royal Pavilion, Libraries & Museums, Brighton & Hove.

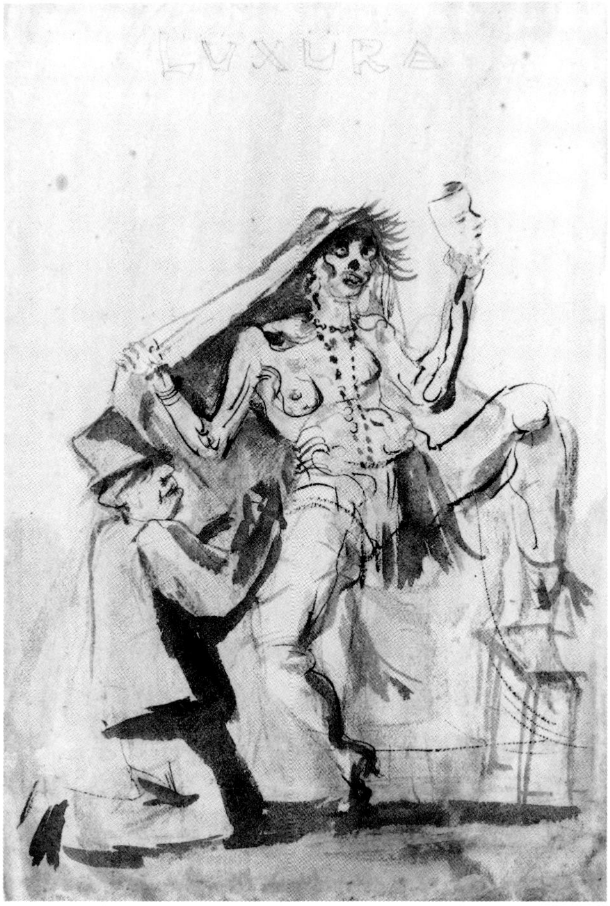

CASPAR NEHER
Design for a banner depicting Luxura [sic] (Lust) in *The Seven Deadly Sins*, 1933.
EJF. Catalogue no. 124.

with disasters. Lifar, aware of his commercial value, threw tantrums and refused to perform, precipitating a civil action brought by James in 1934. The Ballets Russes de Monte Carlo, presenting the more familiar Diaghilev repertoire to a conservative London audience, were a runaway success.

Les Ballets, however, had problems with advance publicity so that the dancers often performed to half-empty houses, a situation that James attempted to remedy by bussing a large contingent of the estate-workers from West Dean to London for the opening night. Critics were luke-warm at best; they liked *Mozartiana* but were baffled by *Anna-Anna* and *L'Errante,* which some considered 'very strange'.[15] Others were more charitable, conceding that 'as a piece of abstract form, colouring and motion, it had moments of sheer beauty'.[16] On Wednesday, 12 July, Jasinski (one of only four male dancers) was injured so that Balanchine had to step in to perform his roles. There were other technical difficulties, extensive cast changes among the dancers, and the difficult French conductor de Abravanel was replaced for the London season by Constant Lambert. Further factions had gathered around the temperamental designers Bérard and Tchelitchew, which threatened to tear the company apart. It was hardly surprising, therefore, that Balanchine, who had hitherto remained detached from the in-fighting, swiftly agreed to an offer from the American Lincoln Kirstein to move to the United States to direct a new dance school and ballet company.

As soon as the London season ended, James retired to West Dean to lick his wounds, taking with him nine of the young dancers and their chaperones. There they had a week's pampered holiday and were photographed in posed tableaux, wearing the costumes from *Fastes.*[17] James had failed to revive his marriage with Tilly, was considerably out of pocket at the end of an exhausting season, and had received very little credit and much of the blame for the lack of success in London. For a while, he still had hopes of continuing the company, retaining the rights to three of the ballets and storing the sets and costumes for four of them at West Dean. There, they languished until they were transferred to Brighton Museum in 1974.

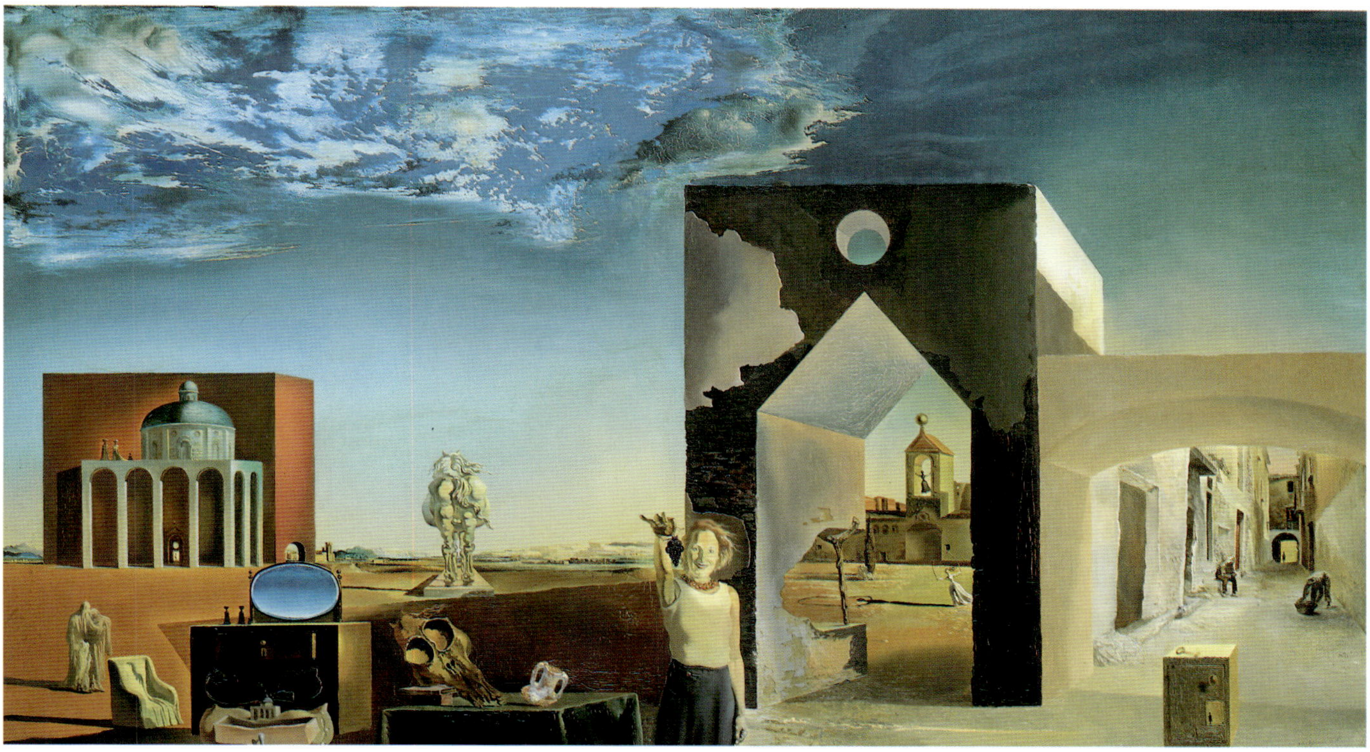

SALVADOR DALÍ
Suburb of the Paranoiac-critical Town: Afternoon on the Outskirts of European History
1936
oil on panel
46.5 x 66cm.
Christie's, London, 31 March 1981.

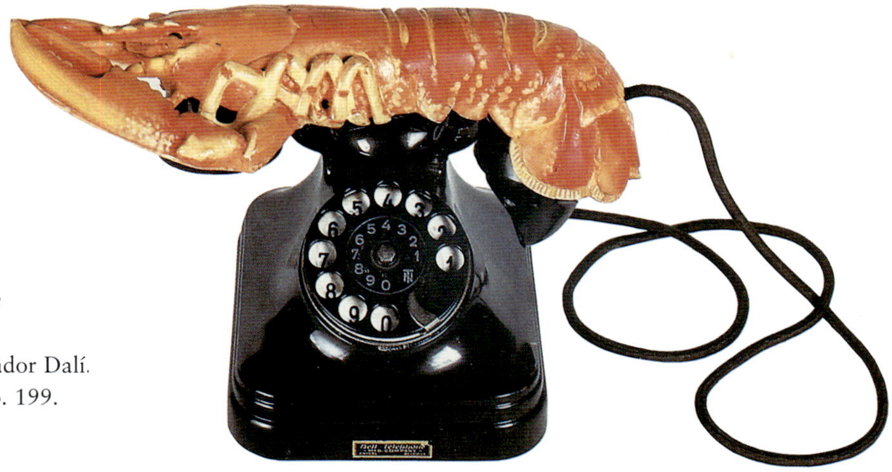

Lobster telephone
1938
Designed by Salvador Dalí.
EJF. Catalogue no. 199.

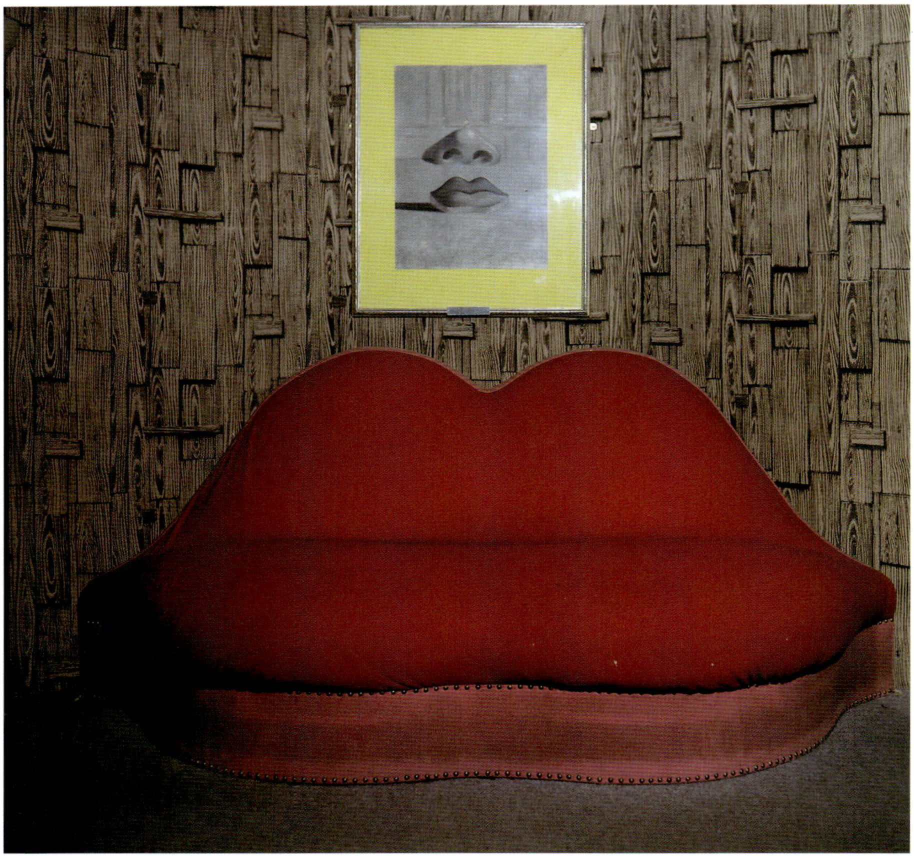

Mae West Lips Sofa
1938
Designed by Salvador Dalí with Edward James.
Royal Pavilion, Libraries & Museums, Brighton & Hove.
Shown on display at Brighton Museum & Art Gallery, 1970s, with Salvador Dalí's *The Birth of Paranoiac Furniture* (1934-35) above.
Catalogue no. 191.

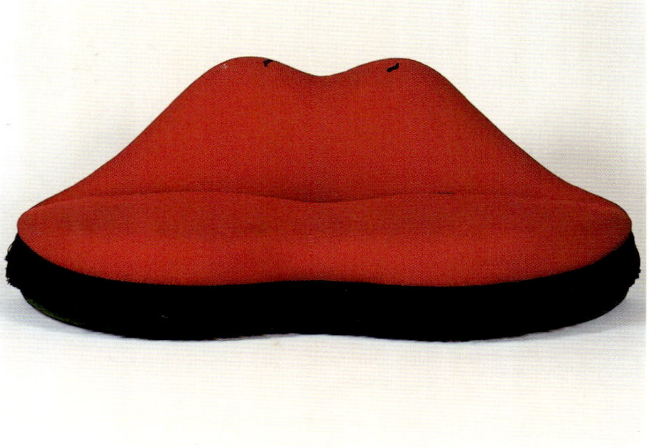

Mae West Lips Sofa
1938
Designed by Salvador Dalí, with Edward James.
EJF. Catalogue no. 192.

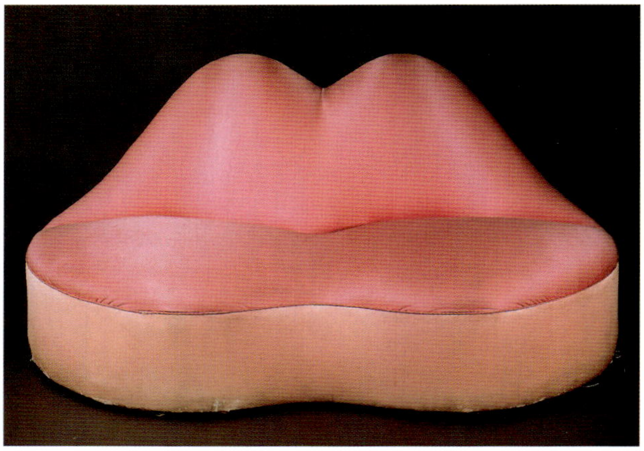

Mae West Lips Sofa
1937–8
Designed by Salvador Dalí, with Edward James.
EJF. Catalogue no. 139.

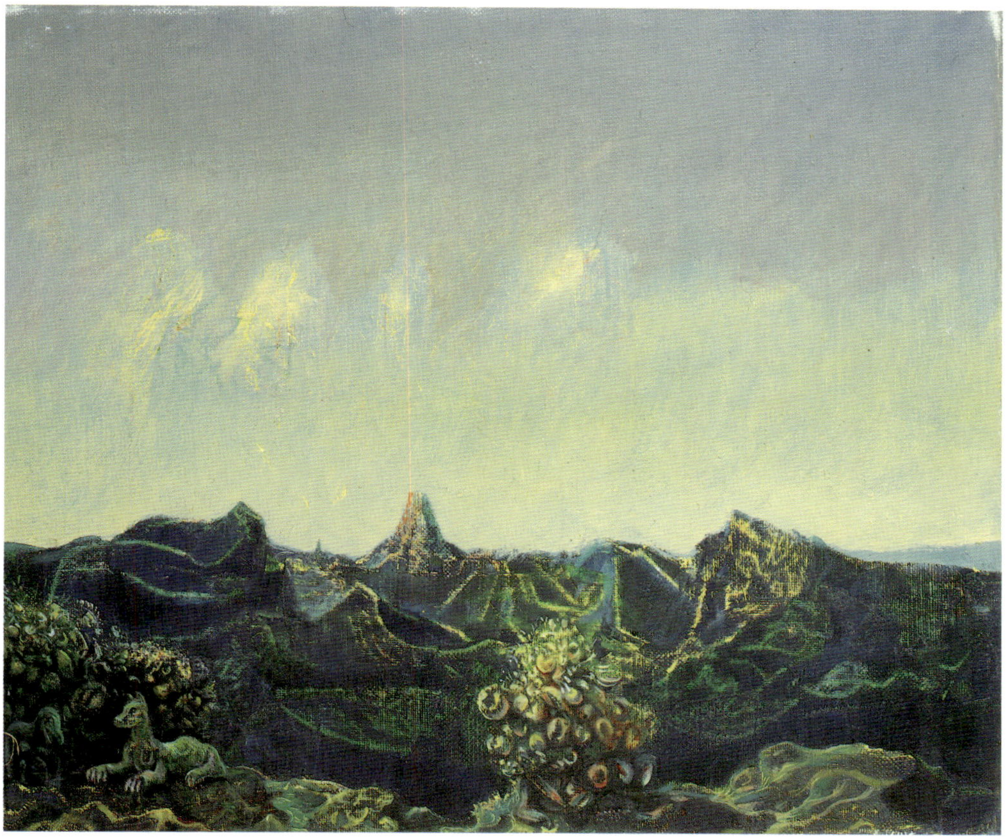

MAX ERNST
Aux Antipodes du paysage
1936
oil on canvas
36 x 45cm.
Christie's, West Dean,
5 June 1986.

SALVADOR DALÍ
Swans Reflecting Elephants
1937
oil on canvas
51 x 77.5cm.
Geneva, private collection.

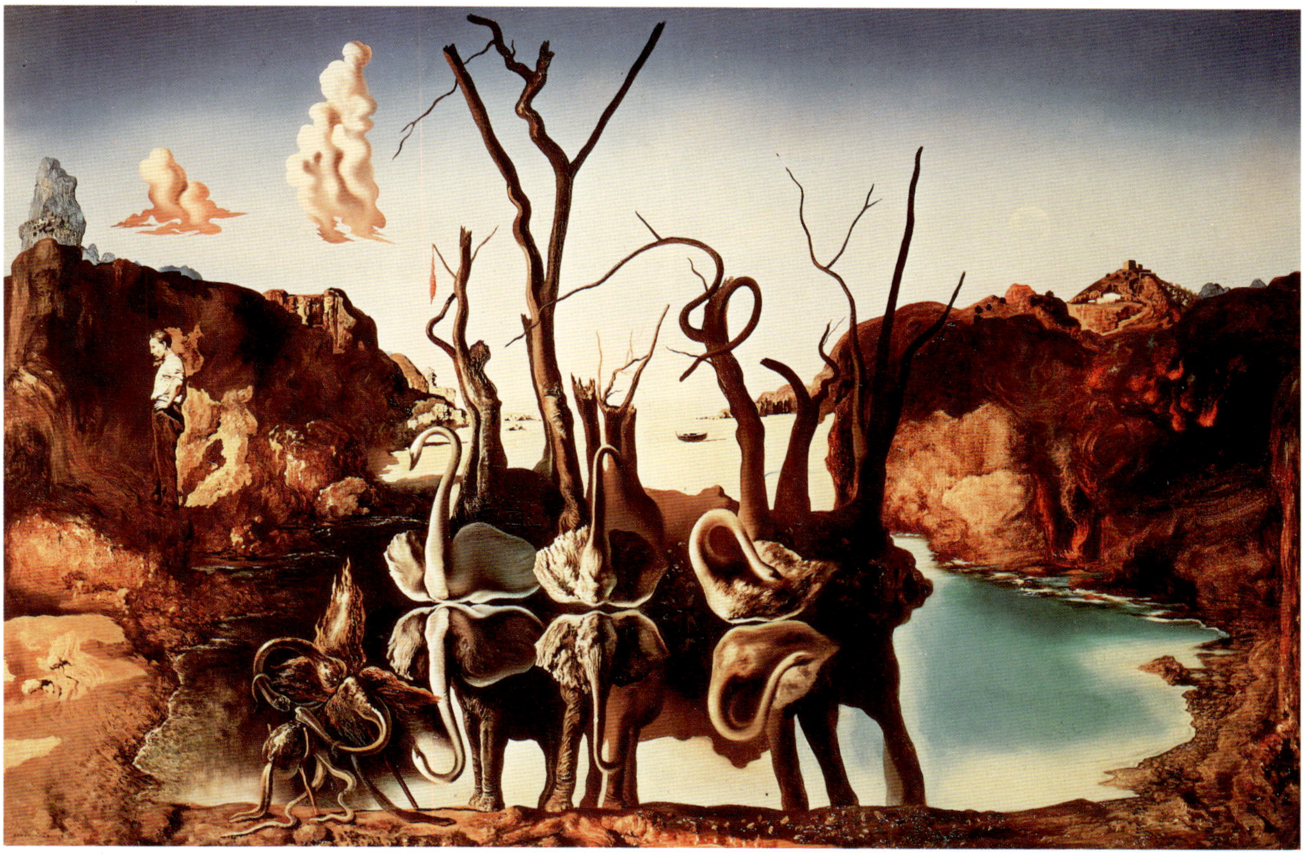

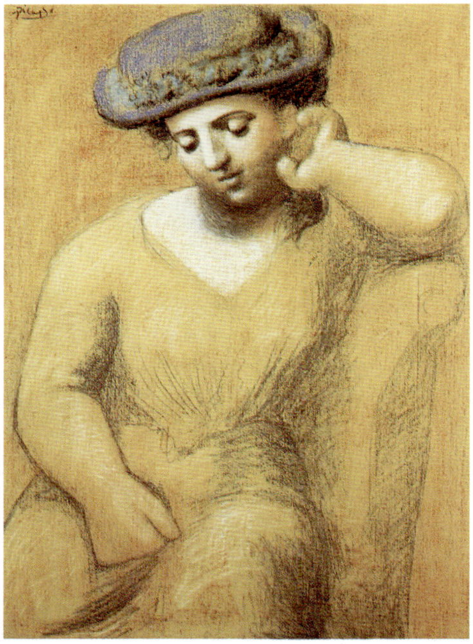

PABLO PICASSO
Femme Assise Au Chapéau
1923
Pastel on unprimed canvas
130 x 97cm.
Christie's, New York, 1984.

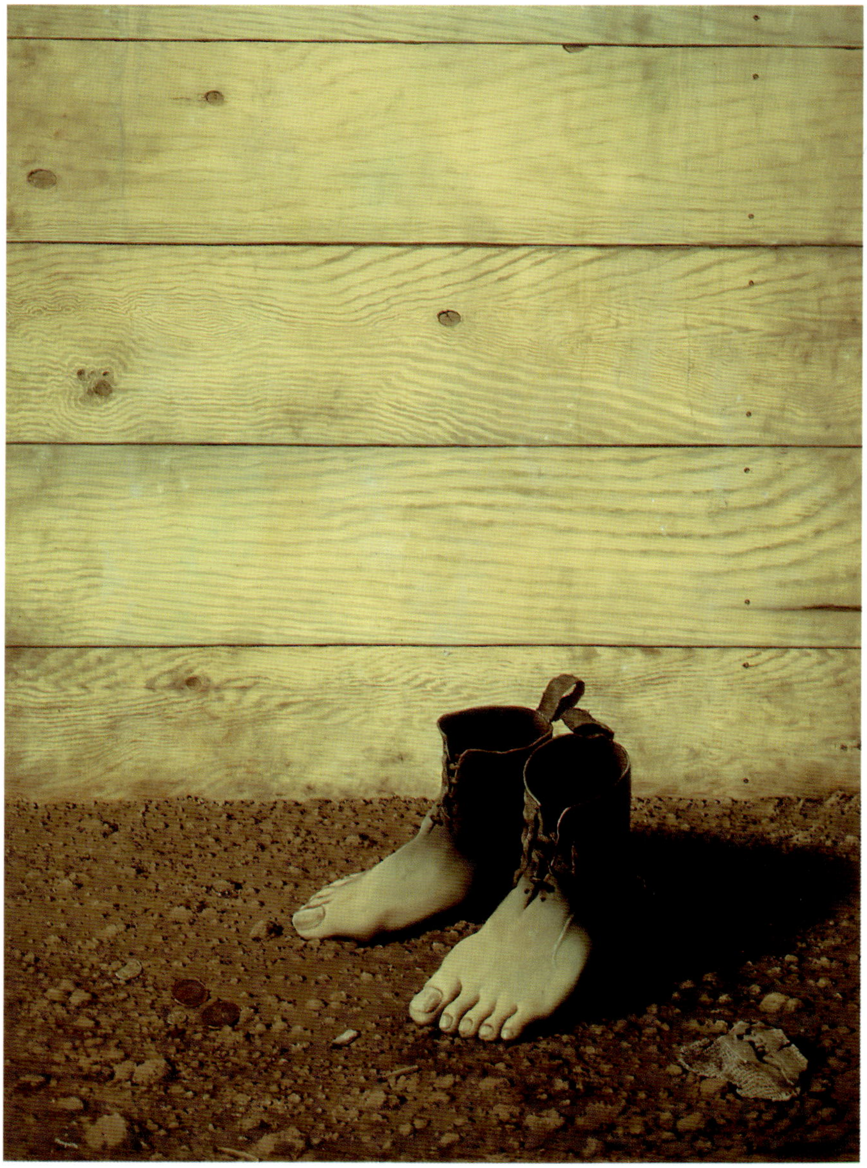

RENÉ MAGRITTE
La Modèle Rouge II
1937
oil on canvas
183 x 136cm.
Museum Boijmans Van Beuningen,
Rotterdam.

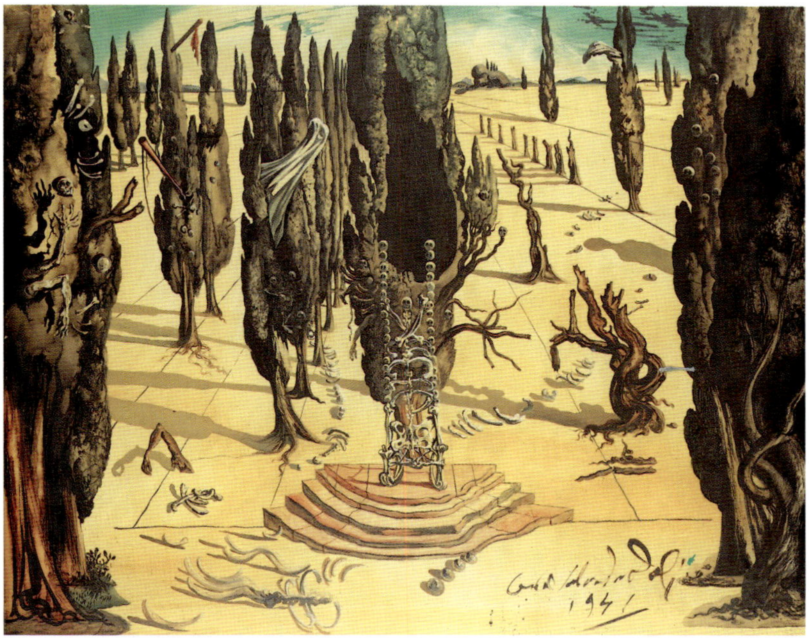

SALVADOR DALÍ
Tristan and Isolde
1941
oil on canvas
64 x 78.5cm.
Geneva, G.E.D. Nahmed.

SALVADOR DALÍ
Paranoiac Face
1935
oil on panel
19 x 23cm.
Paris, private collection.

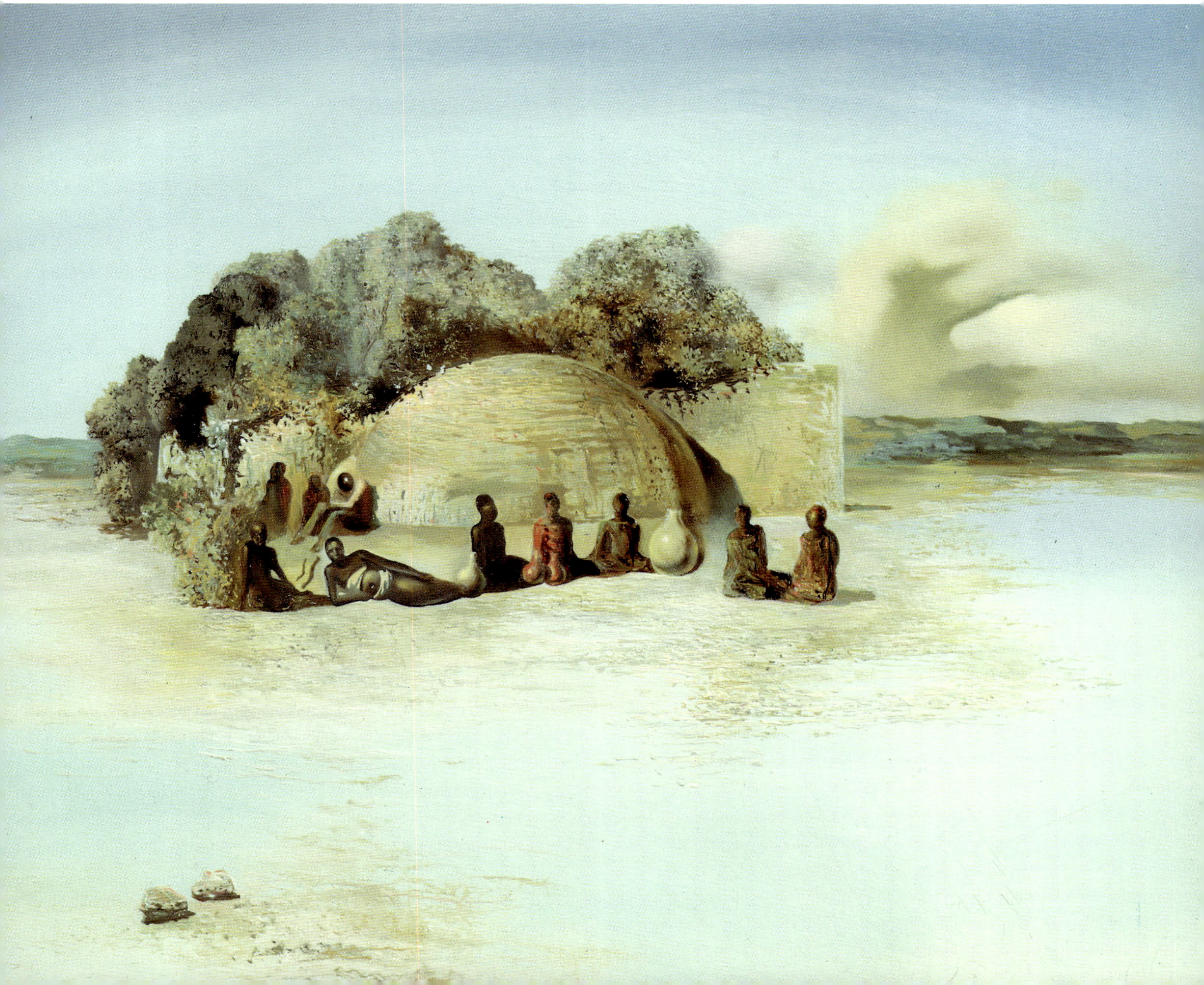

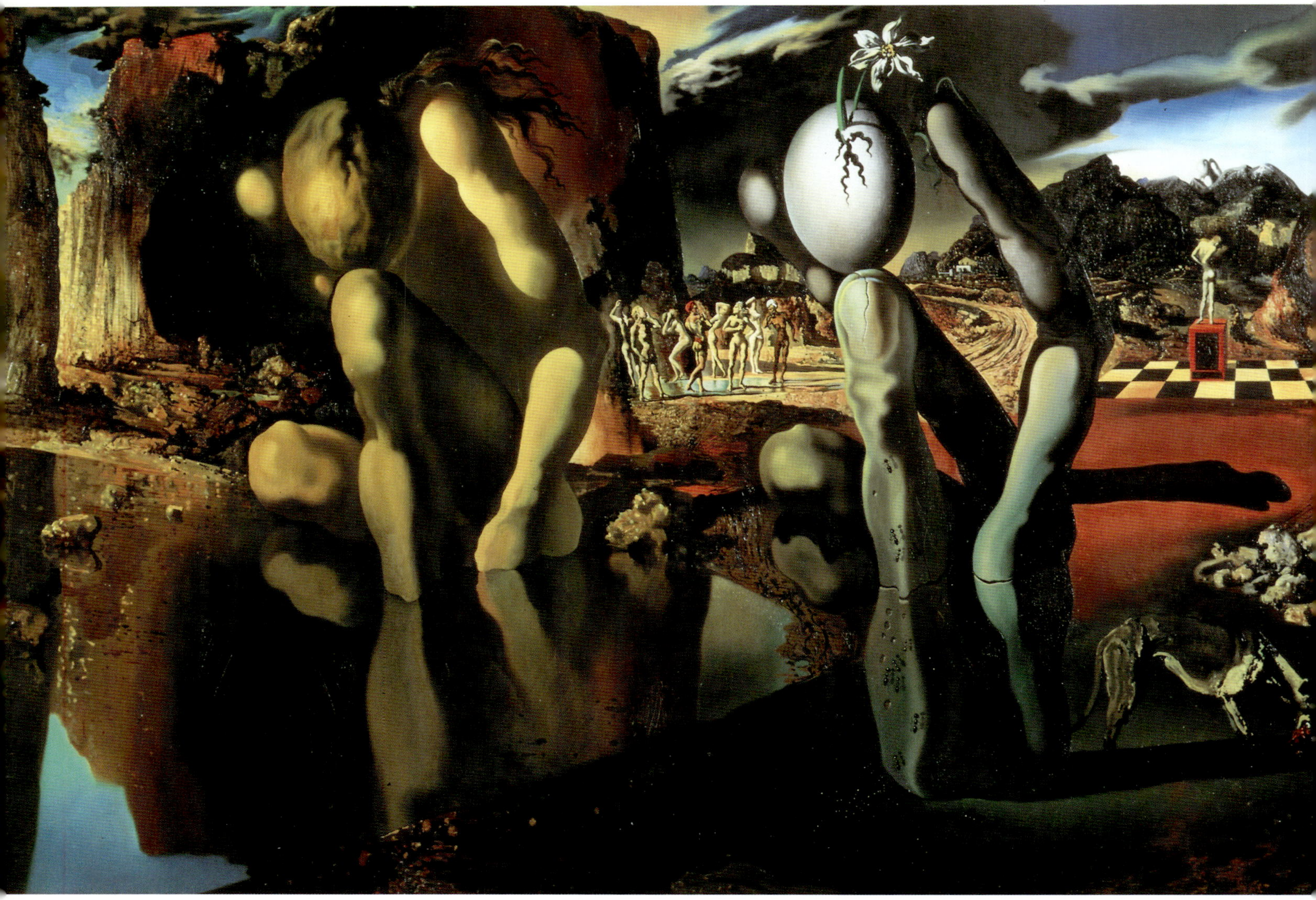

SALVADOR DALÍ
Metamorphosis of Narcissus
1937
Tate Gallery, purchased 1979.
Catalogue no. 144.

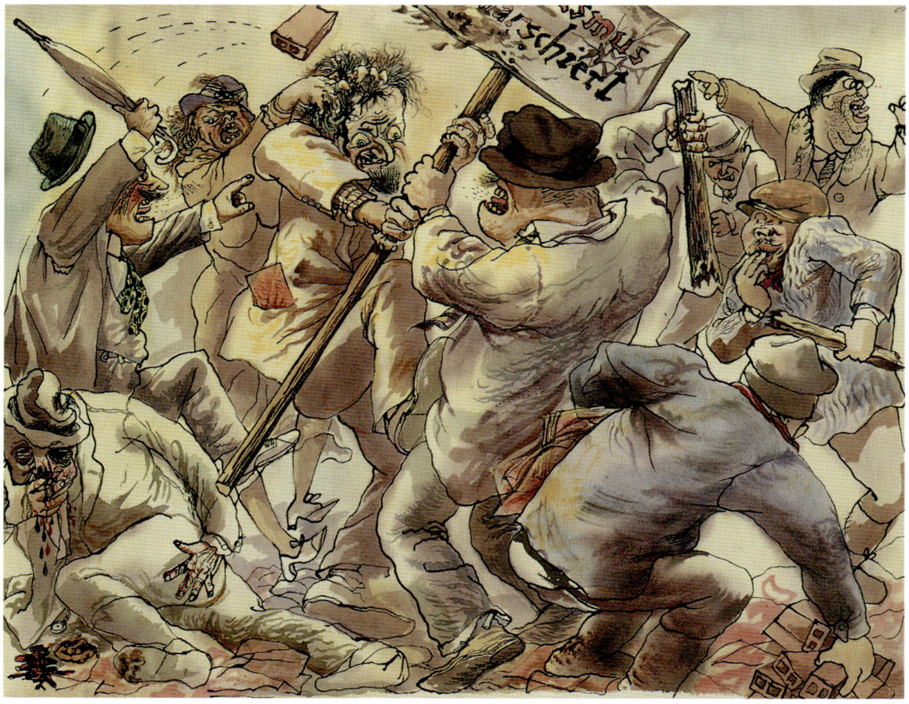

GEORGE GROSZ
Street Fighting
1934
watercolour on paper
45 x 61cm.
Christie's, West Dean,
5 June 1986.

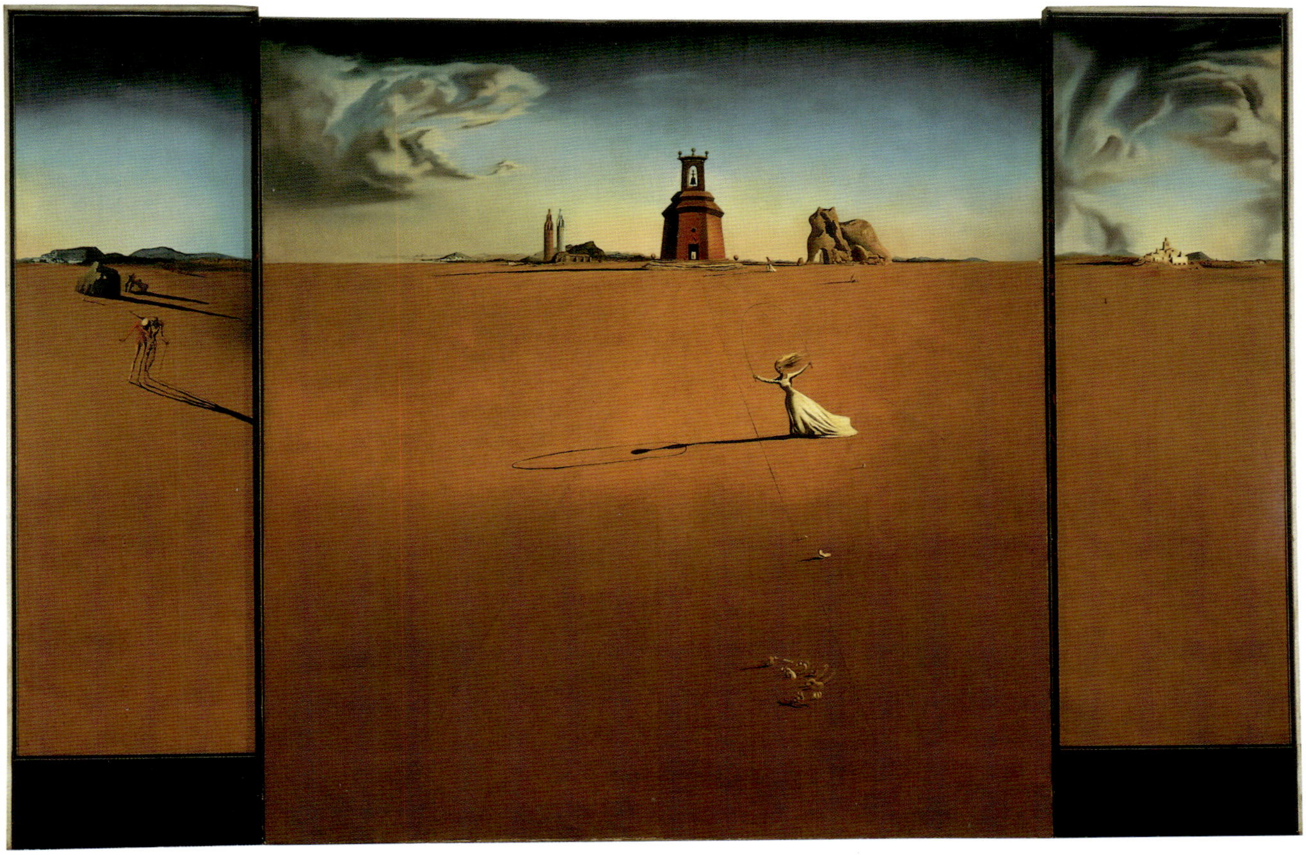

SALVADOR DALÍ
Girl Skipping Rope
c.1936
oil on panel
293 x 280 4cm; 298 x 90 x 7.2cm; 298 x 90 x 7.2cm.
Museum Boijmans Van Beuningen, Rotterdam. This triptych was formerly in the Entrance Hall at West Dean House.

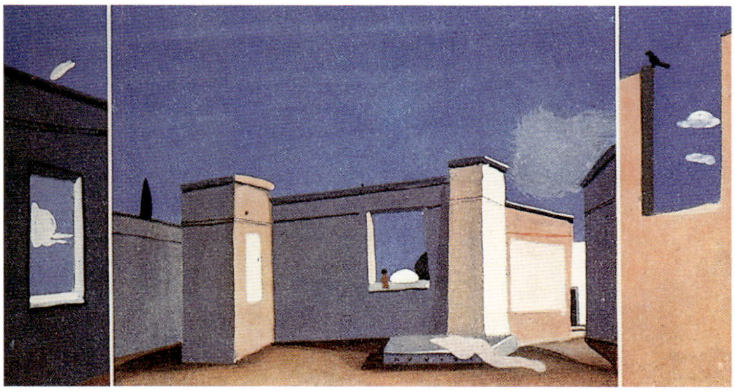

ANDRÉ DERAIN
Set design for *Fastes*, 1933, taken from the original programme.
Royal Pavilion, Libraries & Museums, Brighton & Hove.

ANDRÉ DERAIN
Body mask for a Bearded Genie from *Fastes*, 1933.
Royal Pavilion, Libraries & Museums, Brighton & Hove.
Catalogue no. 100.

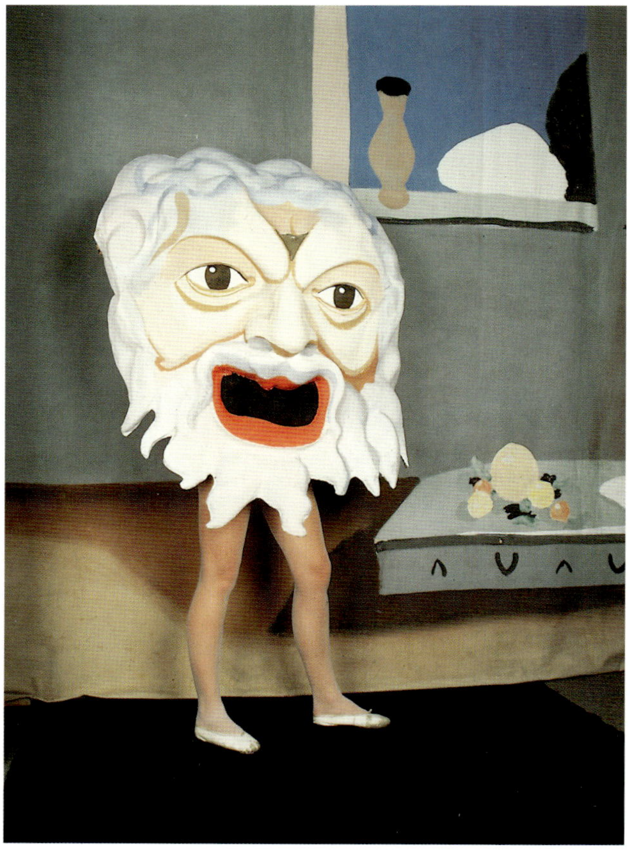

PAVEL TCHELITCHEW
Design for the stage set for the final scene from *L'Errante*, 1933, taken from the original programme.
Royal Pavilion, Libraries & Museums, Brighton & Hove.

LEONORA CARRINGTON
Portrait of the late Mrs Partridge
1947
EJF. Catalogue no. 183.

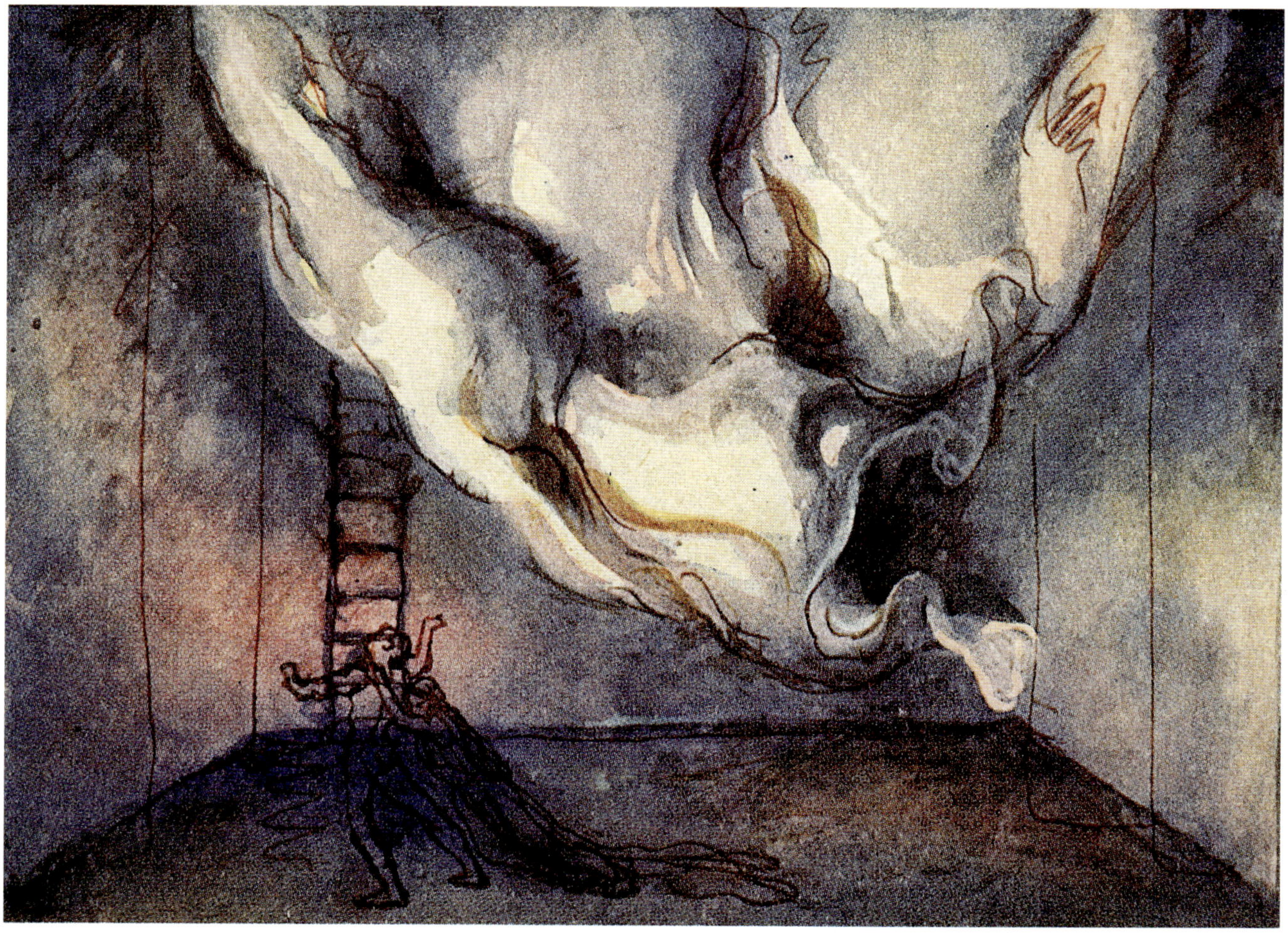

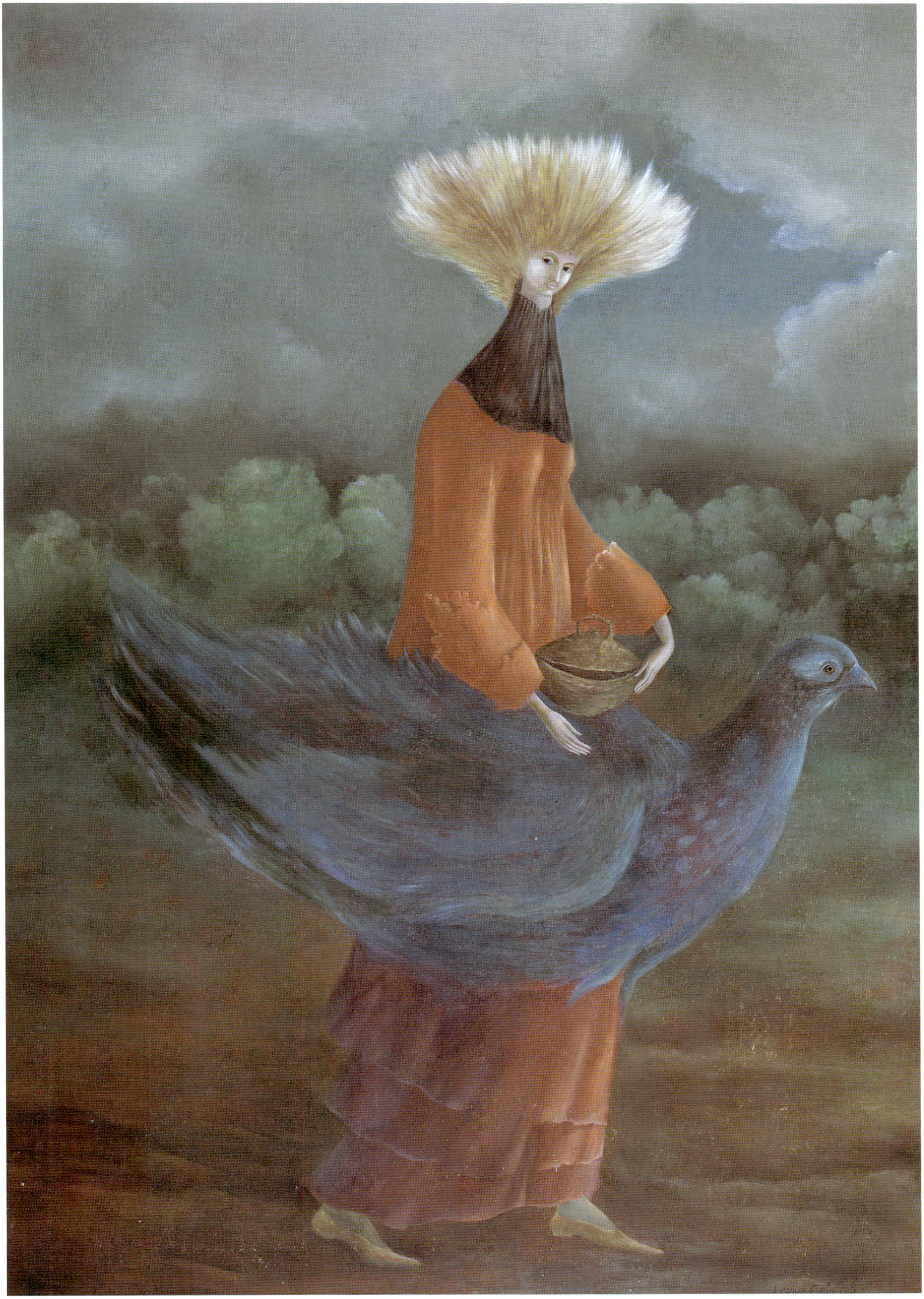

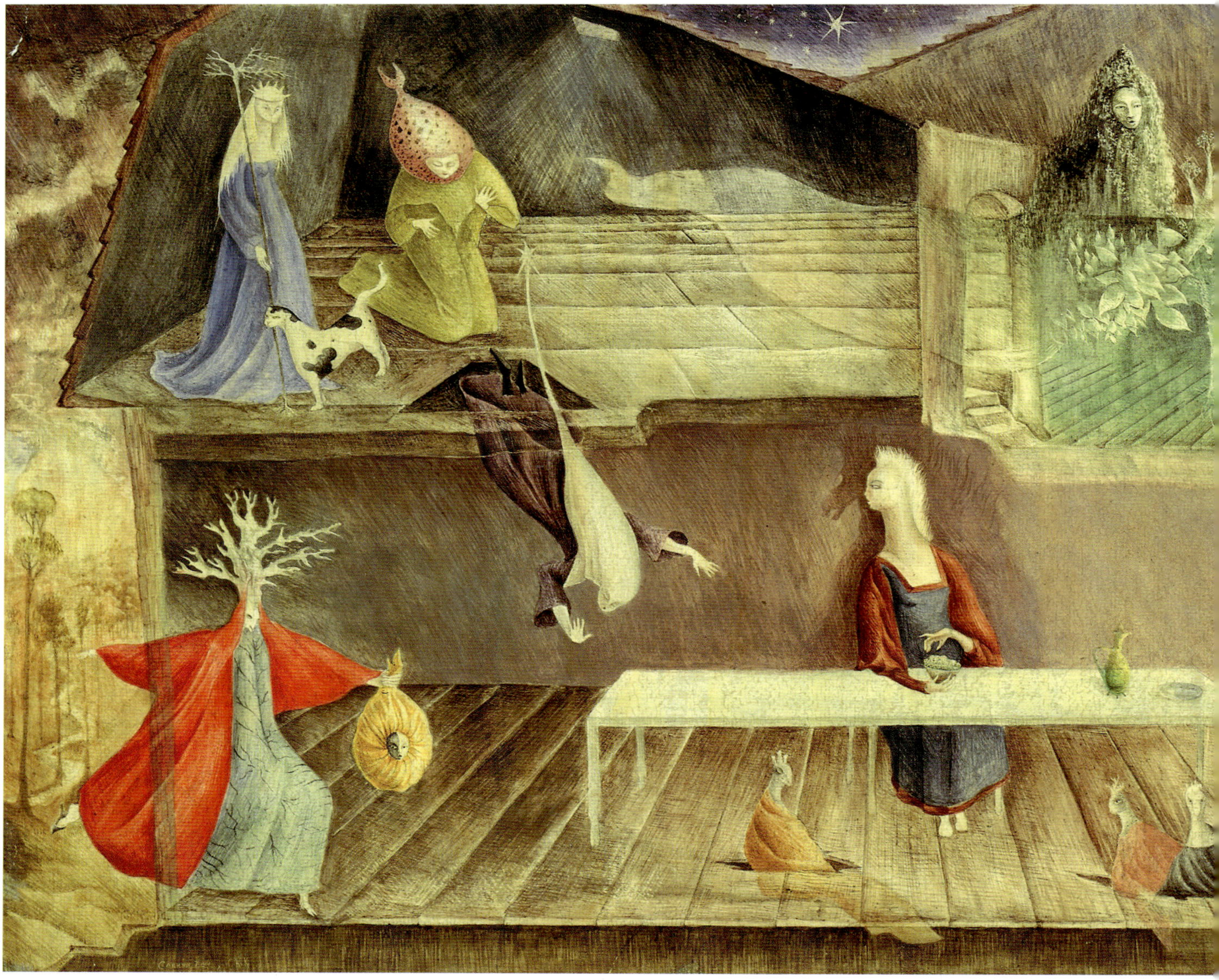

LEONORA CARRINGTON
The House Opposite
EJF. Catalogue no. 184.

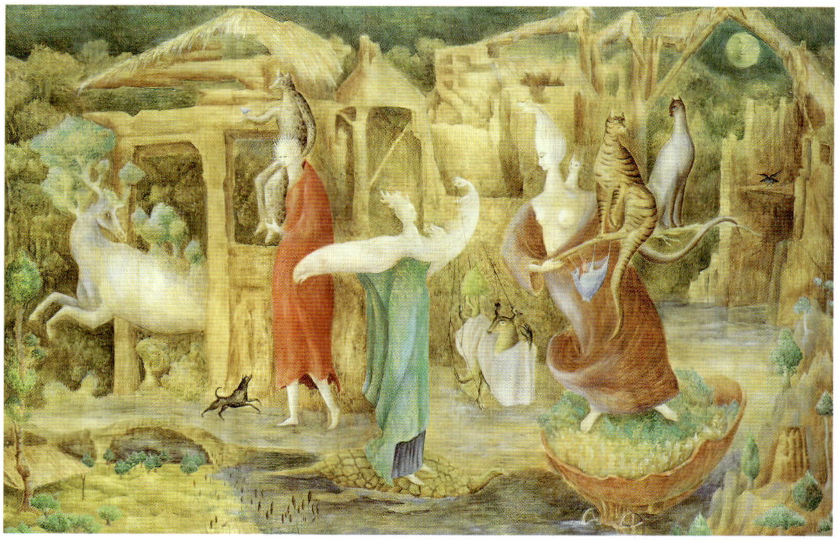

LEONORA CARRINGTON
Tuesday
1946
oil on canvas
53.5 x 82.5cm.
Christie's, New York, 6 October 1988.

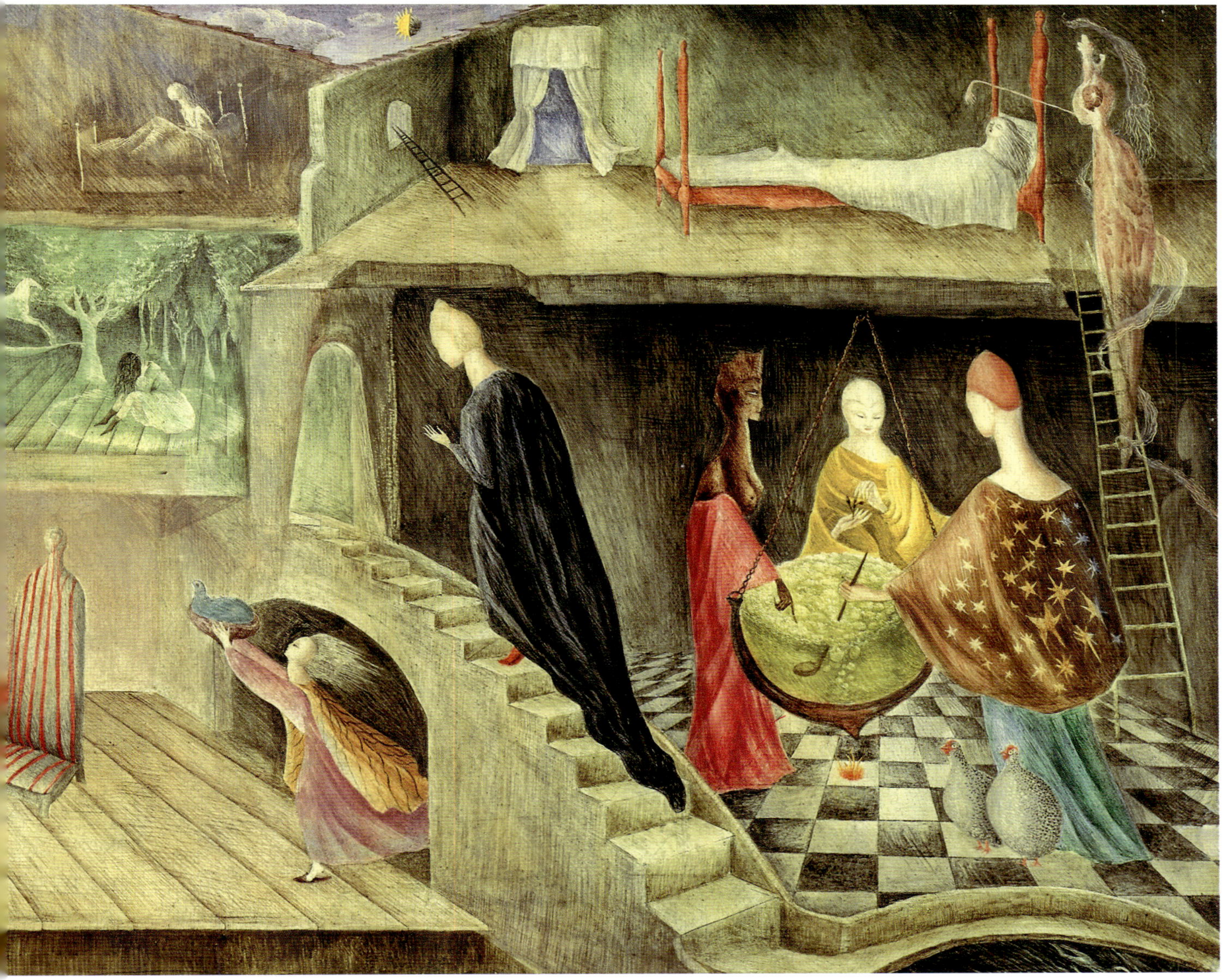

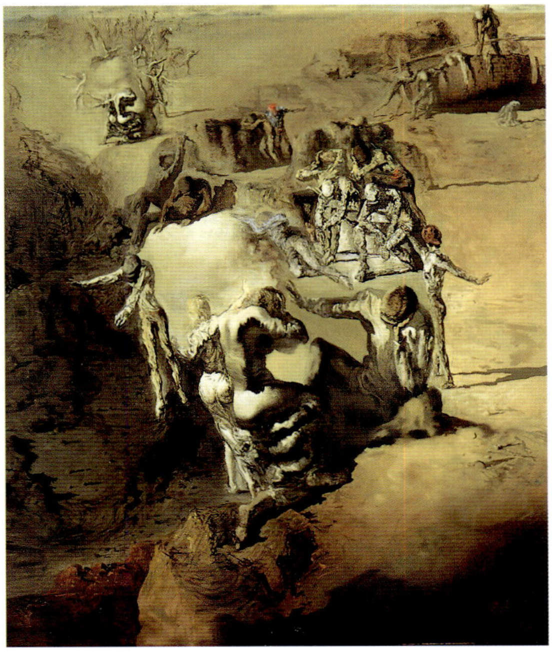

SALVADOR DALÍ
The Great Paranoiac
1936
Museum Boijmans Van Beuningen, Rotterdam.
Catalogue no. 142.

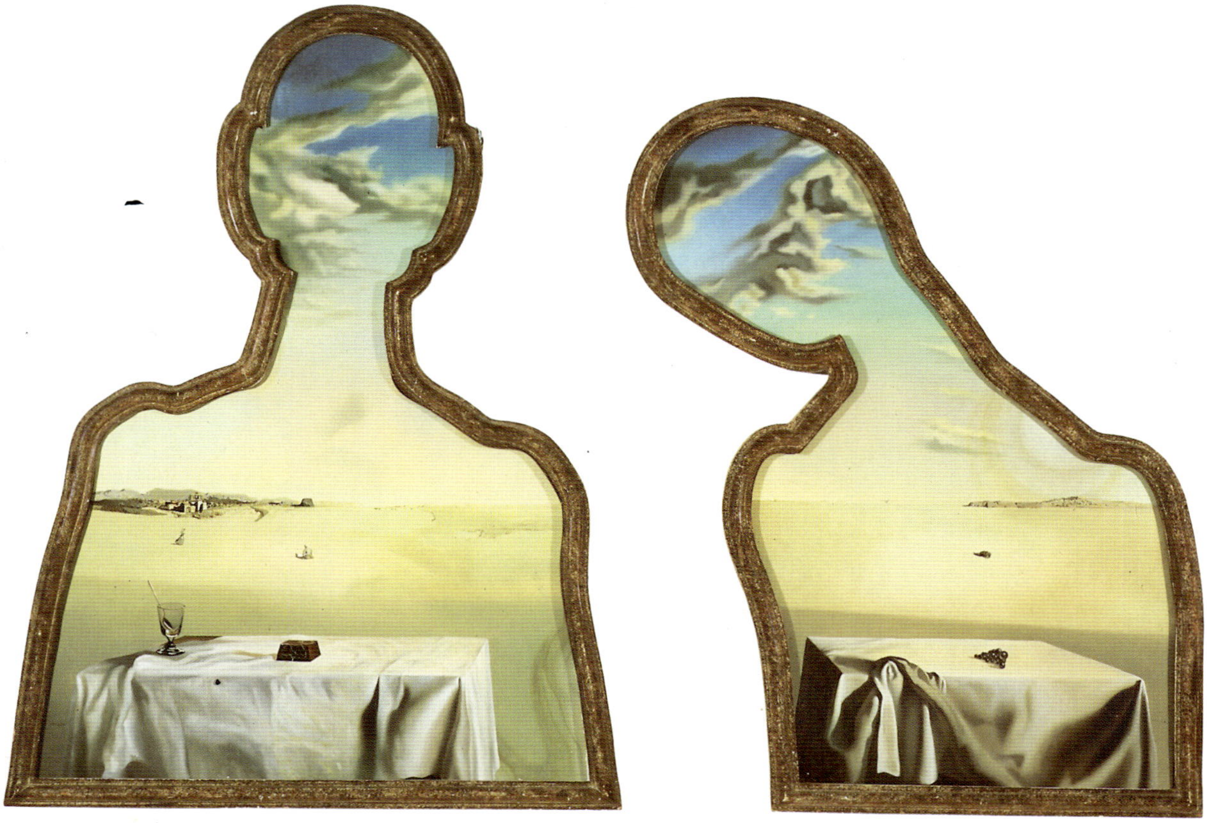

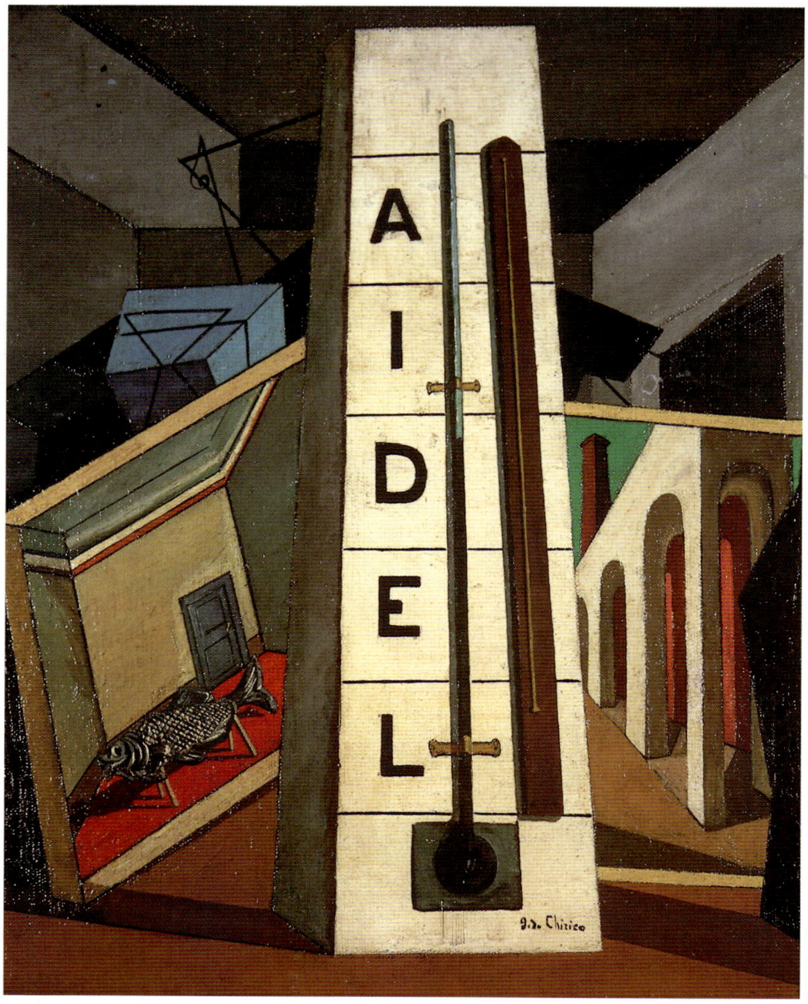

SALVADOR DALÍ
Couple with Their Heads Full of Clouds
1936
Museum Boijmans Van Beuningen, Rotterdam.
Catalogue no. 141.

GIORGIO DE CHIRICO
Dream of Tobias
oil
58 x 48cm.
Private collection.

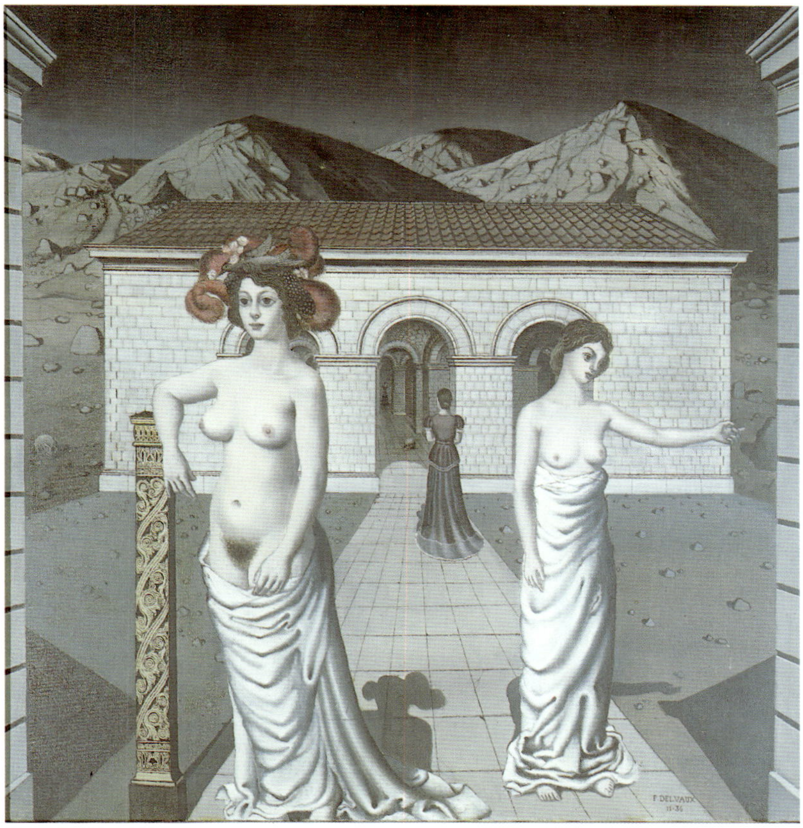

PAUL DELVAUX
Les Belles de Nuit or La Comédie du soir
1936
oil
74 x 99.5cm.
Christie's, New York, 6 October 1988.

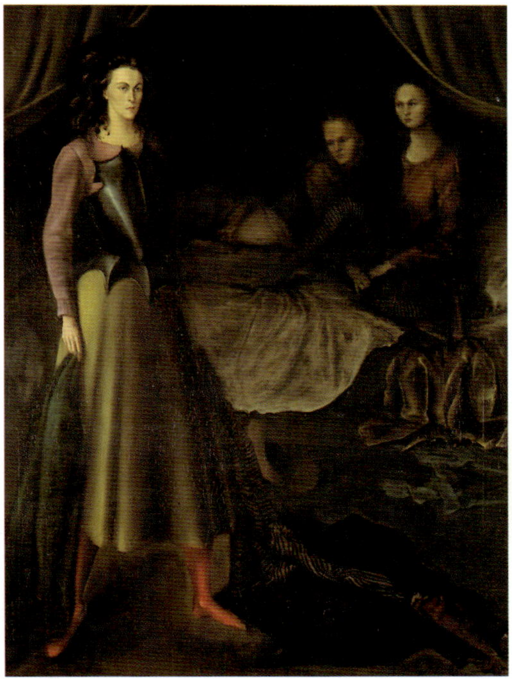

LEONOR FINI
The Alcove
EJF. Catalogue no. 186.

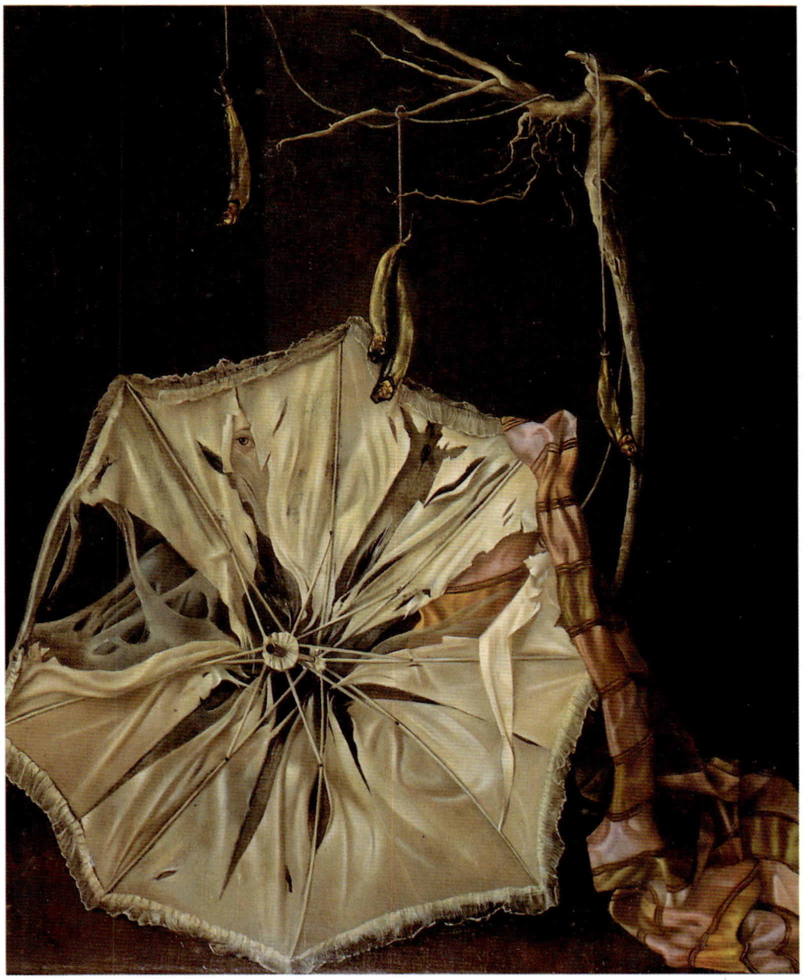

LEONOR FINI
L'Ombrelle No.1
1948
EJF. Catalogue no. 187.

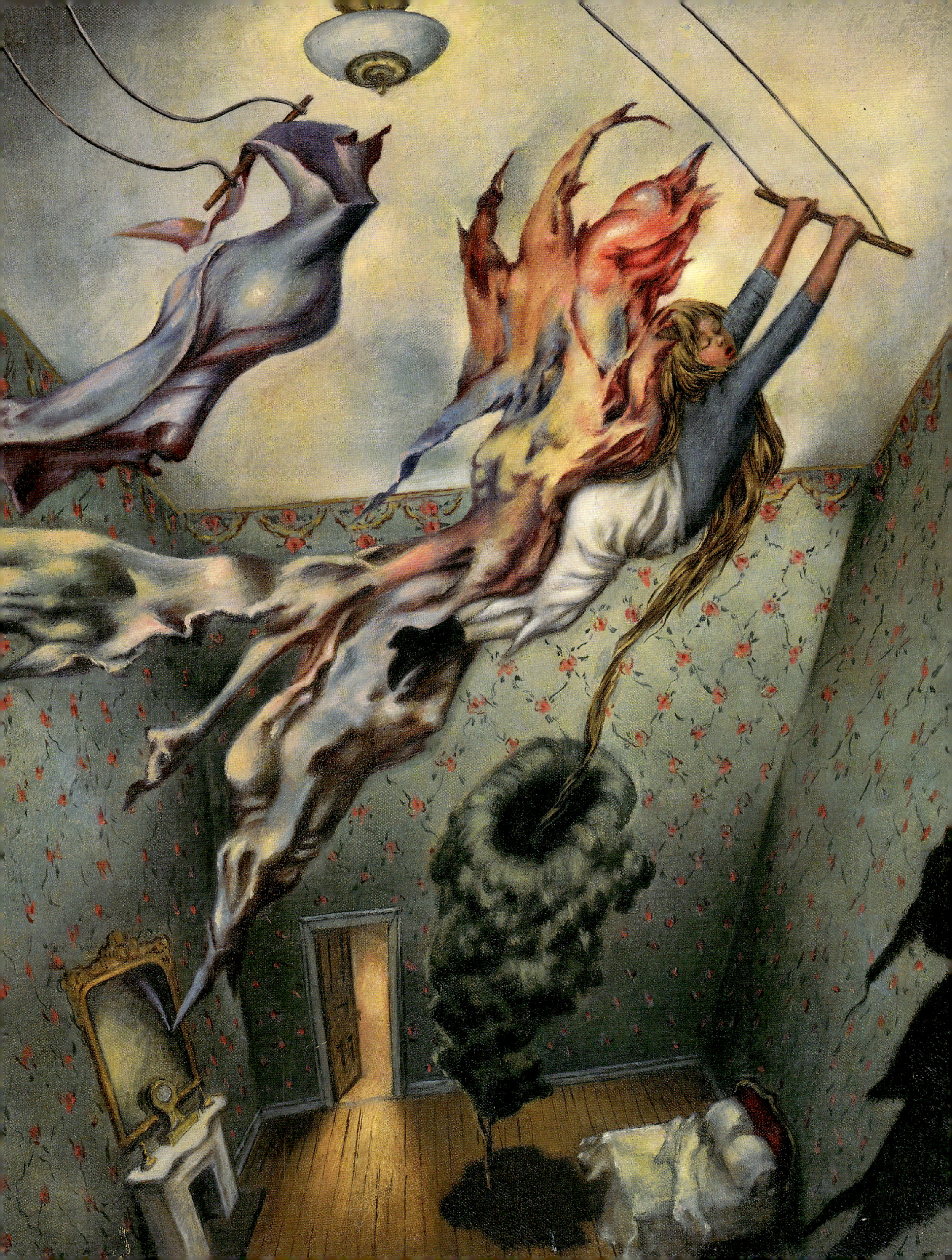

PAVEL TCHELITCHEW
Edith Sitwell
1937
EJF.
Catalogue no. 161.

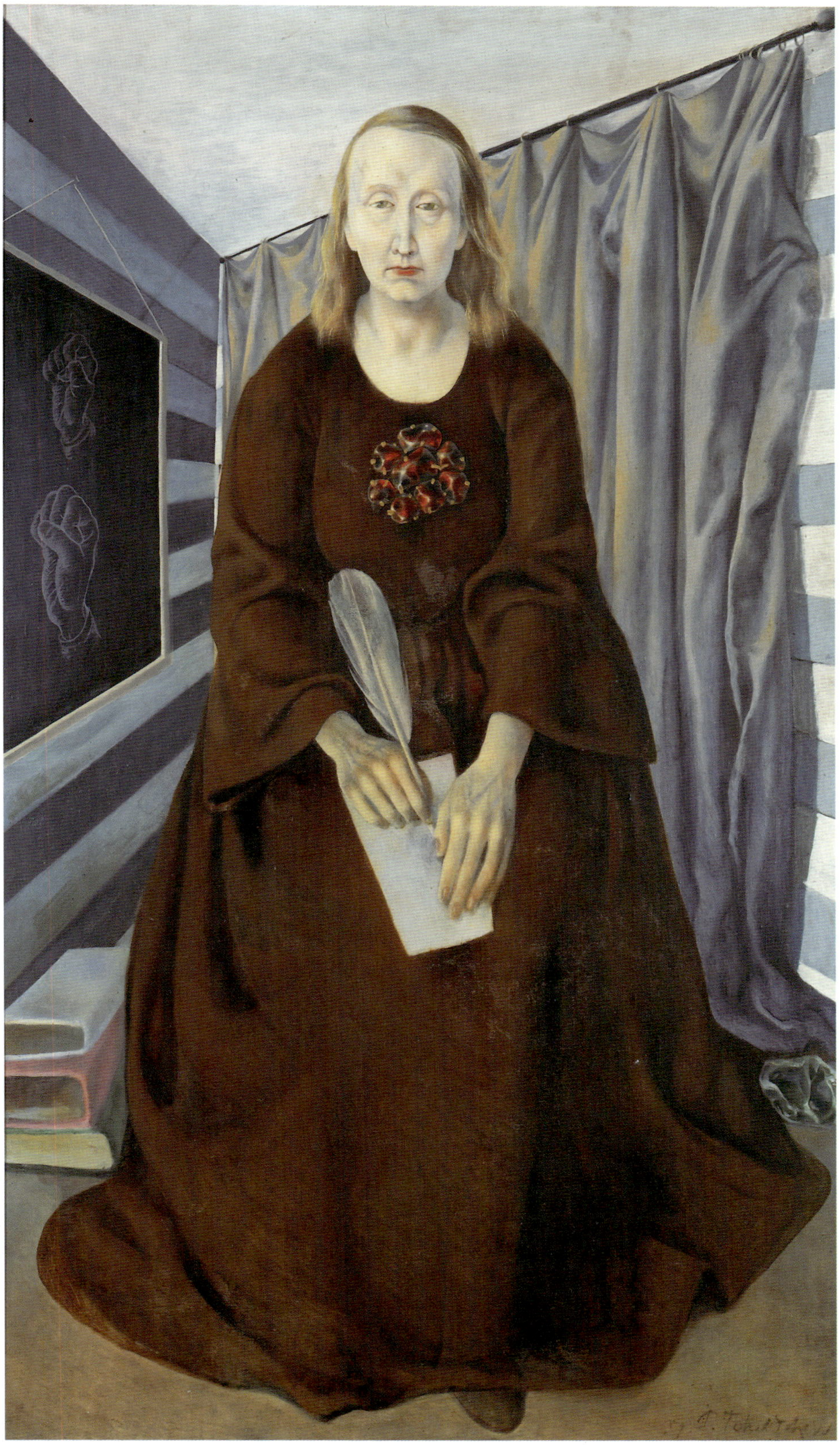

DOROTHEA TANNING
Crepusculum (Concerning Wishes)
EJF. Catalogue no. 160.

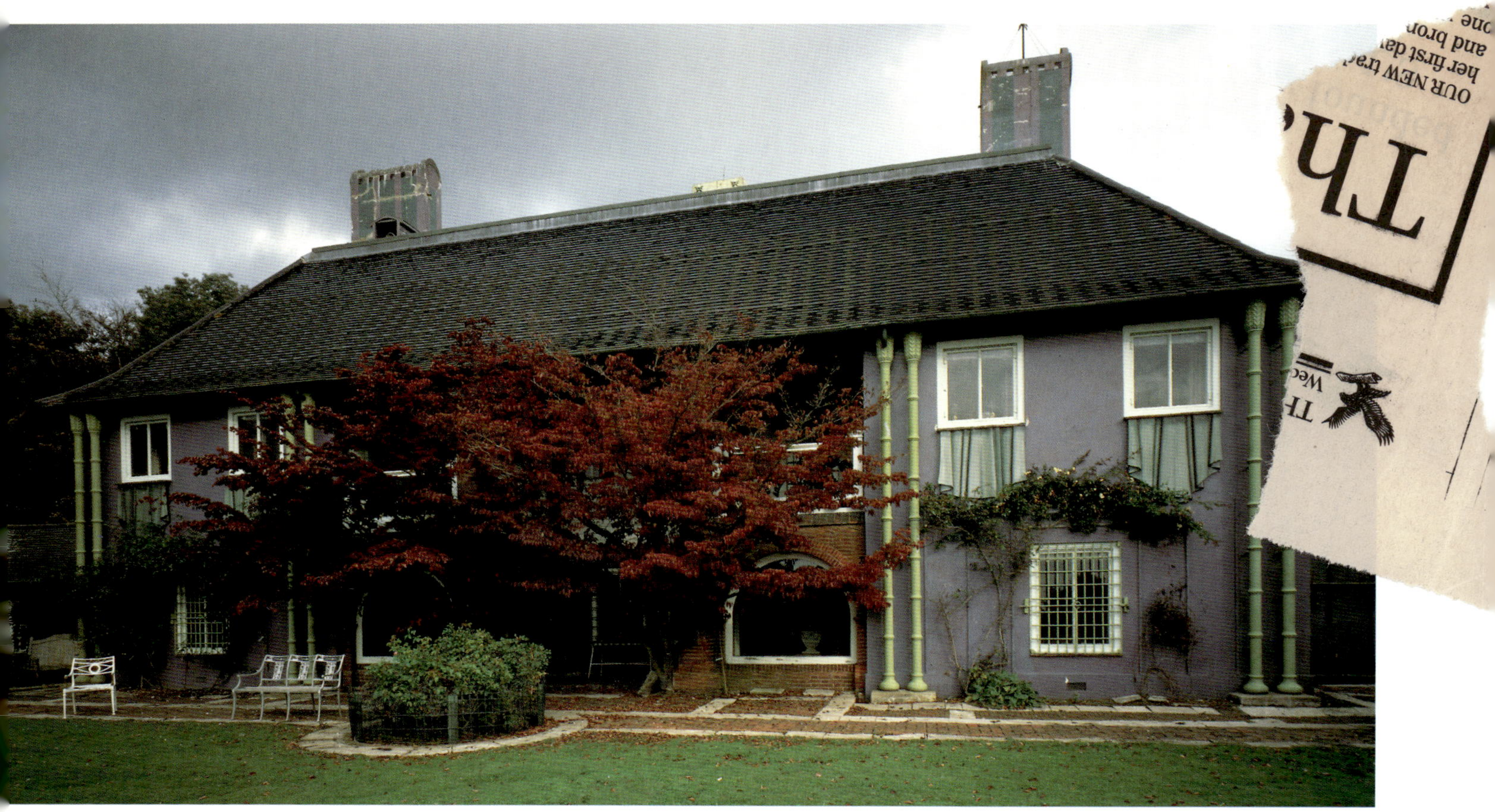

Exterior view of Monkton House.

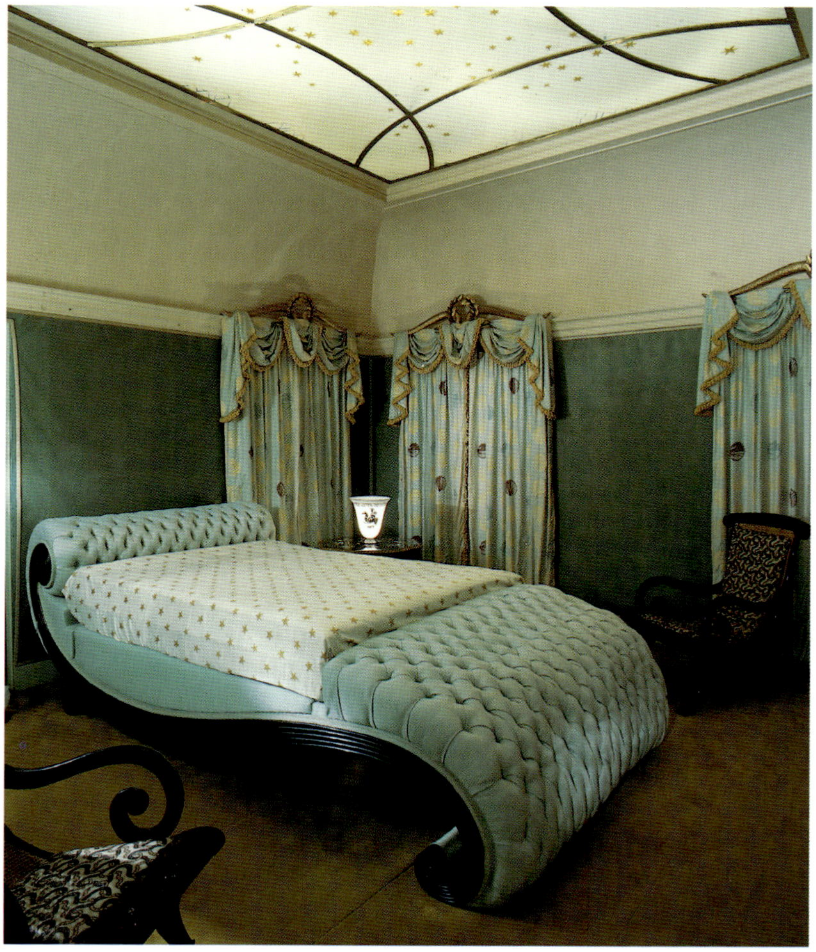

Map Room, Monkton House, 1986.

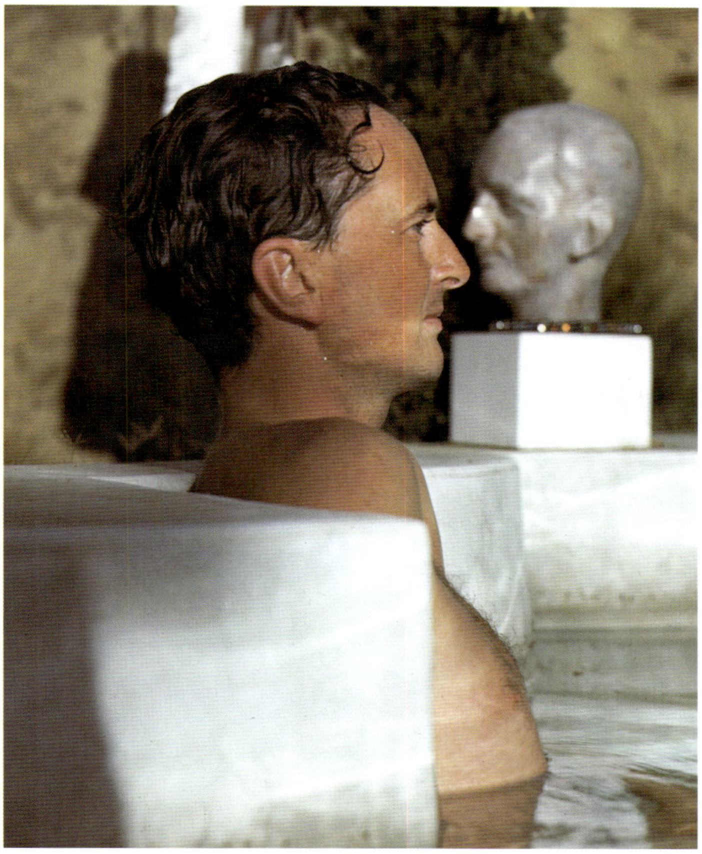

Edward James with bust
by Isamu Noguchi.
EJF. Catalogue no. 53.

TILLY LOSCH
Footprint carpet, West
Dean House, 1995.

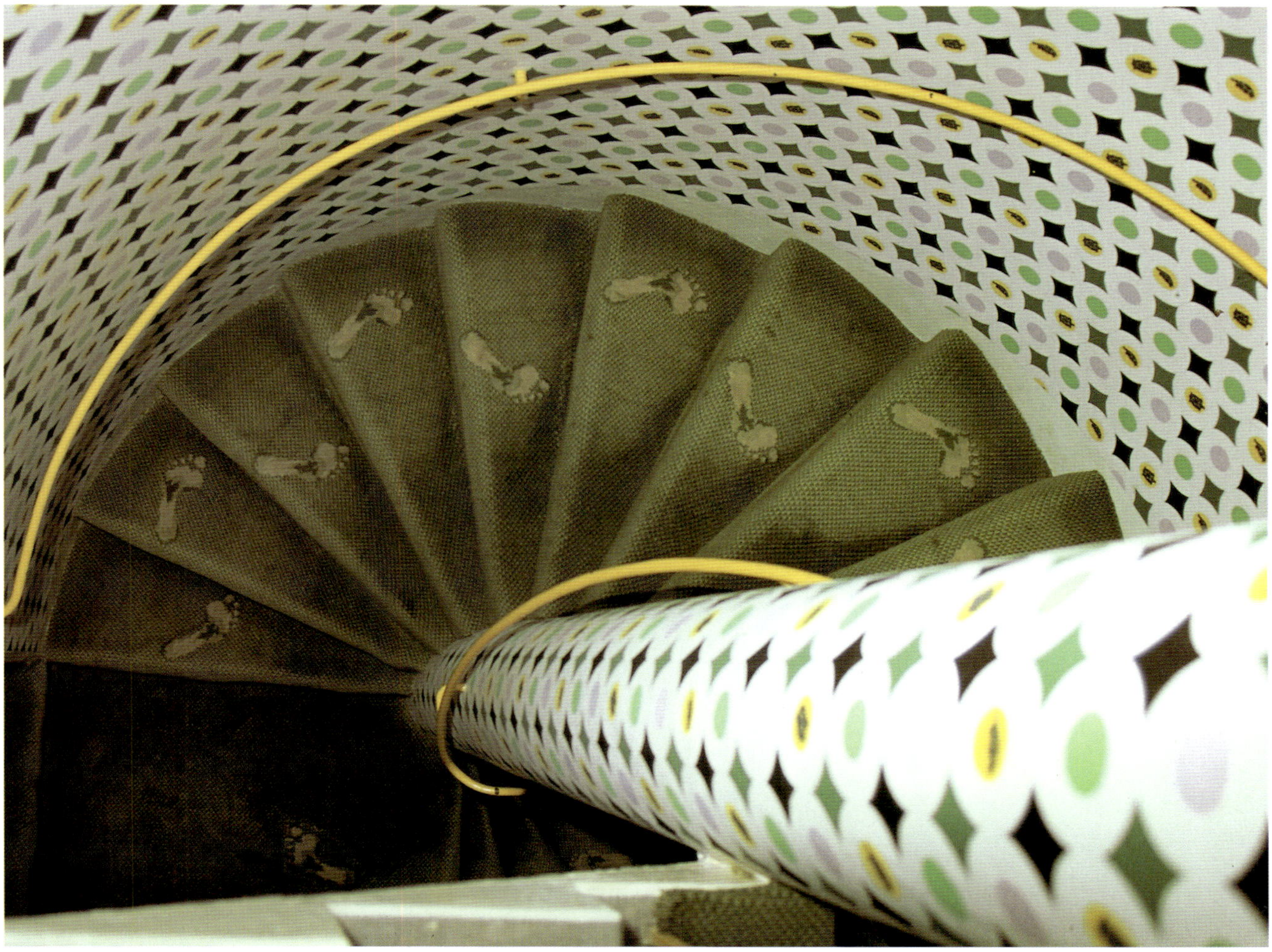

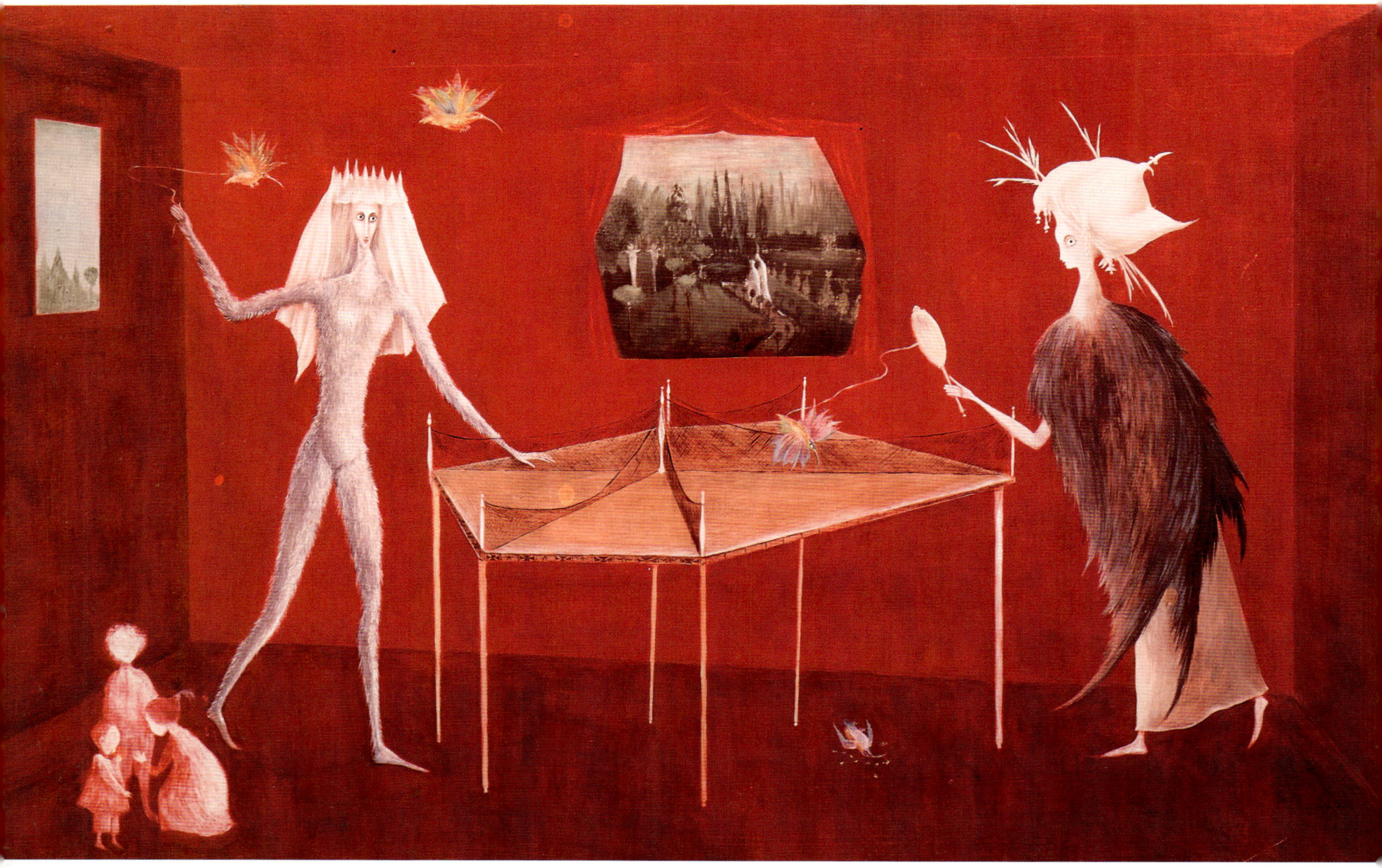

LEONORA CARRINGTON
Bird Pong
1949
Private Collection.
Catalogue no. 185.

SALVADOR DALÍ
Impressions of Africa
1938
Museum Boijmans Van Beuningen,
Rotterdam.
Catalogue no. 145.

Opposite page: *Spain*
1938
Museum Boijmans Van Beuningen,
Rotterdam. Catalogue no. 149.

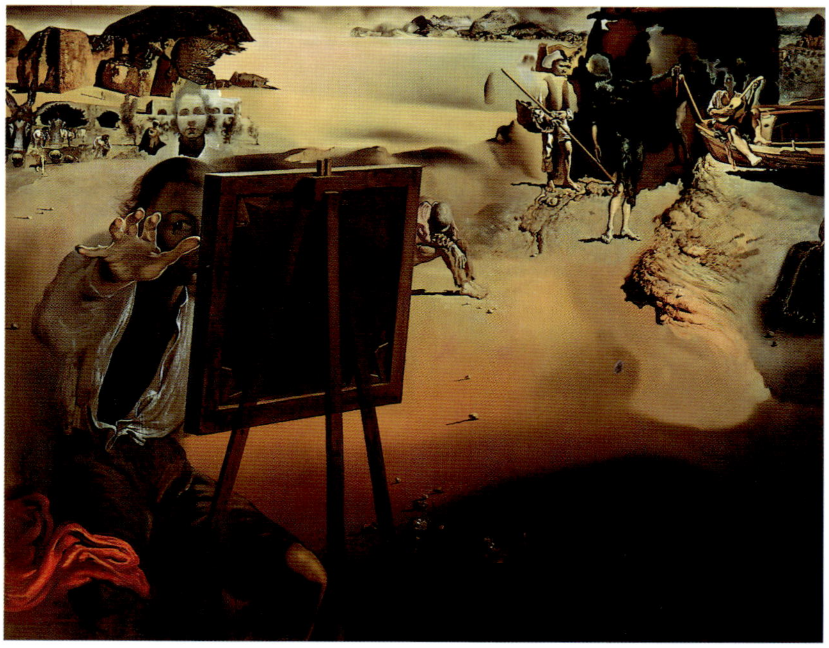

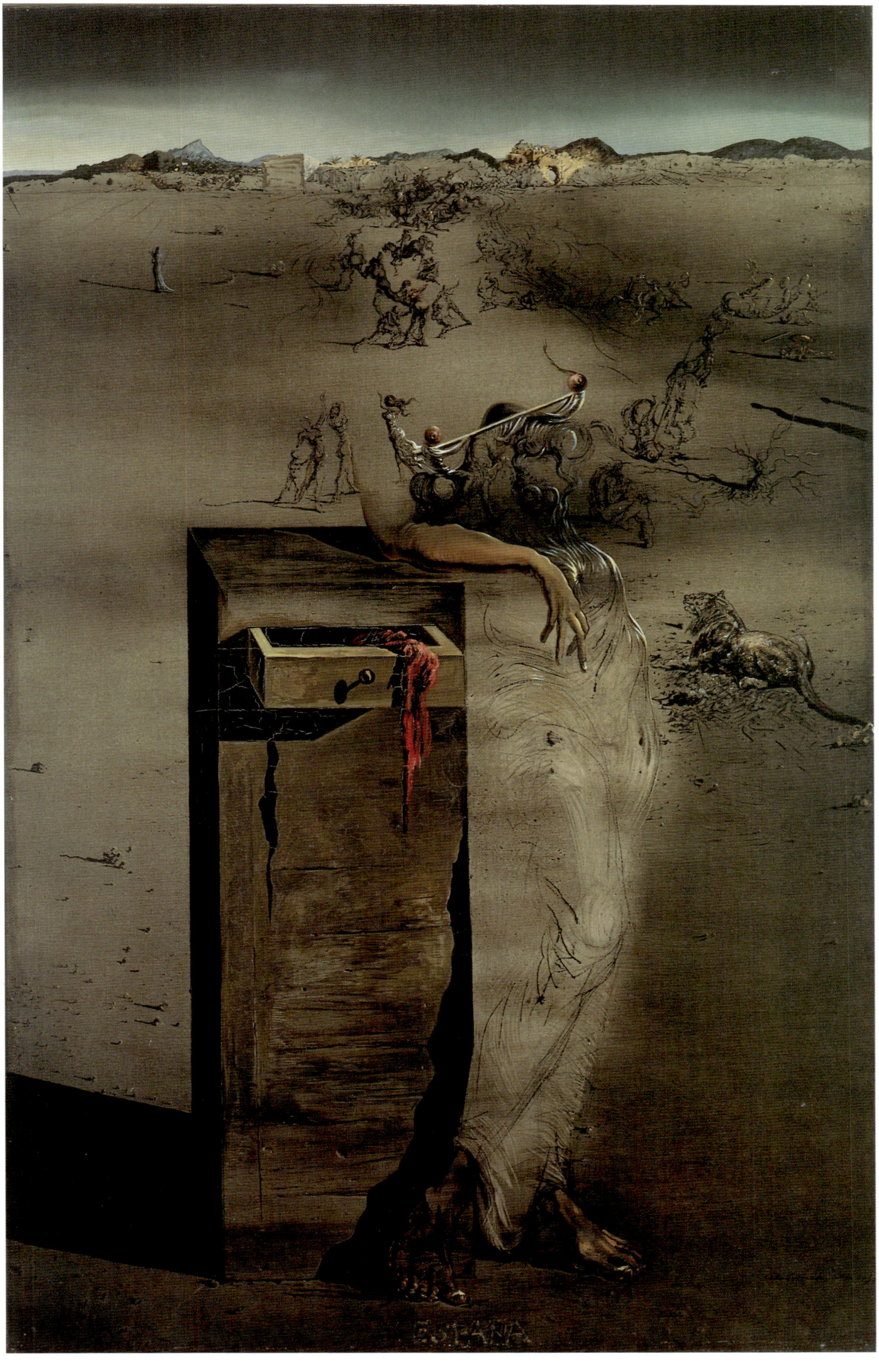

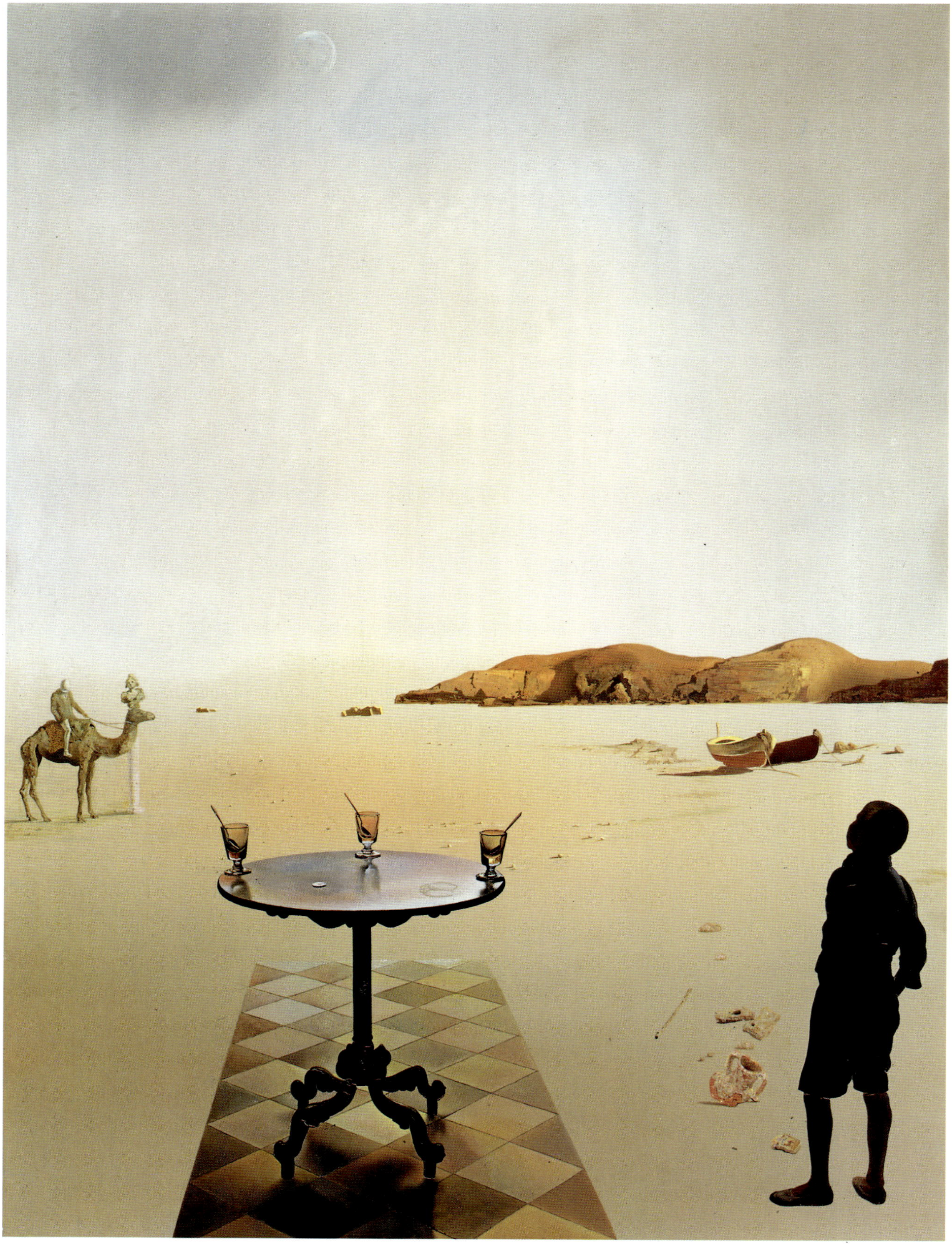

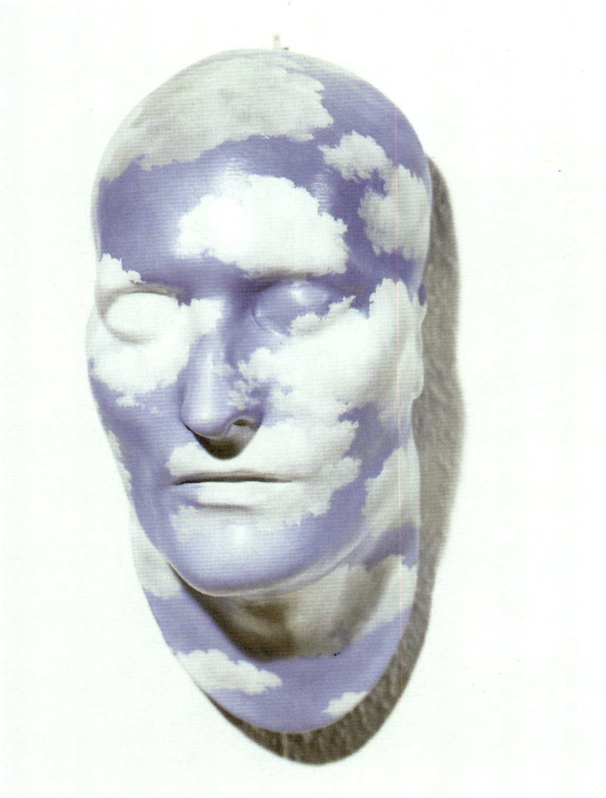

RENÉ MAGRITTE
The Future of Statues
1937
Tate Gallery, purchased 1981.
Catalogue no. 154.

PAUL NASH
Mansions of the Dead
1932
Tate Gallery, purchased 1981.
Catalogue no. 156.

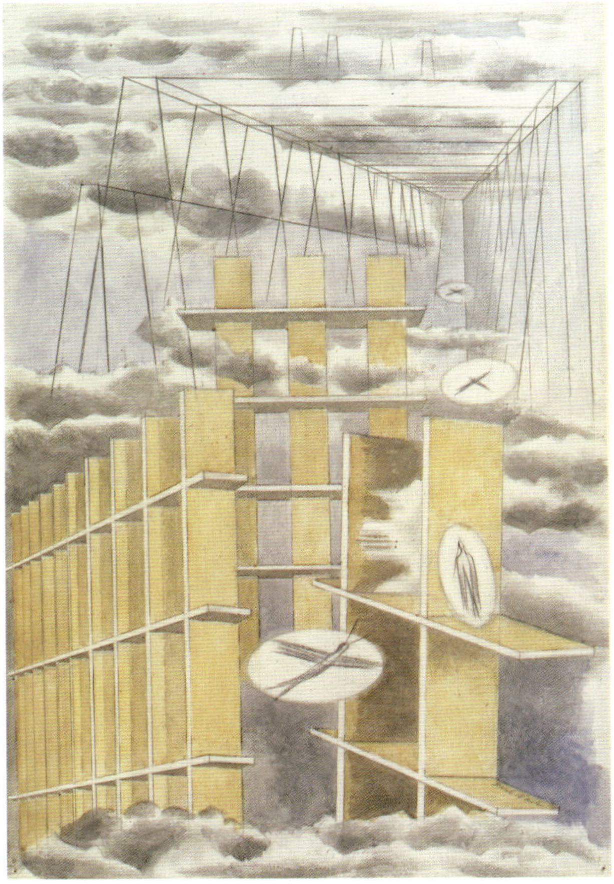

SALVADOR DALÍ
Sun Table
1936
Museum Boijmans Van Beuningen, Rotterdam. Catalogue no. 143.

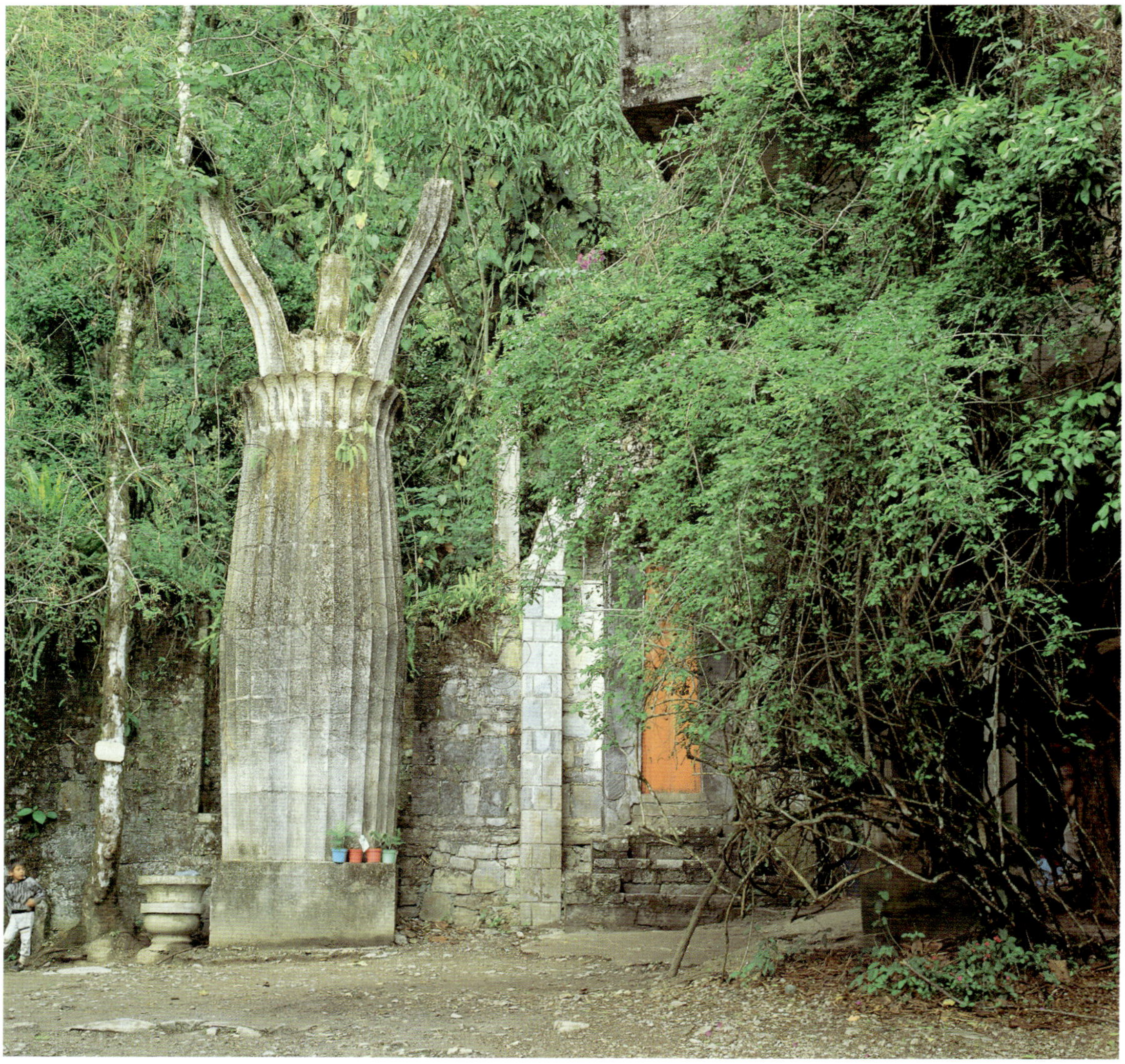

MARIANA YAMPOLSKY
Entrance to Xilitla
1996
The artist.

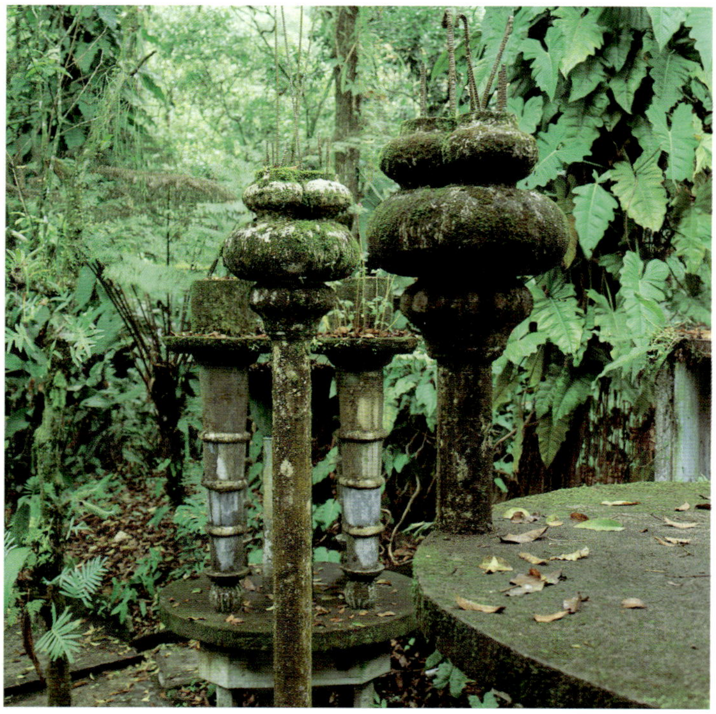

MARIANA YAMPOLSKY
Homage to Max Ernst
Xilitla, 1996
The artist.

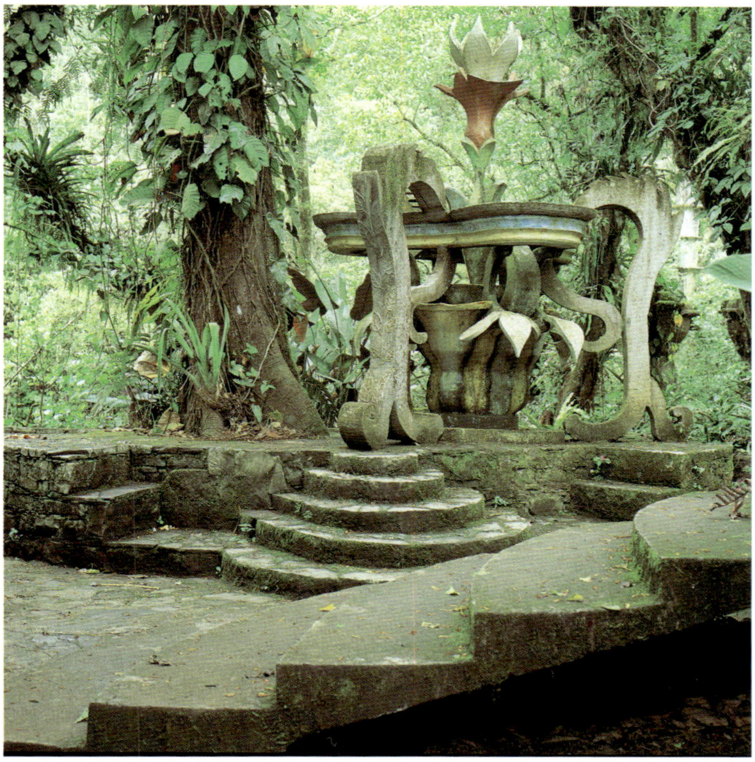

MARIANA YAMPOLSKY
Plaza San Eduardo
Xilitla, 1996
The artist.

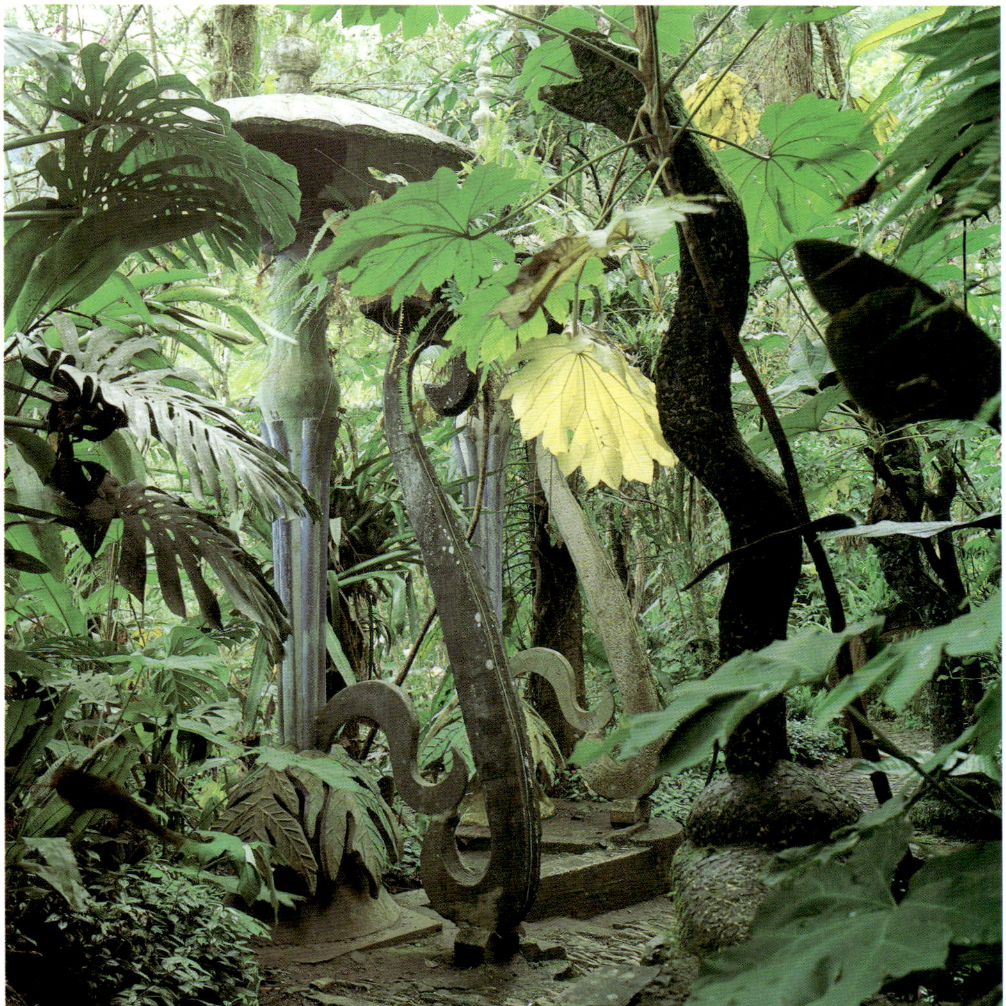

MARIANA YAMPOLSKY
Avenue of the Snakes
Xilitla, 1996
The artist.

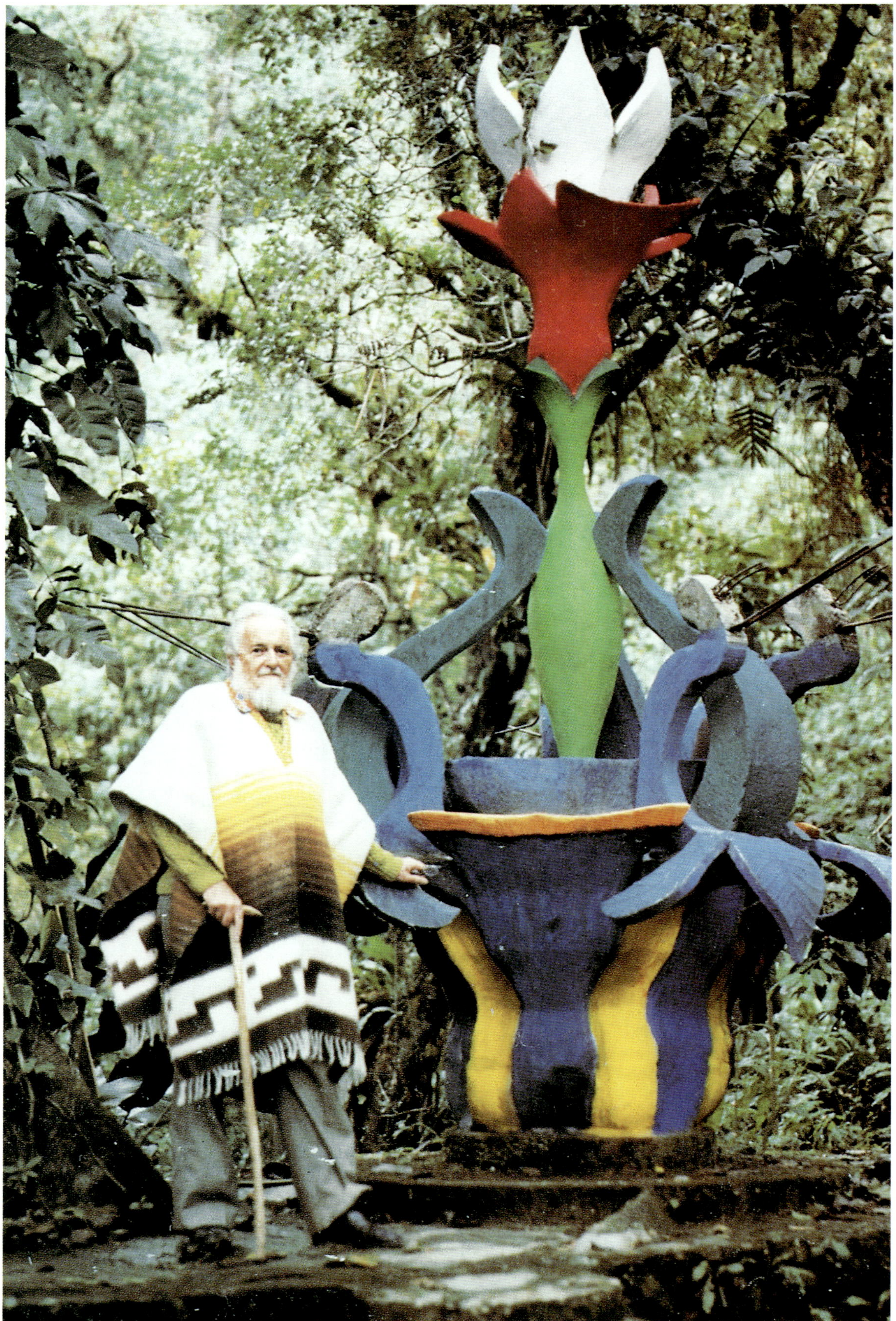

Edward James
in Xilitla.

EDWARD JAMES AND SURREALISM

DAWN ADES

ALTHOUGH MOST famous for his collection of Surrealist pictures and patronage of Dalí and Magritte, Edward James's interactions with Surrealism were ambivalent. A man of complexity and contradictions, he did not acquire these works by virtue of the fact that they were Surrealist, nor did he consider himself a collector and patron. He thought of himself, and wished others to think of him, primarily as a poet and fellow creator.

James had an extraordinary and prescient eye, and passionately loved his paintings, an addiction that apparently stemmed from seeing a de Chirico in a dealer's window in Paris. His collection was the equal of those built up by Surrealist poets such as André Breton and Paul Eluard – though, significantly, richer in work by women artists – and, like theirs, was based on close and intense relationships, often collaborative, with the artists themselves – above all with Dalí, Magritte, Leonora Carrington and Pavel Tchelitchew. But his pleasure in these works was not for the public status they could confer; it was private, and at times almost consolatory. 'When I feel depressed', he wrote to Leonora Carrington, 'and think that I have wasted my life, I go into this little room and realise that I have been able to discover treasures on my own initiative, and this makes a vibration which chases away the sense of futility'.[1] The little room (next to James's bedroom at West Dean) contained her *Portrait of the late Mrs Partridge* (1947, The Trustees of The Edward James Foundation), and two paintings by Dalí, *Metamorphosis of Narcissus* (1937, Tate Gallery, purchased 1979) and *La melancholie diurne*.[2]

It is significant that these works were not only treasures that he had found independently, but were ones with which he had been closely involved at the time of their making; he had found the title for *La melancholie diurne*, had discussed *Mrs Partridge* at length with Carrington, and had watched over the preparation and creation of the *Metamorphosis of Narcissus* almost like a midwife. As he says in a letter to the dealer Julien Levy who wanted to buy it from him: 'I was there when the canvas had its first pencil mark put on it, and even saw the preliminary sketches for the picture before the big canvas was begun at all.'[3] James considered the *Metamorphosis of Narcissus* Dalí's major work to date, and recorded his pleasure that Dalí had by this time left behind 'so many tiresome and unfortunate obsessions'[4]: the anguished sexuality of Dalí's earlier Surrealist paintings like *The Lugubrious Game* (1929, private collection) was probably too overt for him. *Metamorphosis of Narcissus* certainly achieves a new,

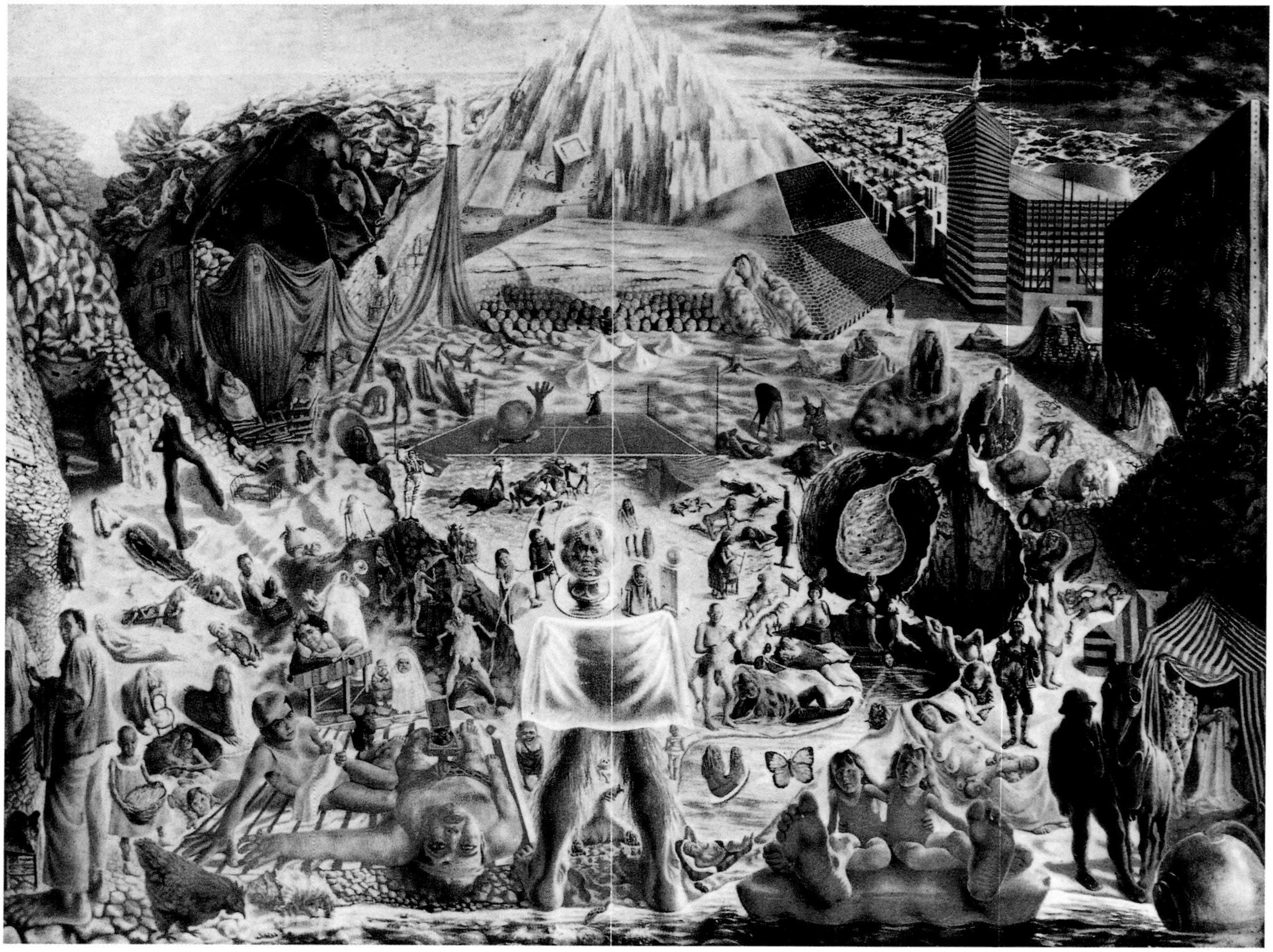

PAVEL TCHELITCHEW
Phenomena
1936–8, oil on canvas
200.5 x 270.5cm.
Collection Tretyakoff State
Gallery, Moscow.

confident expansiveness, with the 'displaced' image of the golden young man gazing at his reflection in the water, repeated and transformed in the configuration of the hand, egg and narcissus. James commented on the way this image evoked for him 'the diamond-like lucency' of the air in the Austrian Alps which he and Dalí had visited one April, where they had seen narcissi blooming in the melting snow.[5]

James also played the role of 'midwife' with Pavel Tchelitchew. In the summer of 1938 the artist stayed with him in a Palladian palace in Venice to finish the large picture *Phenomena* (collection of Tretyakoff State Gallery, Moscow), commissioned by James four years earlier. This apocalyptic vision of the times, with dictator, monsters and toreador, included portraits of James (he told Magritte that he is the boy with two heads) and their mutual friend, the artist Leonor Fini. Tchelitchew, however, was not a Surrealist; he belonged to another circle of James's friends, which included Edith Sitwell and Christian Bérard.

In the summer of 1936 James had signed a contract with Dalí for virtually his entire production, an action motivated not just by an idea that he might act as Dalí's dealer, but by the desire to give Dalí the security and freedom to work uninterrupted. James's collection was an achievement intimately bound up with other purposes: he never set out to make a 'collection'; he bought pictures by 'living artists who possessed more than ordinary talent. Magritte and Dalí turned out to have genius'.[6] They needed his financial help and moral encouragement to launch their careers. Picasso, who became James's close friend around 1934, was the only artist who was already famous when the collector bought his works, but James and Roland Penrose were the first, independently, to bring him to England. James never sought the kudos of a collection – something 'quite different from any true artistic consideration or real aesthetic aim'[7] – and when raising funds for Xilitla, was unwilling to sell the antique works at West Dean in preference to the modern collection. Given that it would be impossible to set up a permanent museum, he preferred to dispense with the Surrealist collection, now valuable and fashionable.

Inviting artists to work at his house and to paint for it brought him into a direct relationship with the living activity of art; the kind of intimacy he sought was not that of patron, organising commissions and devising programmes, but of collaboration and facilitation. It was not inspired by a commitment to the Surrealist cause, and James was never a member of the movement, though there are points of intersection with Surrealist ideas, particularly through the medium of Dalí's distinctive brand of 'paranoiac-critical activity'.

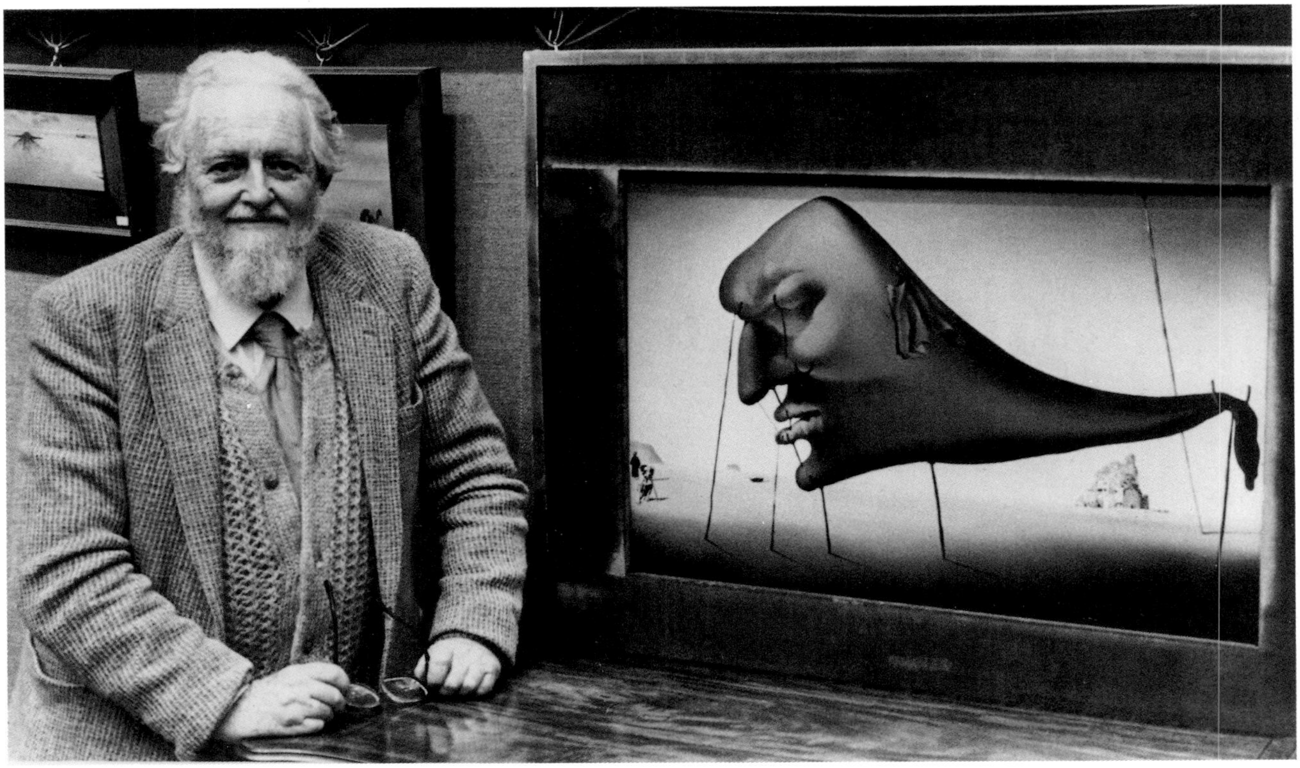

Edward James in front of Salvador Dalí's *Sleep* (1937) at West Dean House.
EJF.

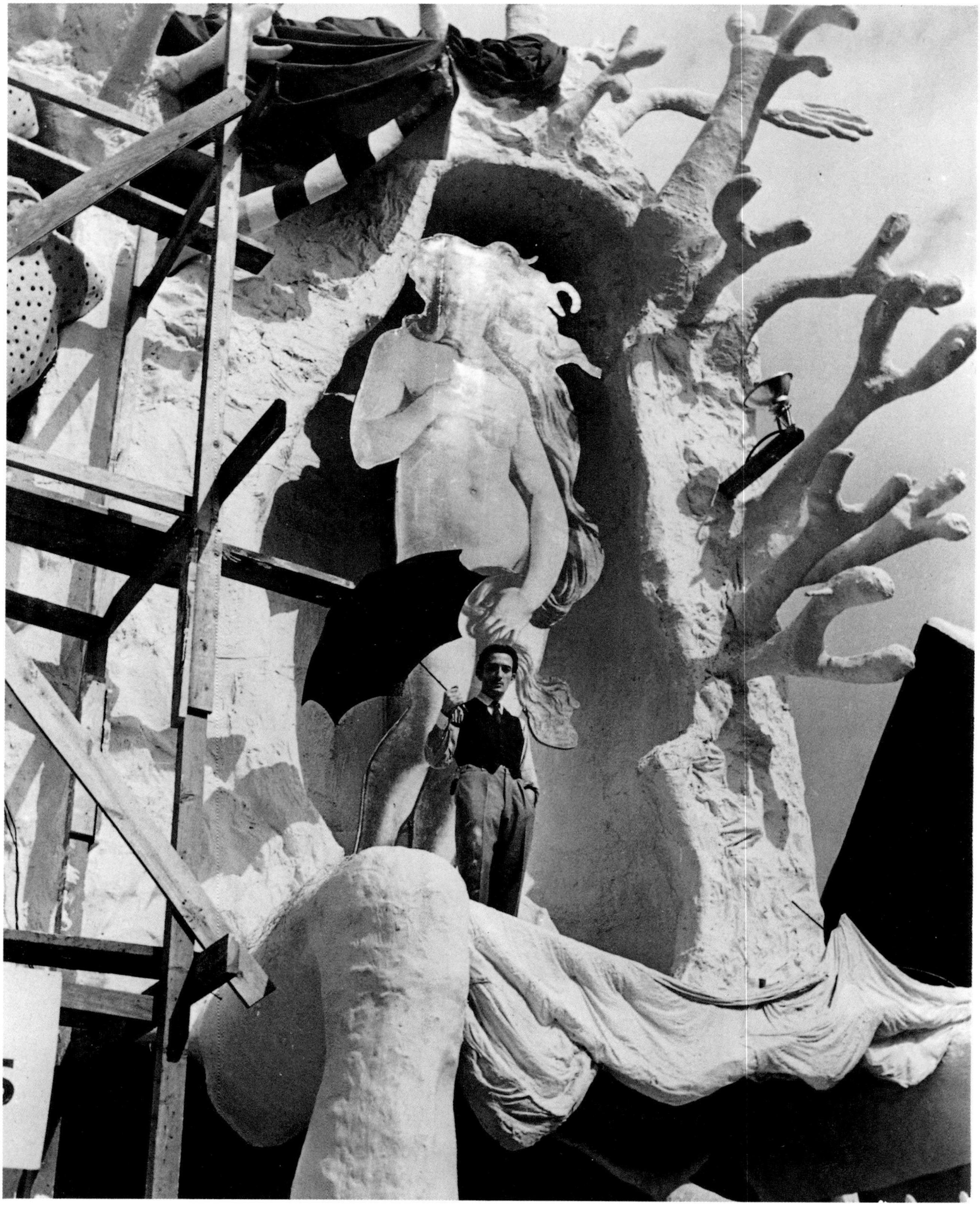

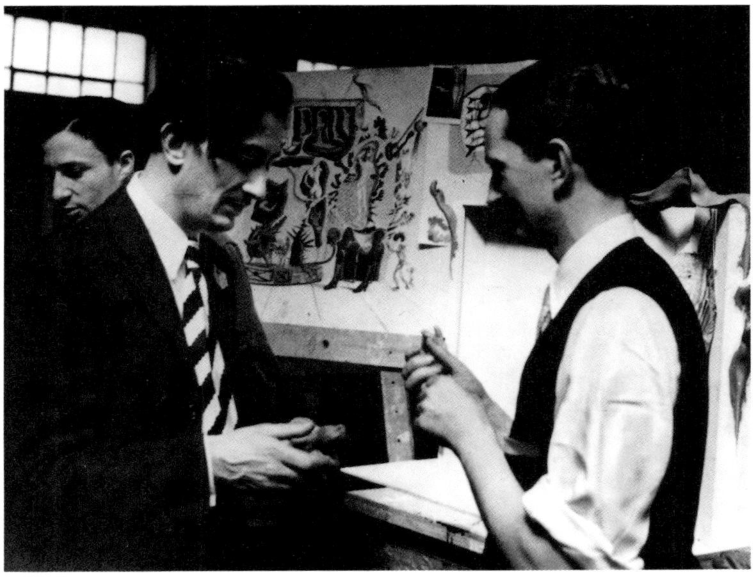

Edward James with Salvador Dalí during the construction of the *Dream of Venus*, 1939.
EJF. Catalogue no. 226.

Edward James with a *Dream of Venus* model, 1939.
EJF. Catalogue no. 225.

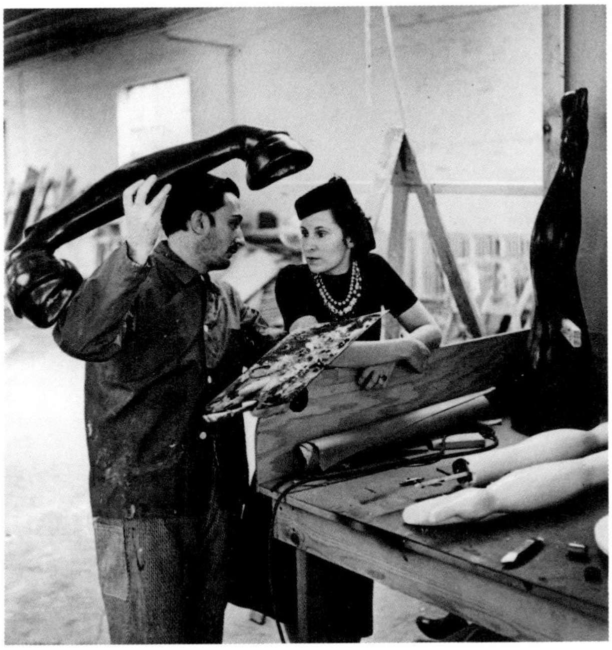

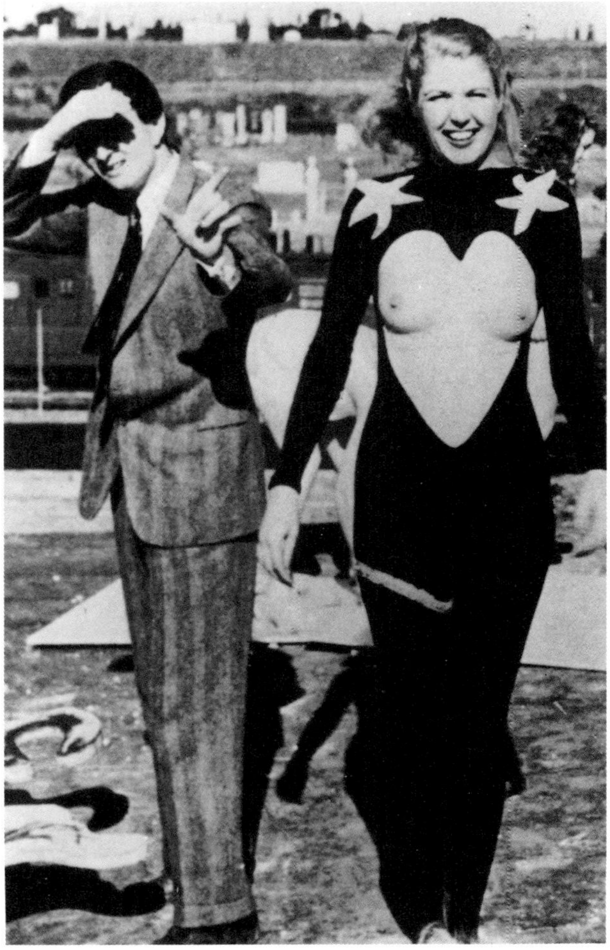

Gala and Salvador Dalí during the construction of the *Dream of Venus*, 1939.
EJF. Catalogue no. 218.

Salvador Dalí standing on the *Dream of Venus* façade, 1939.
EJF. Catalogue no. 211.

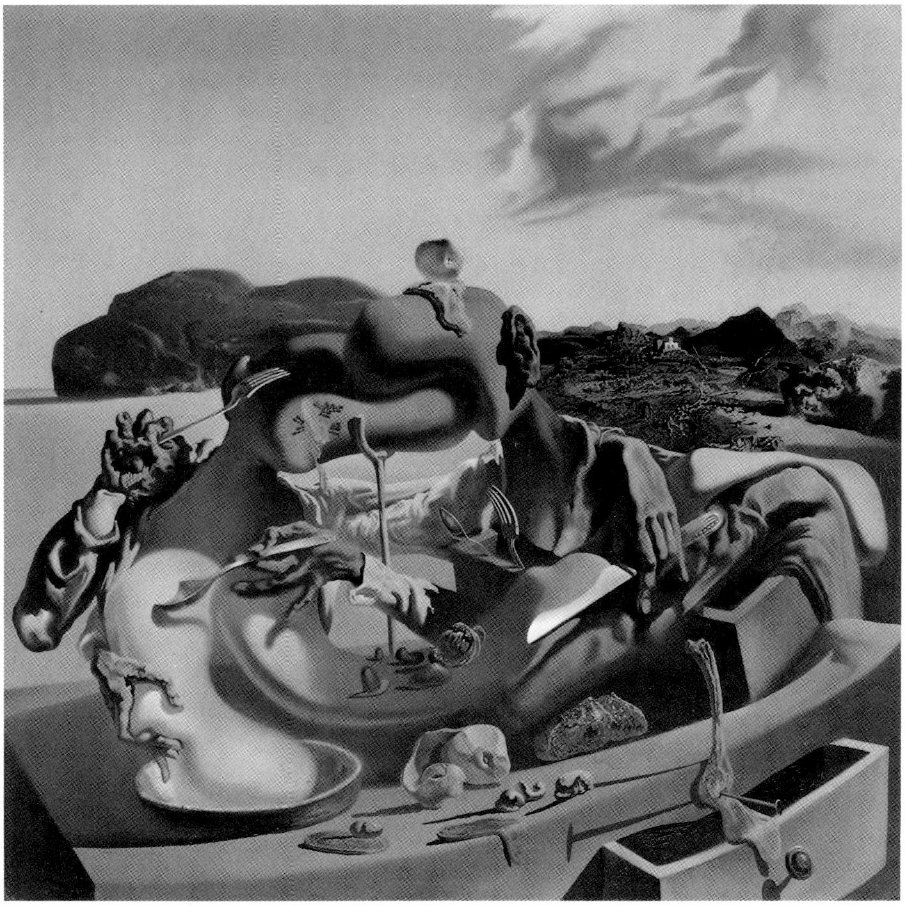

SALVADOR DALÍ
Autumnal Cannibalism
1936, oil on canvas
59.9 x 59.9cm.
Tate Gallery, purchased 1975.

Among the most successful of their collaborations was the *Trois sécheresses*, poems by James and drawings by Dalí, which achieve a remarkable parity of nostalgic disorientation, narcissism and longing. James's translation of Dalí's long poem *Narcissus* in 1937 is, like the original, a remarkable *tour de force*. The *Trois sécheresses* were published in *Minotaure* No. 8, 1936, with a cover by Dalí, and the following issue, No. 9, contained two texts by James, one in French and the other in English. James's brief entanglement with *Minotaure* is illuminating – a financial agreement in 1936 with Albert Skira gave James virtual control of the review. He wrote to John Betjeman asking permission to print poems from the collection he himself had published, *Mount Zion*, and from Betjeman's new book of poems. His plan was, he outlined to Betjeman, to include in the review many more British writers given that two thirds of the subscribers were English speaking; the next issue was to contain, apart from Betjeman's works, humorous poems by Lord Berners and Hilaire Belloc, in keeping with *Minotaure's* 'eclectic spirit of vitality'.[8] A Surrealist editorial board set up for the next issue put paid to this plan, but it demonstrates the degree to which James's literary affiliations were distant from Surrealism, even if his visual sensibility was so close to it: the inclusion of work by Belloc in a Surrealist review would be unthinkable.

The extent of James's involvement in the projects of the artists close to him is well demonstrated by the pavilion for the amusement area of the New York

RENÉ MAGRITTE
Time Transfixed
1938, oil on canvas
146 x 97cm.
The Art Institute of Chicago,
The Joseph Winterbotham
Collection.

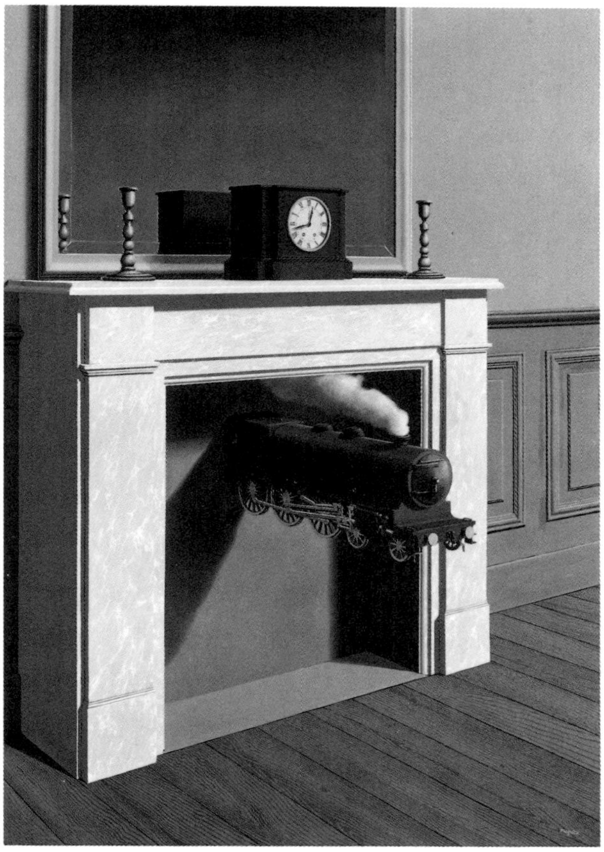

World's Fair of 1939, Dalí's *Dream of Venus*, a 'three-dimensional phantasmagoria' with a large tank in which live 'mermaids' would swim amongst surrealist objects. James not only paid the bills but maintained a close watch on the process of construction to make sure Dalí's elaborate ideas were correctly realised. The façade of the building bristled with plaster corals and large-scale reproductions of Botticelli's *Venus* (c. 1484, Uffizi, Florence) with a fish's head, and the head of Leonardo's *Mona Lisa* (c. 1508, Louvre, Paris) on the body of his *John the Baptist* (1508–13, Louvre, Paris), with various openings onto the interior, one of which was to create a double image. James described Dalí's sketch for this entrance: 'the archway to give, by means of a curtain, the effect of a hand through which is seen

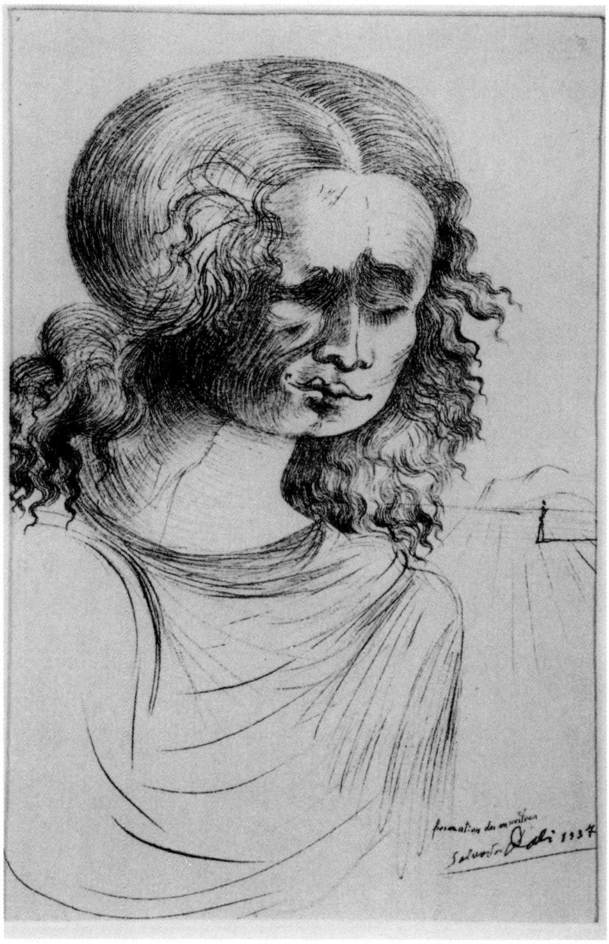

SALVADOR DALÍ
Creation of the Monsters
1937, ink on pink paper
23.5 x 16cm.
Chicago, Mrs Edwin A. Bergman
Collection.

RENÉ MAGRITTE
On the Threshold of Liberty
1937, oil on canvas
255 x 204cm.
The Art Institute of Chicago, Gift of Mary and Leigh Block. The photograph shows the painting after it was discovered rolled up in the stables at West Dean in the 1960s.

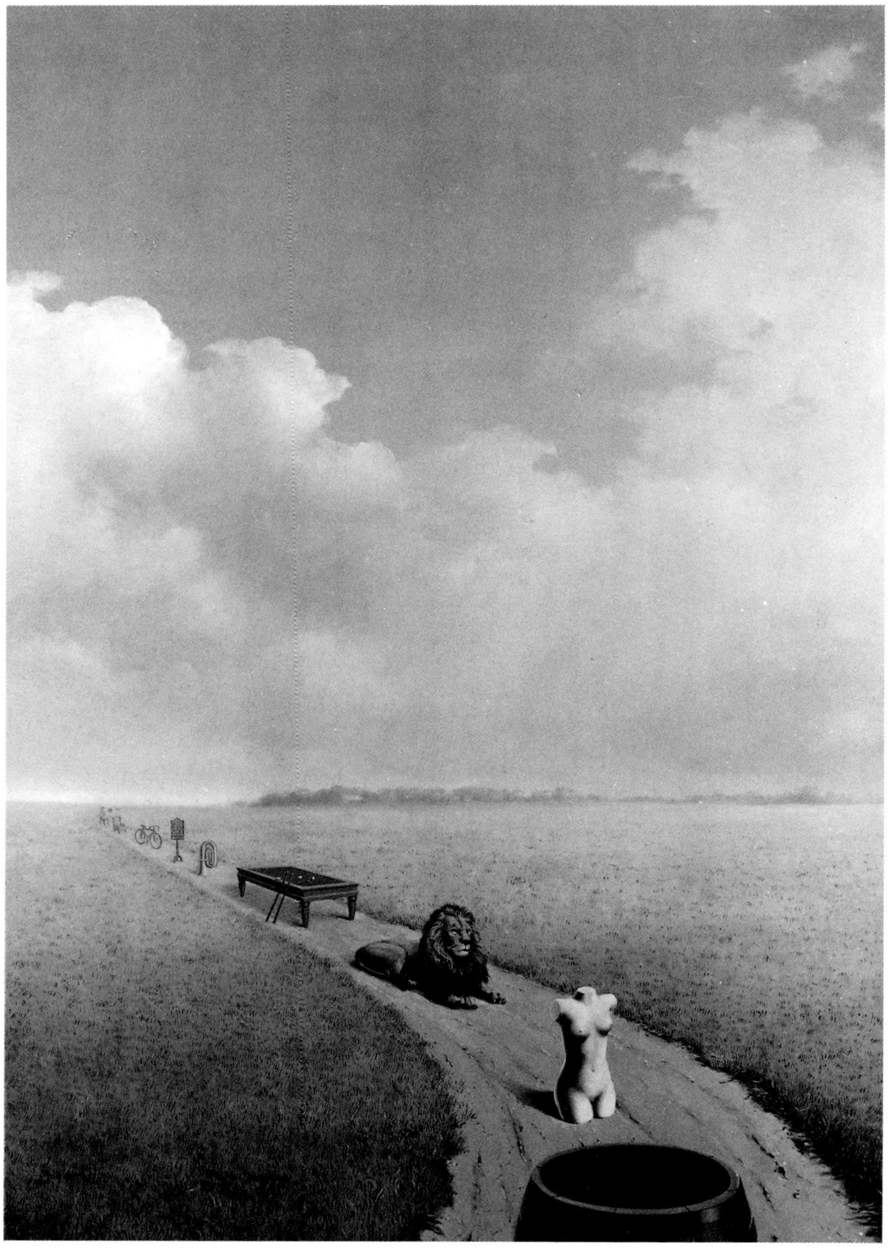

RENÉ MAGRITTE
La Jeunesse Illustrée,
1937. Museum Boijmans Van Beuningen, Rotterdam.
Catalogue no. 152.

an Egyptian head, the features of which are formed by objects on a table in the tank'.[9] To James's despair, the builders destroyed the illusion by making the archway too low, involving him, as so often, in additional expense to rectify the problem. The company putting up and co-funding the pavilion (Gardner Displays) and the Dalí camp were always at loggerheads. The former disliked the façade because it was not representative of the pavilion's interior, which they planned to be '60% under-water mermaid show and 40% a surrealist show' adding 'why then should the façade be all surrealist: men's passions to spend a quarter will not be aroused by a girl with a fish's head but by a suggestive mermaid ...'.[10] In protest, Dalí published his manifesto

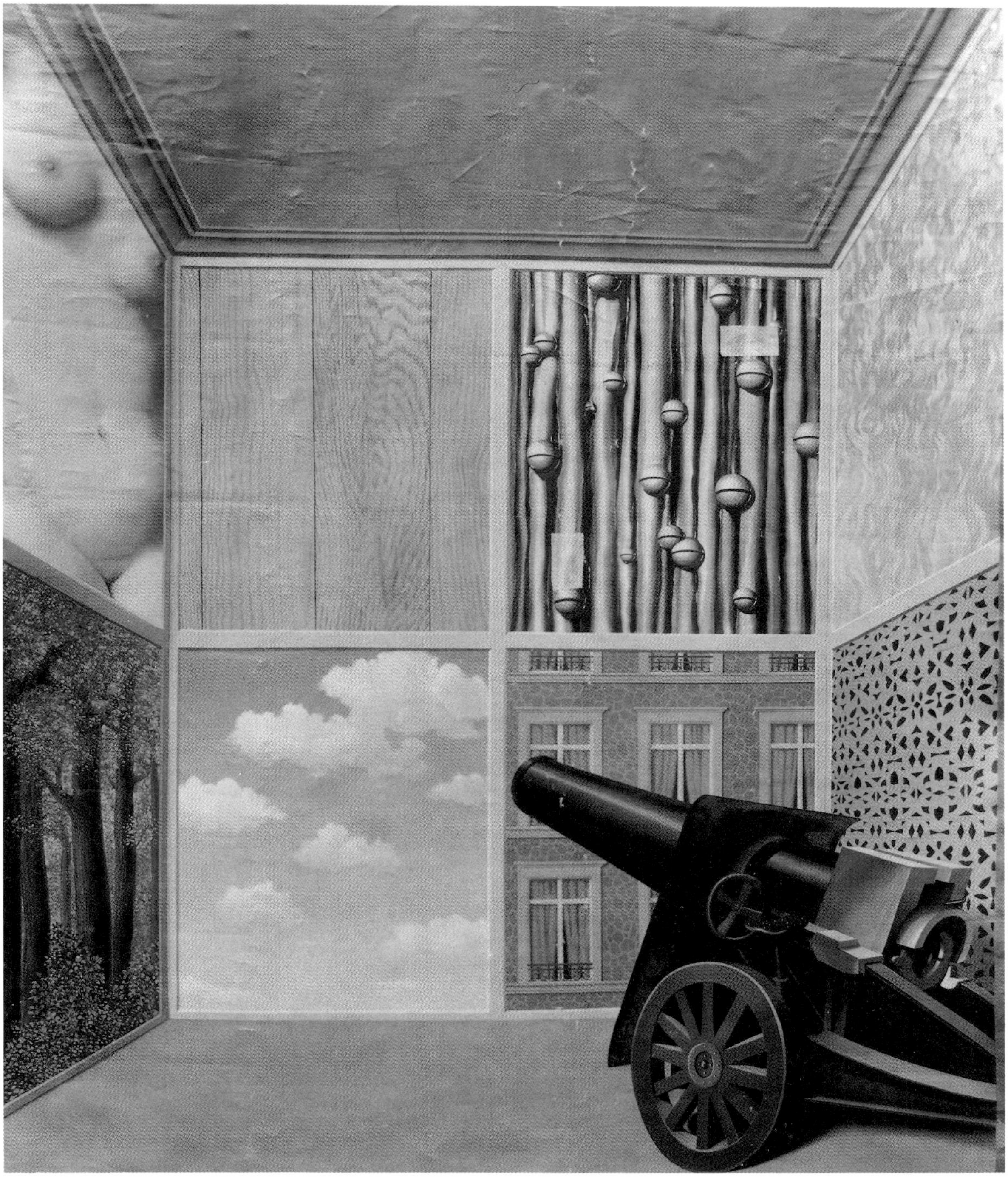

'Declaration of the Independence of the Imagination and the Rights of Man to His Own Madness', raging that every profoundly original idea was 'systematically rejected, diminished, mutilated, chewed up, spat out... and reduced to the most monstrous mediocrities'.[11]

Dalí left for Paris before the opening of the pavilion; James stayed to witness the final disaster. By the end of August the whole installation was completely changed, Botticelli's *Venus* with fish head removed, 'the façade covered with unbelievable writing explaining Surrealism according to Gardner's ideas, the tank filled with false Walt Disney fish and rubber sirens...'.[12]

With René Magritte too, who came to London early in 1937 to paint for the Wimpole Street house,

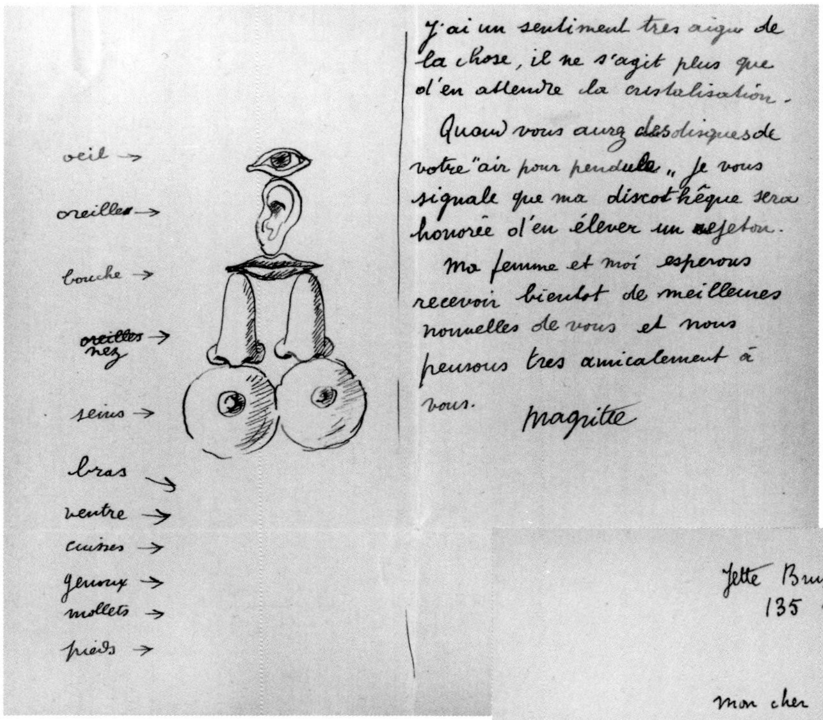

oeil →
oreilles →
bouche →
~~oreilles~~ nez →
seins →
bras →
ventre →
cuisses →
genoux →
mollets →
pieds →

J'ai un sentiment très aigu de la chose, il ne s'agit plus que d'en attendre la cristalisation.

Quand vous aurez des disques de votre "air pour pendule" je vous signale que ma discothèque sera honorée d'en élever un rejeton.

Ma femme et moi espérons recevoir bientôt de meilleures nouvelles de vous et nous pensons très amicalement à vous.

Magritte

Letter to Edward James from René Magritte, 18 August 1937, with sketch for *The White Race* (1937).
EJF. Catalogue no. 247.

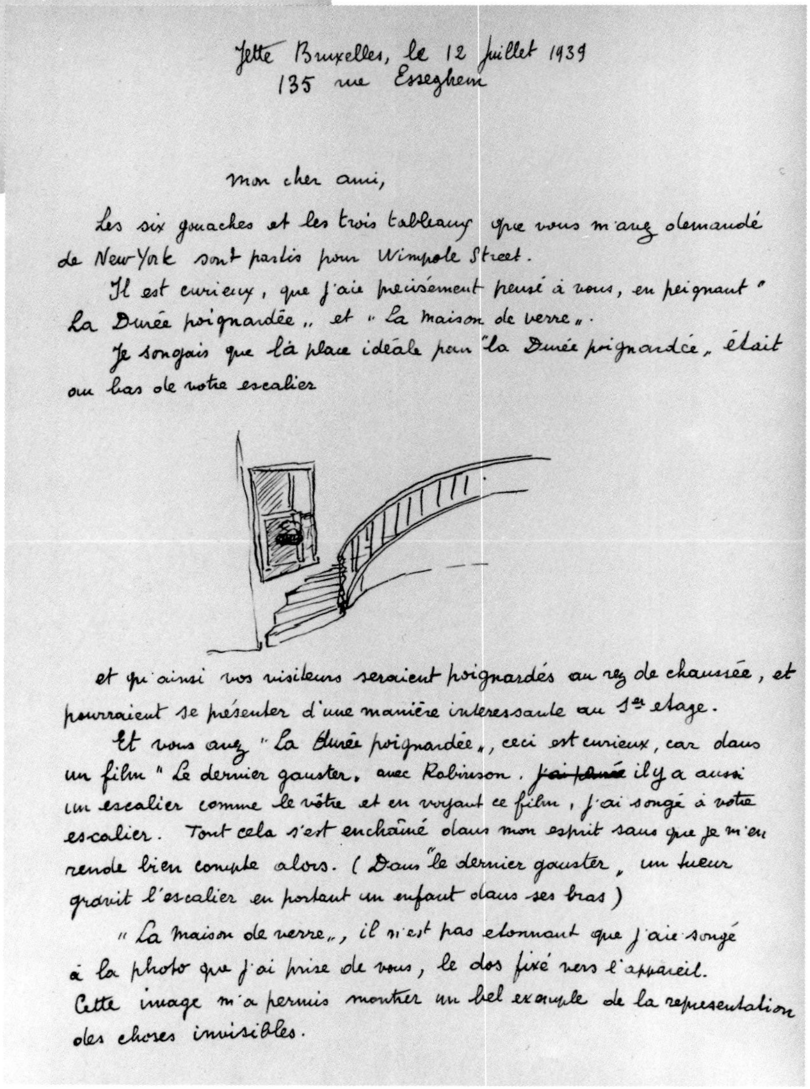

Jette Bruxelles, le 12 juillet 1939
135 rue Esseghem

Mon cher ami,

Les six gouaches et les trois tableaux que vous m'avez demandé de New York sont partis pour Wimpole Street.

Il est curieux, que j'aie précisément pensé à vous, en peignant "La Durée poignardée" et "La maison de verre".

Je songeais que la place idéale pour "La Durée poignardée" était au bas de votre escalier

et qu'ainsi vos visiteurs seraient poignardés au rez de chaussée, et pourraient se présenter d'une manière interessante au 1er étage.

Et vous avez "La Durée poignardée", ceci est curieux, car dans un film "Le dernier gangster" avec Robinson, ~~[illegible]~~ il y a aussi un escalier comme le vôtre et en voyant ce film, j'ai songé à votre escalier. Tout cela s'est enchaîné dans mon esprit sans que je m'en rende bien compte alors. (Dans "le dernier gangster", un tueur gravit l'escalier en portant un enfant dans ses bras)

"La maison de verre", il n'est pas étonnant que j'aie songé à la photo que j'ai prise de vous, le dos fixé vers l'appareil. Cette image m'a permis montrer un bel exemple de la représentation des choses invisibles.

Letter to Edward James from René Magritte, 12 July 1939, with sketch showing *Time Transfixed* (1938) on the stairway at 35 Wimpole Street.
EJF. Catalogue no. 253.

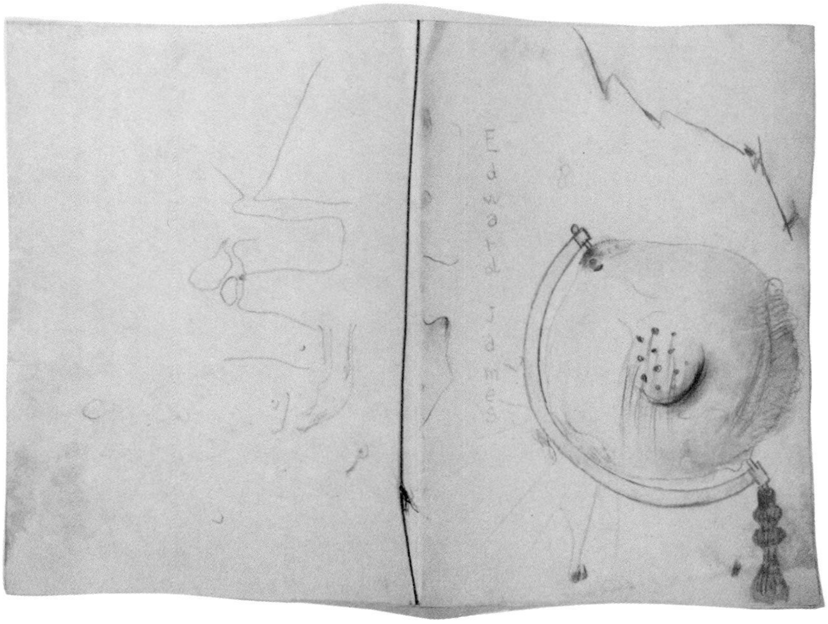

Front cover of handmade album dedicated to Edward James, 28 March 1937, with poems by Paul Colinet, Louis Scutenaire and his wife Irène Hamoir and Georgette Berger-Magritte, and illustrations by René Magritte. EJF. Catalogue no. 79.

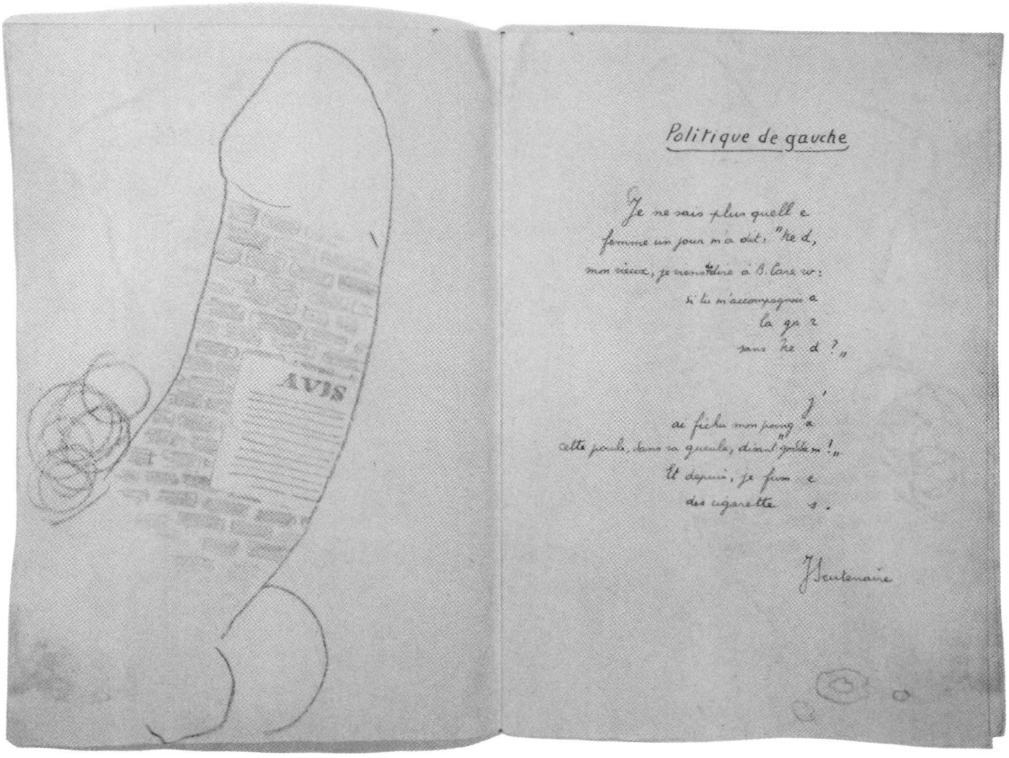

RENÉ MAGRITTE

Illustration for 'Politique de gauche' by Louis Scutenaire, from a handmade album dedicated to Edward James, 28 March 1937, with poems by Paul Colinet, Louis Scutenaire and his wife Irène Hamoir and Georgette Berger-Magritte, and illustrations by René Magritte.
EJF. Catalogue no. 79.

James had a close relationship. Wishing to appear to Magritte as a poet not a collector, he sent the artist a rare copy of his poems (*Your name is Lamia*), and talked of translations of his novel. Magritte often wrote with little sketches of new pictures or of 'problems' he hoped to solve. This was not just for the purpose of whetting James's appetite to purchase his paintings; he was sharing his thought process with James, who responded eagerly: 'You are a poet in painting. More perhaps than a painter, if I dare say so, but a great poet.'[13]

Magritte clearly thought of the Wimpole Street house as an appropriate site for his inventions: *Time Transfixed* (1938, The Art Institute of Chicago, The Joseph Winterbotham Collection), he suggested, would make a good picture for the stairwell – 'visitors will be transfixed on the ground floor'.[14]

The intimate, personal relations between James and Magritte's Belgian Surrealist group, which included E.L.T. Mesens and Louis Scutenaire, are expressed in the small hand-made album or booklet they sent in 1937 to cheer him up during one of his periodic illnesses. A collaborative effort with poems by Paul Colinet, Georgette Berger-Magritte, Louis Scutenaire and his wife Irène Hamoir, and drawings by Magritte, the cover is a multi-coloured *cadavre exquis*, with each contributor adding to the drawing without seeing the whole.

There was, however, a temporary hitch in their relationship when Magritte wrote an extraordinary letter to James, proposing that, as the latter had more money than he needed, and he himself had considerably less, they should come to an arrangement whereby James should annually pay him £100 in exchange for whatever painting Magritte considered his best recent work. James wrote a biting response mocking Magritte's charming naivety, and revealing his own deep tensions. It was not so much the financial arrangements, which were of a kind James himself could well have proposed, but rather Magritte's assumption of command, and claims to privilege as an important creator. Firstly, James pointed out, Magritte had no conception of the financial responsibilities he bore to his employees as a landowner, and secondly he had a duty to himself as a writer to safeguard his time, which was too often dissipated in having to write letters like this.

Within the circles in which James moved as a result of his wealth and international aristocratic connections, Surrealism was a fashion, and moreover, good

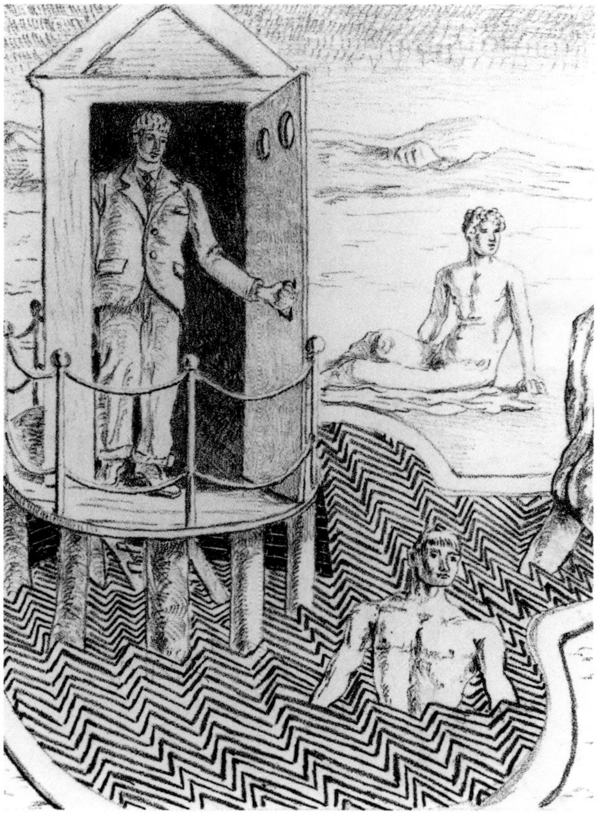

GIORGIO DE CHIRICO
Illustration from *Mythologie*, text by Jean Cocteau, published by Edmond Desjobert, Paris, 1934.
EJF. Catalogue no. 174.

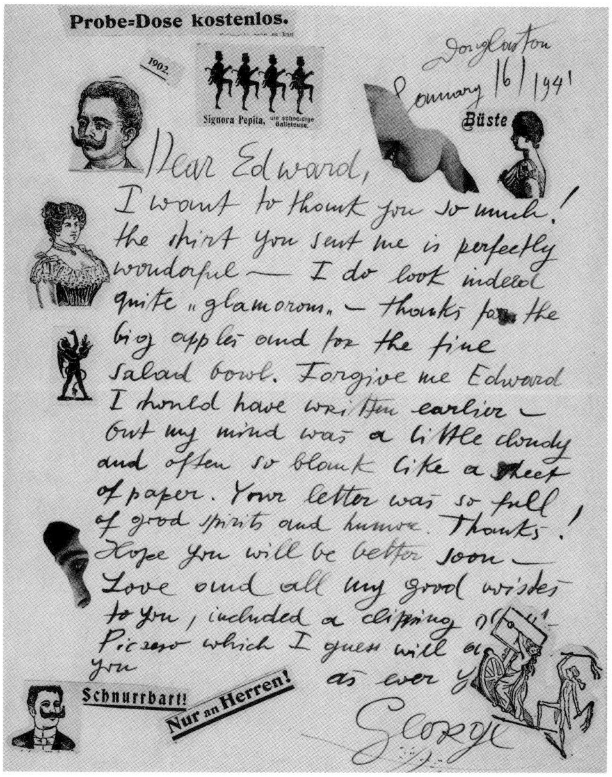

Probe=Dose kostenlos.

1902.

Signora Pepita, die schneidige Balleteuse.

Douglaston
January 16 | 1941

Büste

Dear Edward,
I want to thank you so much!
the shirt you sent me is perfectly
wonderful — I do look indeed
quite „glamorous" — thanks for the
big apples and for the fine
salad bowl. Forgive me Edward
I should have written earlier —
but my mind was a little cloudy
and often so blank like a sheet
of paper. Your letter was so full
of good spirits and humor. Thanks!
Hope you will be better soon —
Love and all my good wishes
to you, included a clipping o
Picasso which I guess will a
you
as ever y
George

Schnurrbart!

Nur an Herren!

Letter to Edward James from George Grosz, 16 January 1941. EJF. Catalogue no. 250.

for scandalising the more conservative sectors of that society, especially in England. He enjoyed telling Magritte of the sensation his paintings had created at the ball he gave in Wimpole Street: 'above all the "human shoes" have softened the young couples dancing in their capitalist heels.'[15]

His novel *The Gardener who saw God* contains some effective satire, both aimed at this high society and at Surrealism. One character is a 'surrealist milord' with a gothic castle in Berkshire, who scatters his garden with grand pianos and plaster ants, and reconstructs a terrace as an operating table with undulating concrete covered in turf like a ruckled green cloth, topped with an umbrella seat. This conceit neatly conflates Lautréamont's famous image: 'beautiful as the chance encounter of a sewing machine and umbrella on an operating table'[16] with English 18th-Century garden follies. A beautiful 'bright young thing' meets a bearded, French, Surrealist poet early one morning, and persuades him to explain to her exactly what Surrealism is while she floats in the swimming pool. The explanation is hardly that of a Surrealist, though it certainly has echoes of Dalí: 'I am altogether *pour* a good ripe decadence ... Like the sturgeons we swim at the mouths of the rivers between the fresh sweet waters of art and the cold salt tide of science, the vast material ocean'.[17] There is a strong autobiographical element in this novel: James invests a young heir with his own wealth and position but with a totally different personality. The fictional character is interested only in such things as hunting, not at all in either art or gardens. The young gardener, by contrast, is much closer to James himself, perhaps suggesting his attempts to find another identity. The gardener finally experiences a vision of the whole of creation, which he interprets as God.

The very fact that this is a novel at all removes it from the central thread of Surrealist writing; it has something in common with Herbert Read's *The Green Child*, but also with a broad tradition of semi-didactic English novelists such as George Meredith. James certainly had a real talent for putting his strong response to scenes and objects into words. Edith Sitwell said of his poems, that they had 'real quality and a fine sense of visual beauty'[18]. (She was 'so glad he was not of the "gas-works" school of poetry'). James also wrote with great fluency about art, as for instance in his text for *Minotaure* (No. 9, 1936), the 'Marvel of Minuteness' on Holbein and Cranach. However, there is also a sense in his more formal poems of the constraints of his education, within a system still gripped by the 19th-

Century nostalgia for a classical world of its own invention. The freedom of the writing in his letters was rarely present in his poems. James's visual sensibility had its roots in a mixture of *fin de siècle* aestheticism, which found expression in the extravagant interiors of his homes, and a love of the natural world nourished by the English Romantic tradition and finally transposed to tropical Mexico.

James's highly developed self-critical and analytical capacity occasionally appears in astonishing passages in his writings such as his description, written in French in a letter to Dalí from a Berlin hotel room, of the significance to him of tissue paper, which dated back to watching his sister unpacking her clothes with tissue paper heaped like snow round the room:

> *I have again been lulled and rocked by the soft sound of the rustling of tissue paper; the muffled sound, invasive and imperial, echoes like a tide in my ears, even though I am no longer touching it. It has the effect of an acoustic mirage, a renewal of sound, an after-taste of hearing, a continuation of memory in my brain.*[19]

There is something here of the sensibility of Joseph Cornell, the maker of intimate, memory-filled boxes, whose work James admired and owned.

The sense of futility to which he referred in the letter to Carrington was almost certainly due to the fact that he never achieved the recognition for his poetry he desired. He reminds correspondents that he is a poet, not a business man, complains that his publishers don't take him seriously because he is so wealthy, but is constantly distracted by his own restless whirl of activities and by increasing legal and financial worries. That there was a loss of impetus is underlined by an anxious letter from Gala Dalí to James in 1940 telling him he must decide between being a talented amateur or a poet seriously devoted to the task in hand.[20] It is not that he settled for the former, but interferences, psychological or material and in the end imponderable, seemed to dog him; perhaps it was his education, or his upbringing, or

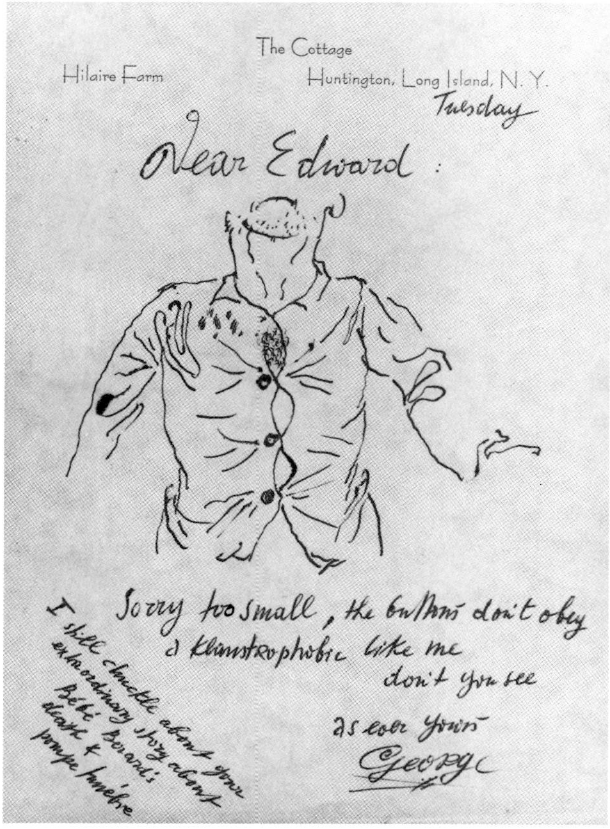

The Cottage
Hilaire Farm
Huntington, Long Island, N.Y.
Tuesday

Dear Edward:

Sorry too small, the buttons don't obey
a klaustrophobic like me
don't you see

as ever yours
George

I still chuckle about your extraordinary story about Bébé Berard's death + pompe funèbre

Letter to Edward James from George Grosz, undated.
EJF. Catalogue. no. 251.

GEORGE GROSZ
Ravaged Landscape
oil on canvas, 51 x 65cm.
Christie's, London
25 June 1985.

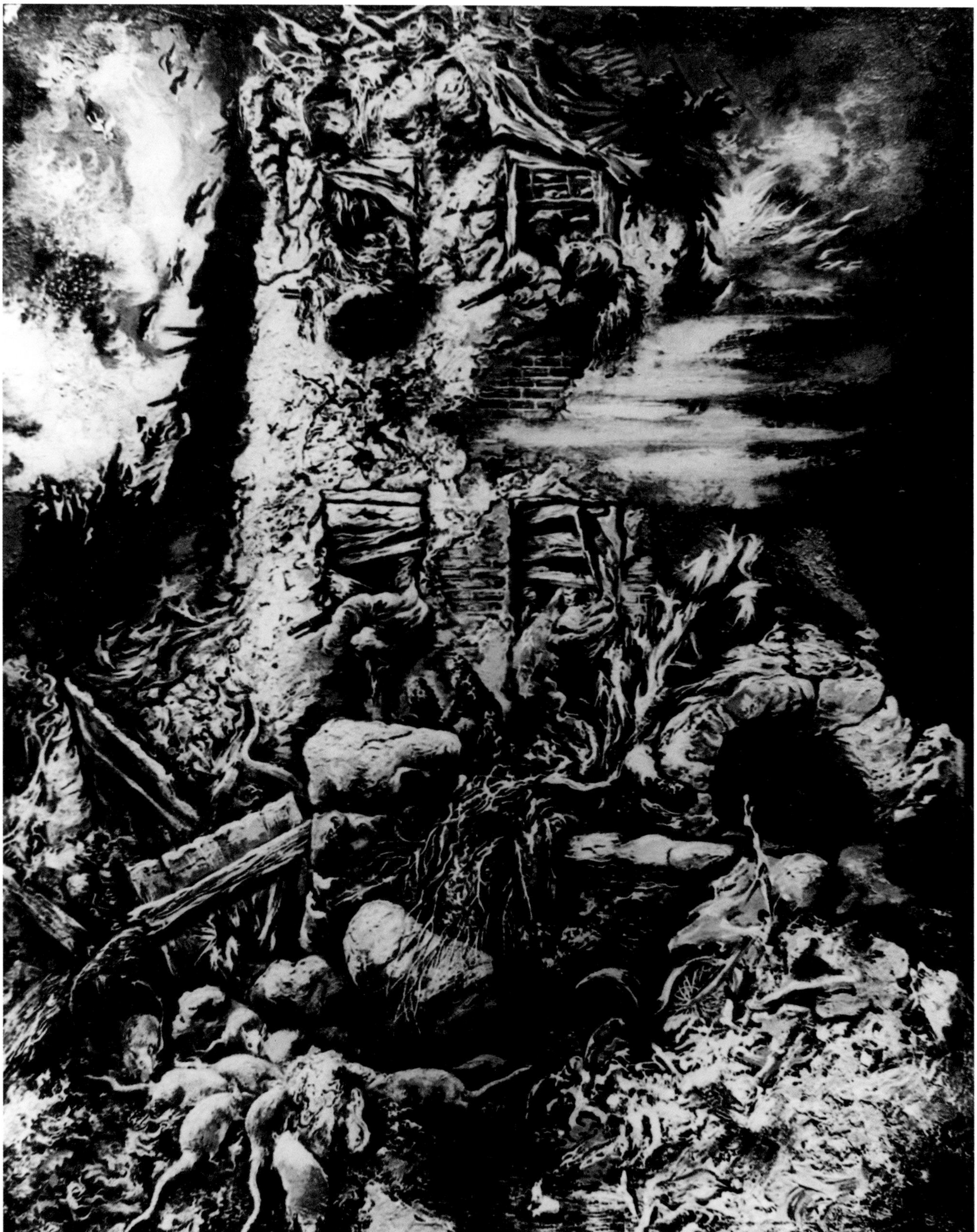

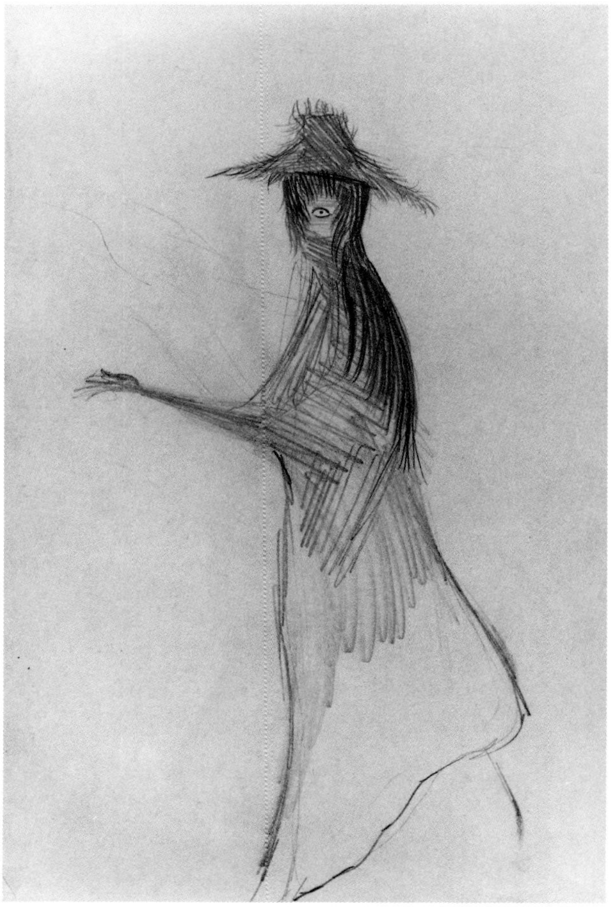

LEONORA CARRINGTON
Drawing from Sketchbook
pencil on paper
23 x 13cm.
EJF.

his wealth, or the disjunctive cultural and social milieu in which he lived.

Henry James had an idea what it meant to be as rich as Edward James. It was not the chief, but the defining characteristic of his heroine Milly Theale in *The Wings of the Dove*:

> *She couldn't dress it away, nor walk it away, nor read it away, nor think it away; she could neither smile it away in any dreamy absence nor blow it away in a softened sigh. She couldn't have lost it if she had tried – that was what it was to be really rich. It had to be* the *thing you were.*[21]

Edward did not want to be thus defined. He published his novels, short stories and poems under a pseudonym, as though this self had to separate from the responsibilities and privileges of Edward James. But his wealth was inevitably the defining feature of his relationship with his artist friends, just as his desire that this should not be so led time and again to bitter disappointment.

The relationship between Edward James and Surrealism raises some basic questions, such as, how is a person or an object to be defined as Surrealist? The real impulses of the movement – which were many and sometimes contradictory – amount to far more than vague notions of the bizarre, unreal or shocking. Membership of the movement is obviously one criterion. This, however, was not always a concern for André Breton, who, in the first Surrealist Manifesto of 1924, designated figures from the past as Surrealist. Swift for example, was 'surrealist in malice', Poe, 'surrealist in adventure' and so on. But if Breton was keen to argue for the possibility of a trans-historical Surrealism, of his own contemporaries complete commitment was demanded. The public's unexpected eagerness to join this new trend and use its terms with freedom disconcerted Breton who sharply closed ranks in the second Manifesto of 1929. Exclusions and excommunications for various failures and compromises were rife. To this Surrealist milieu of intense debate, intellectual and moral solidarity and betrayal, and prolonged visual and verbal experiments, James was a stranger. His humorous description of a visit to Breton in his rue Fontaine apartment, in the summer following the 1936

LEONORA CARRINGTON
Drawing from Sketchbook
pencil on paper
23 x 17cm.
EJF.

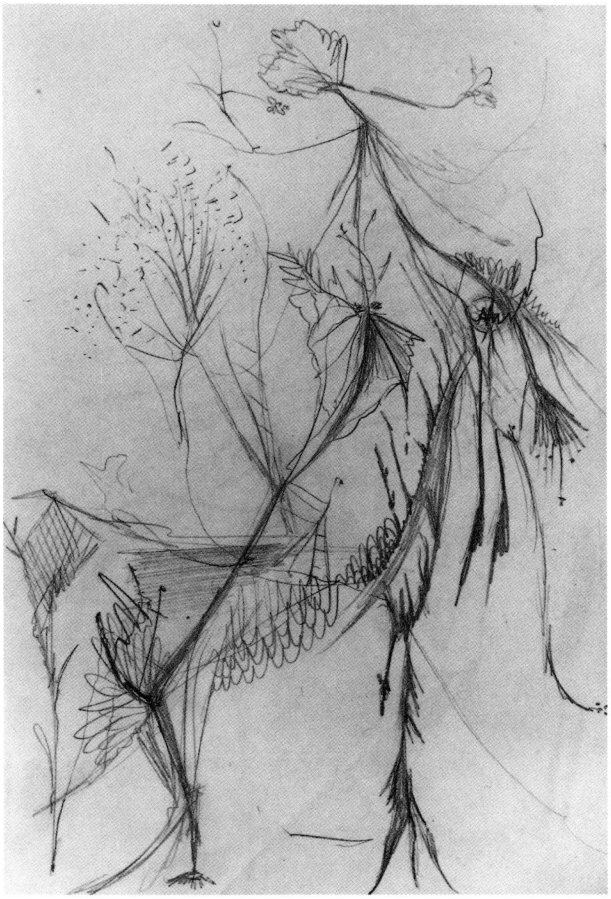

International Surrealist Exhibition in London, is revealing. James found Breton:

> *surrounded by manifestos; this must be fairly typical for him. He signed, made others sign and put into envelopes all these manifestos ... there was a group of signatories of this manifesto who had crossed out their names because they disapproved of something in the text – this was evidently the subject of much discussion, debates in the chosen café and even dramas ...*[22]

James's remoteness from this world is also evident from his relations with the successful satellite group of Surrealists set up in England by Roland Penrose and David Gascoyne with the distinguished recruit, Herbert Read. His correspondence with Penrose was friendly but formal, largely limited to questions concerning the loan of his pictures to the 1936 exhibition. Present at such events during the exhibition as the lecture Dalí gave in a diving suit, James was described by Paul Ray in his study of the Surrealist movement in England as 'Dalí's English manager'.[23]

James relied entirely on his own judgement in his purchase of pictures: he chose according to his own aesthetic sensibilities, and not in relation to any given code, extra-pictorial ideas or set of principles. Many of the artists whose work he bought were not Surrealists, and indeed, several who were aligned with the Surrealists in the public imagination, like Jean Cocteau, were anathema to Breton. Tchelitchew, Berman and Bérard were 'Neo-Romantics', and James collected work by de Chirico from the period subsequent to his abandonment of the metaphysical style that had so engaged the Surrealists. In New York in the 1940s he also became intimate friends with George Grosz and his wife, buying a number of Grosz's paintings and watercolours of the period. Some of these are romantic landscapes, but others, like *Ravaged Landscape* (oil on canvas, 51 x 65cm, Christie's, London, 25 June 1985) have an apocalyptic savagery in which there are still echoes of the old Dadaist – a side of Grosz that surfaces in the collage-letters he sent James.

The artist with whom he had most in common was Leonora Carrington; though her revolt against her background was more fully realised than his own, it was one he understood. He remembers first meeting her in

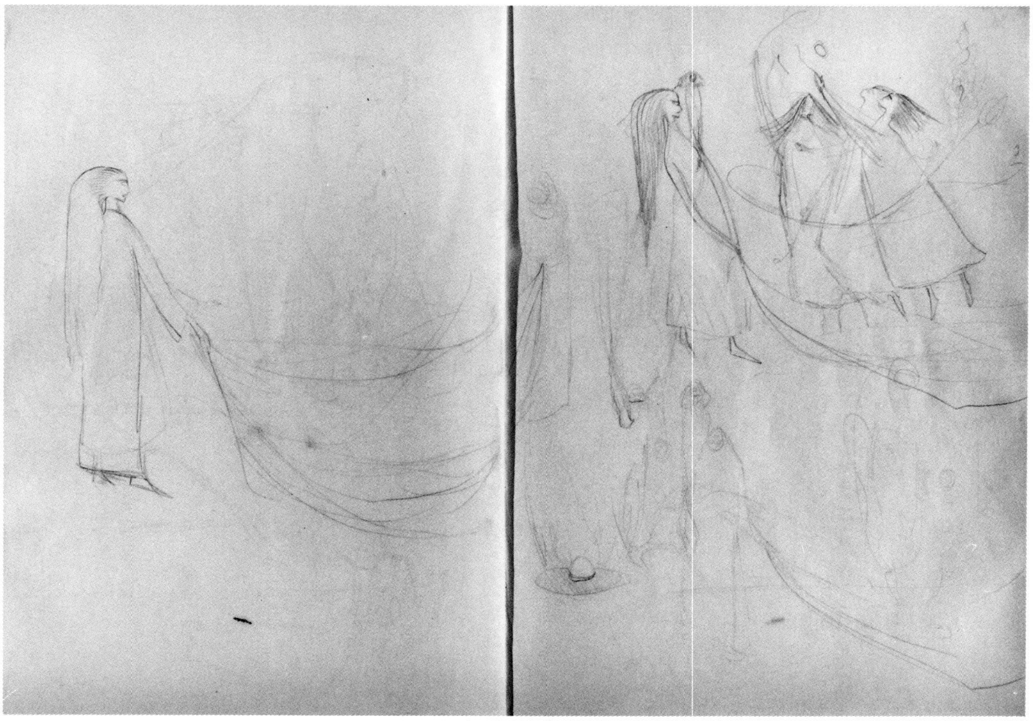

LEONORA CARRINGTON
Drawing from Sketchbook
pencil on paper
23 x 34cm.
EJF.

Acapulco in 1944, where he recognised her quality of being 'permanently in revolt against authority. (So with me also)'.[24] They share memories of a lonely childhood, a country house fearsome with sporting trophies and 'county' characters around whom they could construct humorous and ironic tales.

Mrs Partridge, the imaginary squire's wife, is, James wrote, 'a peculiar personage, but not a whimsical one ...'. Leonora replied: 'She lived highly respected, and is still remembered as the "better half" of poor Colonel Partridge ... when she died the neighbours sighed, she was fay but she was county'. This light reference to the intricate British class system was relished by James, and he owned several of Carrington's paintings that transform the Edwardian tea party or hunting scene into a medieval alchemical world, such as *Again the Gemini are in the Orchard* (1947, oil on board, 91 x 60cm, Christie's, West Dean, 5 June 1986). But he also pointed to a general affiliation with Irish folk mythology and what he described in his introduction to her retrospective exhibition in New York in 1976 as a 'wondrous Celtic feeling'.[25] He was sensitive to the accusation levelled at Surrealist painters in the 1950s that they were 'literary', and insists that hers is not a literary painting: it is not illustration of fairy tales, 'rather they are pictures distilled in the underground caves of libido, vertiginously sublimated. Above all (or below), they belong to the Universal subconscious'.[26]

Unfortunately, the book about women artists that James once contemplated writing was never realised, but it would have explored the multiple traps and obstacles experienced by the female creator. James was constantly trying to extract Carrington from the domesticity that he felt distracted her from her art. A part at least of James must have identified with the opposition she so graphically expressed to the civilisation of western man: 'There are so many questions and so much Dogmaturd to clear aside before anything makes sense and we are on the point of destroying the earth before we know anything at all.'[27]

EDWARD JAMES'S INTERIORS

STEPHEN CALLOWAY

EDWARD JAMES belonged to an intriguing international coterie of rich young men who, between the two World Wars, made the pursuit of beauty, the patronage of avant-garde art and the creation of extravagant interior decorations the abiding passions of their elegantly chic, and often highly eccentric lives. Like the Sitwell brothers, Osbert and Sacheverell, poets and aesthetes whom he initially admired and sought to emulate, James cast himself from the outset in the role of a thoroughly modern Maecenas.

Born into an Edwardian world of almost unlimited wealth and luxury, James was marked to some degree, at least in his earliest visual tastes, by the style of living adopted by his parents, but much more importantly, if rather less tangibly, by the very fact of the opulence – extreme even by the standards of the day – of their great house at West Dean. Accustomed from an early age to an overwhelming richness of furnishing, to a profusion of pictures and sculpture, arrays of hunting trophies and other bric-à-brac, he was always aware of, and sensitive to his mother's often less than subtle striving for effect, her constant search for the reassurance of social position that overtly sumptuous furnishings could provide.

As a result, in later life James seems always to have sought to define himself by the accumulation of pictures and other more unusual treasures, to validate his much desired artistic role through the formation of his collections and the exercise of generous and enlightened patronage, and perhaps most importantly to realise his own fantasies in the creation of bizarrely furnished rooms or, finally, in the building of his unfinished dream palace deep in the jungles of Mexico.

The earliest manifestation of James's desire to create an idiosyncratic style of interior, and thereby make a statement of his own rapidly developing sense of 'apartness' from the ordinary run of things, is to be discerned in the description he left of the college rooms that he had decorated during his brief time at Oxford. Although he went down without taking a degree, his sojourn at Oxford was relatively enjoyable when compared with the unhappiness of his schooldays at Eton. Through an old acquaintance of his mother's, a Professor Lindemann, he secured one of the biggest and best sets of rooms in college, and with what he himself described as 'an enormous allowance'[1] he created a memorable decorative ensemble. His sybaritic bedroom was lined, he recalled, with:

spread silk on the walls, silver and grey
crossed in a diamond-pane weave. The living-

room was full of imitation 17th-Century verdure tapestry which I had bought, and thick pile carpets ... I had very nice William-and-Mary design red curtains, with beige in them ... the one thing that was unusual was that I painted the ceiling very dark purple, and I had a frieze of lighter purple about eighteen inches deep all round this rather high-ceilinged room, with a quotation from Seneca in gold lettering going round it: ARS LONGA VITA BREVIS SED VITA LONGA SI SCIAS UTI ...'[2]

Perhaps warned by some vague Oxford legend of the days when Oscar Wilde and other devotees of the Aesthetic cult had had their rooms sacked by the 'hearties', James decided that he did not want to have 'any good pictures' for fear that they would be 'smashed'. Instead, he chose to hang gently modernistic LNER and Underground Railway posters by Ben Nicholson. Such brash images must have added an intriguing note, spicing up the overall decorative effect, and distancing the look from the conventional richness of Edward's background by the means that would become second nature in everything he did: the juxtaposition of unlikely elements. 'For Oxford it looked very extravagant', admitted the precocious creator of this opulent *studiolo*.[3]

James's circle of friends was an intriguing one: Evelyn Waugh had already gone down from Oxford, but remained much in evidence, whilst Harold Acton, the aesthete and writer, and his brother William, a gifted painter who died tragically young, Michael Ross, Bryan Guinness and John Betjeman were also part of this select group. All these talented men shared a curious mix of aesthetic predilections that happily embraced both avant-garde English and continental art, and the newly fashionable taste for the baroque. In addition, Acton, Ross and Betjemen (as well as the Sitwells and others in the larger fashionable world beyond Oxford) were all beginning to flirt with an, initially at least, self-consciously camp interest in the 19th Century. They relished in particular some of the more bizarre or even surreal qualities that they perceived in Victorian things. For James this strange, but increasingly chic taste would prove highly influential when he first began to think in earnest about playing with the interiors of West Dean or planning the arrangements and decorative effects of a London town-house on the grand scale.

On his twenty-first birthday James inherited the very substantial fortune of more than a million pounds left to him by his Uncle Frank, and on reaching the age of 25, by the terms of his father's will, he at last became master of West Dean. Though free, his actions now unfettered by trustees and guardians, he seems at first to have made no sweeping plans for any alterations either at West Dean or to the London house, 35 Wimpole Street. West Dean must by this time have already appeared as something of a period piece. Edward's father had acquired the house and its vast estate in 1891 and immediately had the interiors entirely remodelled by the highly fashionable architectural practice of Ernest George and Peto, specialists in the grandest, most comfortable, historicising domestic manner. Equally extensive exterior renovations were initiated in 1895 and a new *'tous les Louis'* library, added in 1902, finally expunged the remaining traces of the house's earlier Wyatt gothick appearance. The house was fitted out with every possible luxury, including electric lights (powered by generators), food lifts, a steam laundry and other innovative devices.

Edwin Lutyens, who observed the main house during many visits to the estate occasioned by the building of Monkton House, a sort of *petit trianon* set in the grounds for the family to use as an escape from the oppressive grandeur of their social life, recorded that

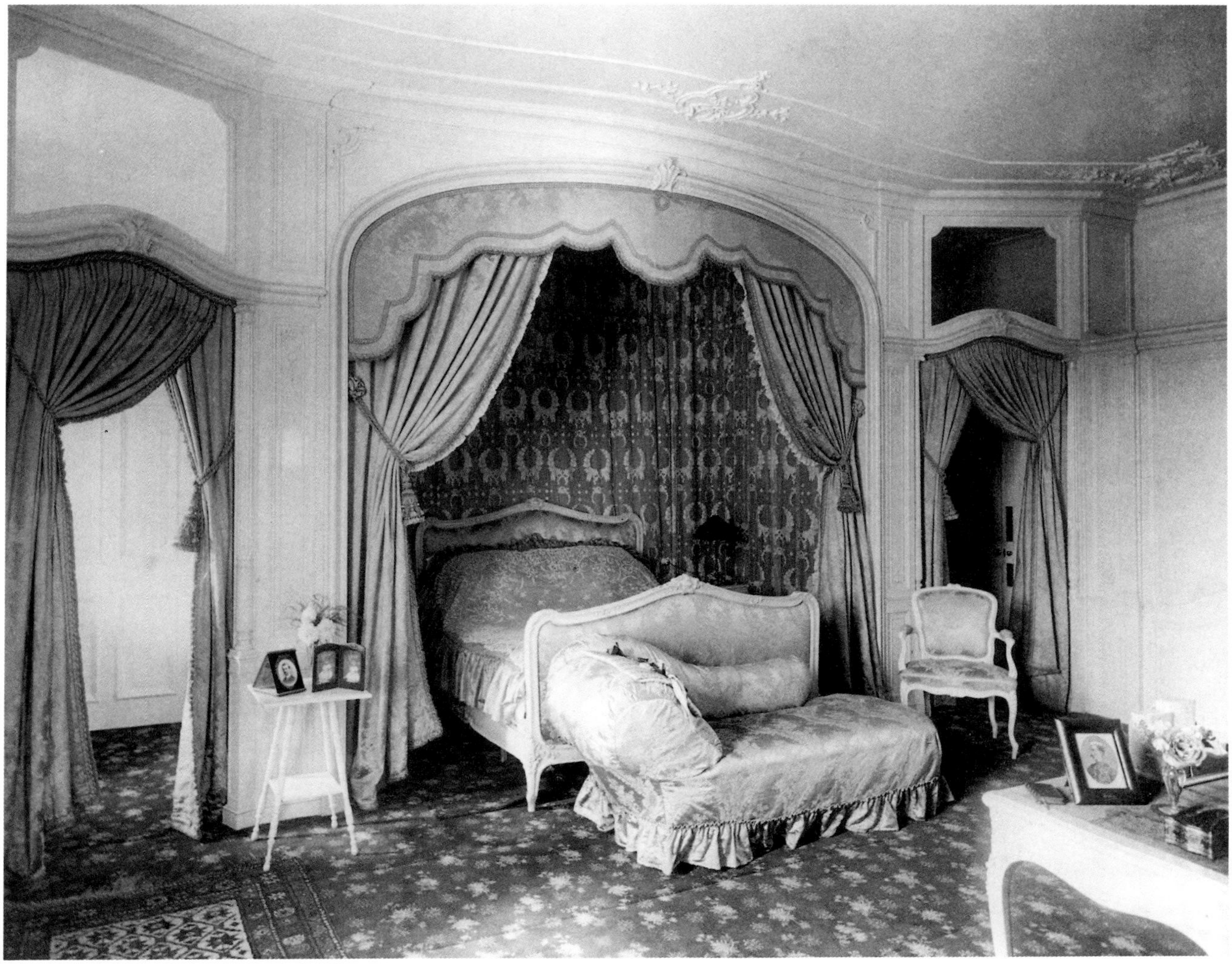

Evelyn James's bedroom,
West Dean House.
EJF.

West Dean appeared to him 'very smart and luxurious ... lots of beautiful things – and a ping-pong table etc. No untoward evidences of Royal favours ... '.[4] The furnishings had been bought from many sources and included some fine things from the Hamilton Palace sale. There were all kinds of continental and 'Old English' pieces as well as plenty of opulently comfortable contemporary upholstery, but also much good 18th-Century satinwood furniture that was very much to chic Edwardian taste. A number of the best pieces were illustrated by the influential early furniture connoisseur Percy MacQuoid in his seminal volume, *Age of Satinwood* (1908).

James's first attempt to add to this already heady mix was in an appropriately fanciful, eclectic style. He commissioned from Rex Whistler designs for a number of carved overdoors, intending to have them carried out in fruitwood by Austrian craftsmen, whom he felt would naturally be able to capture the slightly saccharine-sweet, almost tongue-in-cheek quality of the artist's rococo-revival style.[5]

At this stage James was already exploring certain tentative literary ambitions and increasingly moving in intriguing artistic circles, but his aspirations as a collector and patron were for the most part confined to the acquisition of individual objects. His genius for the creation of the amusing ensemble was yet to emerge. Then, in 1931 he married the exquisite yet cruel dancer, who would quickly break his heart. For the moment, though, with the arrival in his life of Tilly Losch, like a nest-ornamenting bower-bird, James seems to have begun to think in far greater earnest about the decoration of his surroundings, principally aiming to please his beautiful new wife by creating the most lavish settings possible for her. With plans to carry out considerable works at Wimpole Street, he took a smaller house in Culross Street to serve as a temporary base; ironically it was to prove the one place that the difficult-to-please Tilly Losch actually liked, perhaps, as it was said, because someone had pointed out to her that a classic Mayfair address was smarter than one north of Oxford Street.[6]

The first phase of new decorations at Wimpole Street, carried out at the time of his marriage, reveals James's taste in a moment of transition. Still in a sense 'traditional' and grand, the rooms were hardly more than freshened up; such personal touches as were introduced only begin to hint at the more fanciful and surrealistic extravagances to come. Moreover, the one truly extraordinary room in the house, Tilly Losch's glass bathroom, was not one that was generally seen; however, both from a small number of photographs published at the time and perhaps even more by word of mouth, it gained a considerable degree of celebrity and came to be considered as undoubtedly one of the key interiors of the decade, although preceded by Oliver Hill's glass bathroom for Lady Mount Temple, designed in 1930–32. James was clearly motivated by the desire to persuade his wife of the desirability of life in the Wimpole Street house by commissioning a scheme from the painter and designer Paul Nash, which would combine every possible technological innovation of the day with a use of novel materials to create the most startling statement of the Modernist decorative domestic ideal.

The walls of this room were entirely sheathed in coloured glass and mirrors, variously described as being almost black, slate-pink, purplish or mulberry-colour. The six-millimetre 'cathedral' glass panels were finished with a dimpled surface contrived so that their look was not spoiled by the effect of steam and condensation. The dark mirror elements gave a richly lustrous feel to the room; it was, noted that perceptive observer of the era, the Vogue journalist Madge Garland, so very different from the commonplace appearance of the kind of peach glass that became widely popular in suburban 'Deco' bathrooms and bedrooms of the later 1930s. With its modern chrome fittings, neon tube lights, inset electric fire and elegantly laddered dance exercise barre, this was, declared Miss Garland, 'the *ne plus ultra* in bathrooms'.[7]

Edward James's own bathroom, refitted at this date too, is less well-remembered, but was also highly stylish. It was ornamented with trompe l'oeil architectural mural decorations in a modernistic Pompeian manner by Geoffrey Houghton-Brown. A talented young painter, he had recently completed, to considerable acclaim, the jazz-modern style decorations of the smart London restaurant, The Blue Train, a rendezvous much favoured by the Bright Young Things. Houghton-Brown was one of a number of painters who was featured at the celebrated

NORMAN PARKINSON
Edward James on the stairway of 35 Wimpole Street, late 1930s.
EJF. Catalogue no. 63.

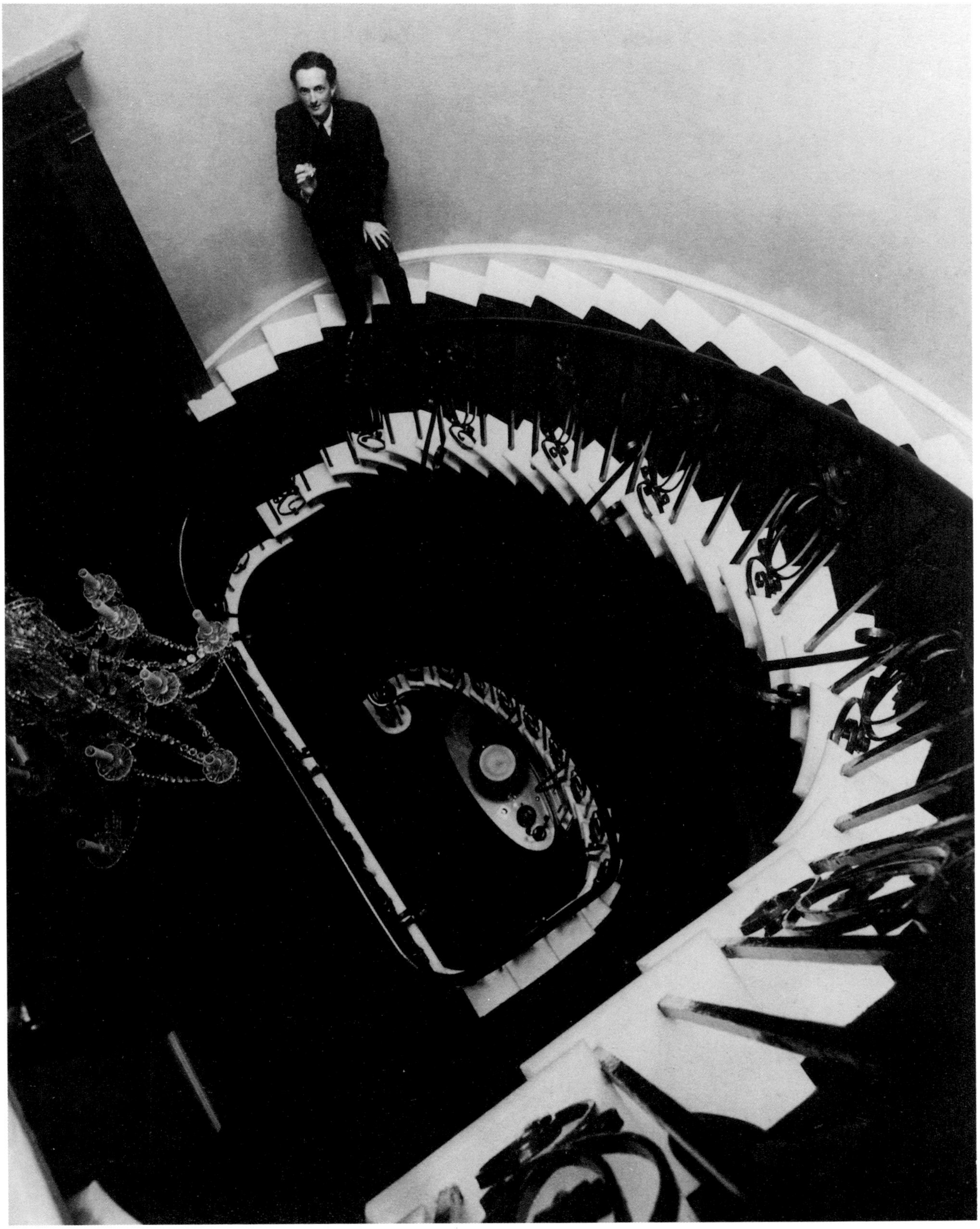

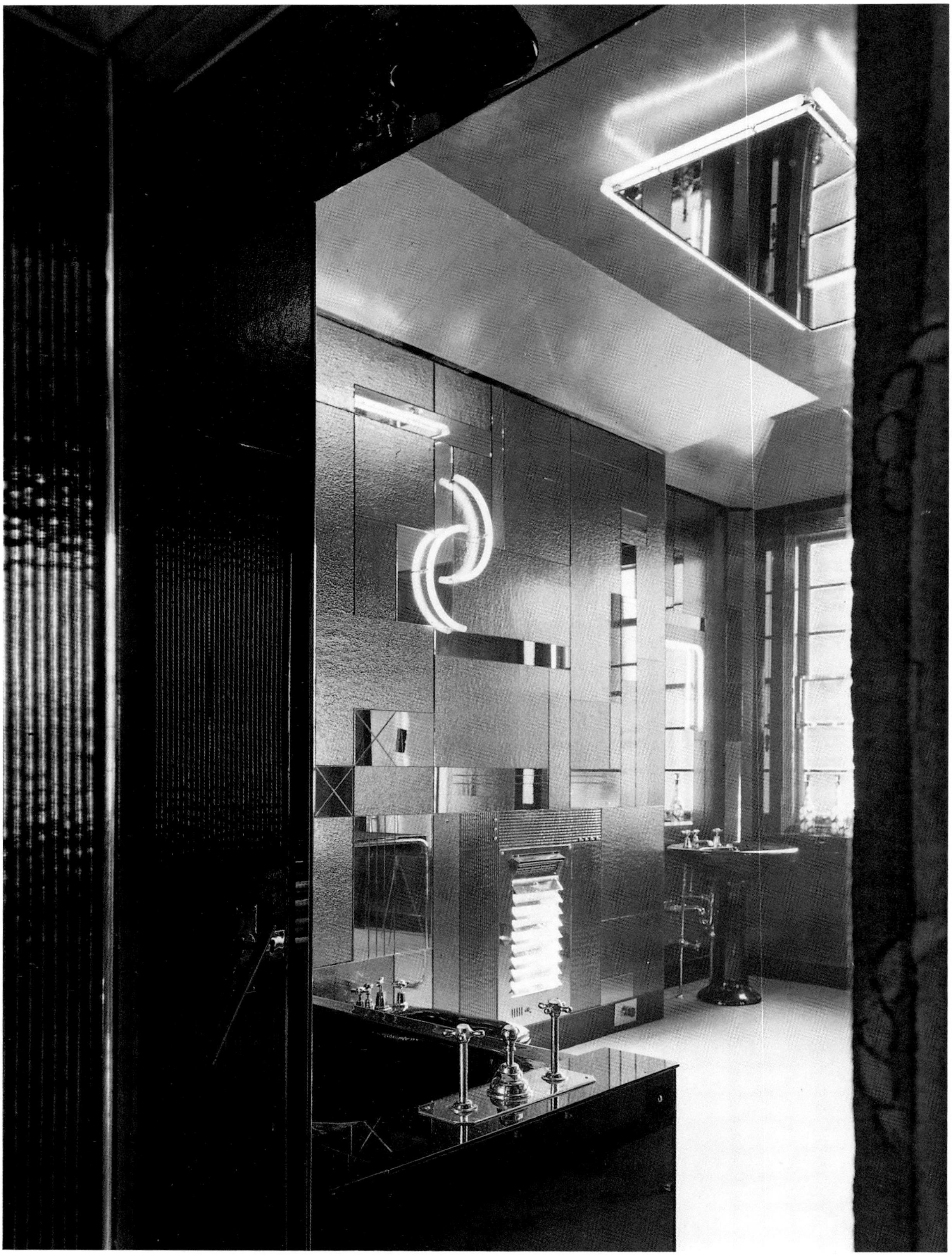

Dorland Hall show of decorative arts in 1933, where his work was prominent among the examples of 'modern traditional' decoration selected by his friend the interior decorator Ronald Fleming. Drawings for the walls of James's bathroom survive, revealing an elaborate scheme in which the false perspectives, visual ambiguities and spatial conundrums of Pompeian decoration are cleverly adapted; this cunning re-vamping of ancient visual tricks must have had considerable appeal for James, who always relished revelations of the irrational in the arts.

Like many a rich man considering schemes of decoration, James had flirted with a number of designers and interior specialists. One, however, would prove crucial. Norris Wakefield, the junior partner in the small, but highly successful firm owned and run by that great stylist Mrs 'Dolly' Mann, recalled that he first met James at a party when they talked about cushions. Although he recognised later that it was 'the watershed' in his decorating career, James's subsequent first visit to their shop – at a moment when Mrs Mann was away, leaving Wakefield, then just 24 years old, in charge – gave little real intimation of what was to come. Initially James merely asked about the possibility of ordering four cushions, tentatively wondering if they could be ready by the weekend; thus began one of the most extraordinary episodes in the history of 20th-Century interiors. The cushions were completed and James, finding Wakefield an interesting and sympathetic young man invited him to go down with him the following weekend to the country in order to discuss 'further possibilities'. According to Wakefield's recollection, they were driven at great speed in James's luxurious Rolls, but had already, by the time they arrived at West Dean, thought up several amusingly extravagant ideas.[8]

One of the first to be realised was the famous carpet designed specifically for the stairs that led to Tilly's bathroom at West Dean, woven with a repeating pattern like her delicate little wet footprints. The effect entranced Edward, who used the carpet in several places. Years later Norris Wakefield mused upon the idea that he should have contrived the footprints to appear only on the treads and not on the risers of the stairs; that final sophistication did not, he said, occur to him until too late. A second version of the design, substituting the footprints of Edward's favourite dog, was also woven. With the all-too rapid failure of his

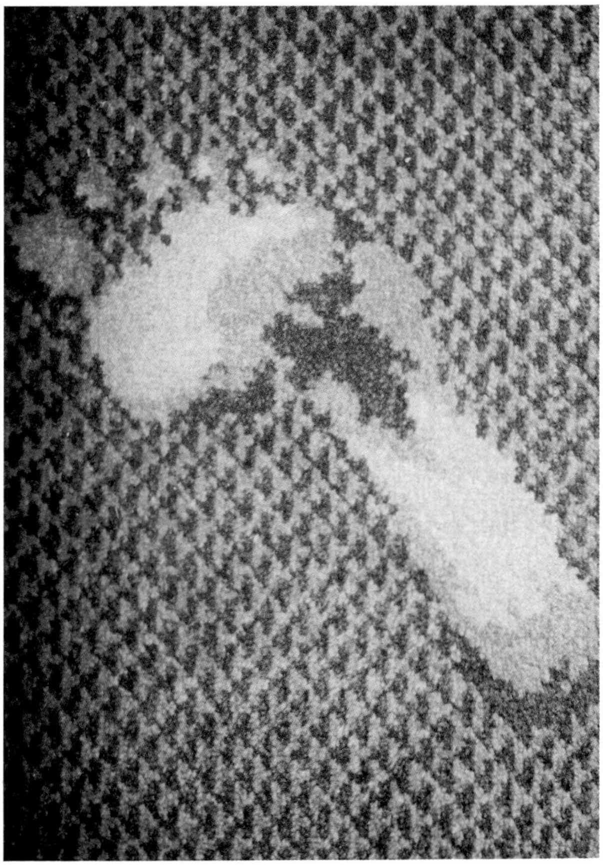

Bathroom designed by Paul Nash for 35 Wimpole Street.

Detail of Tilly Losch footprint carpet, early 1930s. Catalogue no. 87.

marriage, Edward would come to reflect ironically that this second carpet represented a more faithful friend.[9]

With the departure of Tilly, far from giving up his decorative schemes, Edward threw all his enthusiasm into the creation of what can inevitably be read as an emotionally 'safer', more private world of the imagination, a world in which collecting and the realisation of fantasies through decoration was to prove both a distraction from pain and an all-absorbing passion. His schemes at this time encompassed both making changes to many of the rooms at Wimpole Street to make them reflect his now more fanciful tastes, as well as the decision, taken towards the end of 1935, largely to abandon life in the big house at West Dean and to concentrate on making the little Lutyens house, Monkton, the embodiment of his dreams and the ideas of his new, surrealist friends Dalí, Magritte and Tchelitchew.

In London, particularly with the advent of Dalí who stayed with Edward frequently in these years, most of the rooms at 35 Wimpole Street generally became more bizarre in aspect. In spite of Dalí's strange plans for surreal dinners served by dwarfs, and other drolleries,[10] the vast dining room, one of the first great decorative set-pieces of the house, remained perhaps least changed. It was a *tour-de-force* in the sophisticated Vogue Regency manner first popularised a few years earlier by decorators and collectors such as Lord Gerald Wellesley. By co-incidence, Wellesley was a close friend of Mrs Mann, who as one of a handful of crucial taste-making 'lady decorators' of the period, became the commercial doyenne of the style. She and Wakefield supplied the large and superb suite of late 18th-Century painted furniture, a speciality for which the firm was principally known. The colours of the chairs – predominantly sea-green and blue-grey with touches of brilliant coral – found an echo in the enormous pictorial carpet, one of James's single greatest decorative commissions, woven to the curved shape of the room and designed by Rex Whistler. Depicting a florid baroque Neptune seated in an aquatic triumphal car surrounded by jolly mermaids, sea-nymphs and sportive dolphins, its background of conventionalised wave motifs was enclosed by a broad border in the form of a massive *trompe-l'oeil* gilded frame with cartouches bearing the initials 'E.J.'.

In contrast to this still formal grandeur, elsewhere in the house far more unusual effects were gleefully introduced. For example, many of James's newly acquired Surrealist pictures, including his fine group of exquisitely finished small oils and elaborate drawings by Dalí, were displayed in a cleverly contrived system of sliding panels, which lit up as each was opened and its picture revealed. Dalí also from time to time created other individual fantasy objects for the house such as his celebrated *Lobster Telephone*. James's study, previously a sober enough room, was also now theatrically transformed by the introduction of a set of massive semi-precious marble columns with gilded capitals all-but engulfed by vast, billowing draperies held back by ropes and tassels. Norman Parkinson's well-known photograph of James seated at his beautiful, Italian neo-classical desk in this room, private editions of his own poems carelessly strewn before him, clearly reveals the extent to which the study interior reflected the style of Tchelitchew's decorations for *L'Errante*, one of the most visually arresting of the productions staged by Les Ballets 1933.

It was at Monkton, however, that James's desire to create a complete Surrealist house was to be most wholeheartedly pursued and successfully realised. Guided to some extent by the artistic vision of Dalí the complete transformation of the previously earnest Arts and Crafts house as designed by Lutyens was effectively the work of the architect, Christopher 'Kit' Nicholson (and his assistant, at that time, Hugh Casson) and of Norris Wakefield, who spent at least

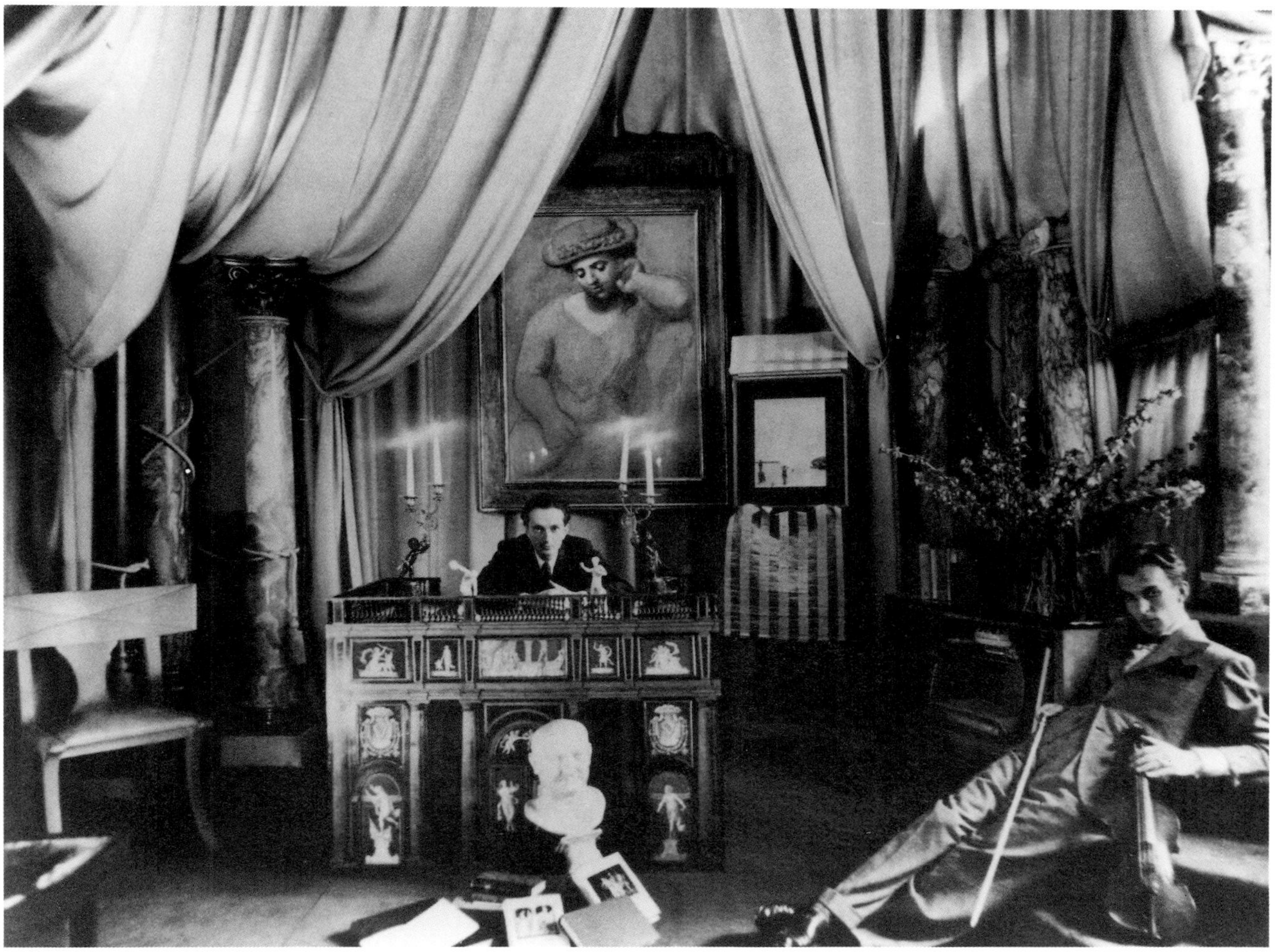

one day a week there for a period of some four years.[11] Before commencing work, James had consulted Lutyens's son Robert out of politeness to ascertain his reactions to the planned changes. Hardly in any position to raise objections, he gave the project his blessing; in the event almost all trace of the original character of Lutyens's house was ruthlessly obliterated.[12]

The exterior of the house was radically altered by the addition of fanciful 'bamboo' drain pipes, elaborate palm-tree columns flanking the central doorway and by curious swags beneath the windows that played on classical allusions whilst also suggesting the more light-hearted notion of towels hung out to dry. Dalí is said to

NORMAN PARKINSON
Edward James and Igor Markevitch in the 'Tent Room' at 35 Wimpole Street, late 1930s.
Edward James is seated behind the desk; the composer Igor Markevitch is seated in the foreground. Pablo Picasso's *Femme Assise Au Chapeau* (1923) and Salvador Dalí's *White Calm* (1936) are in the background.
EJF. Catalogue no. 65.

have suggested these motifs, in which Surrealism subverts a more classic 'English' sort of exoticism, as well as prompting the choice of the extraordinary purple colour with which the masonry is rendered, an effect so unusual in the English countryside as still to cause shock today. Nicholson's alterations to the interior structure mainly focused on certain essential improvements such as the modernisation of the bathrooms, but also, more importantly, the creation of a new, very 'thirties', cast-concrete sweeping staircase, replacing Lutyens's original hand-crafted woodwork.

Beyond this, almost all of the extraordinary effects were realised by Norris Wakefield using both traditional and novel decorative techniques. His recollection was that most of the actual ideas came from James himself. Characteristically, each discussion would begin with an enquiry such as: 'Wakefield, what about this quilting nonsense, do you think you could quilt the walls?' However far-fetched the suggestion, generally, if at times tentatively, Wakefield answered that things were possible; to which James would invariably reply 'Good, let's do it then'. As a result of such precipitous enthusiasm many of the problems posed sent Wakefield scurrying off to question his friends and colleagues. Fortunately in those creative inter-war years his immediate circle was part of a widespread network of talented people, or as he described it 'a sort of brotherhood of artists, decorators and fashion people ... with grasshopper brains' who could work out how to realise even the most unlikely, theatrical ideas. Nothing, according to Wakefield, was actually particularly expensive to do.[13]

One extravagance was the special creation of a boldly patterned cloth, widely used on the walls throughout the house, which combined elements of Hispano-moresque or medieval Siennese style with an essentially jazz-modern insistence of pattern. This enlivened the entrance hall, in which Nicholson's staircase had the added attraction of a porthole affording a view into a tall, columnar fish tank, which rose towards a fish-themed bathroom above, and in which tropical fish, sea-anemonies and other exotica were to be seen. Various odd objects were gathered here including some Victorian items, perhaps used ironically, as well as fashionable artifacts such as African wooden sculptures.

James's study was decorated with a startling colour scheme based upon a highly original notion of his own to line the walls with the same blue serge fabric as his suit. This novel effect was relieved by upholstery and other notes in the brilliant cowslip yellow of his favourite buttonhole. A further amusing conceit was the idea of concealing the door completely; it had no visible handle and could only be opened by operation of a hidden tab and a pedal set in the floor. One of the other most important rooms at Monkton was the drawing room, where all the walls and even the concealed door were upholstered, in this instance in softly luxurious diamond-quilted fabric. The effect curiously recalls James's first excursion into whimsical decoration in the sitting room of his college rooms at Oxford, which was also diamond-paned in silk. Here Edward hung many of his best pictures, whilst extravagant Chinoiserie cabinets, thought to have come from the Royal Pavilion at Brighton, and a more sober Marion Dorn key-patterned rug completed the effect.

James's own bedroom was dominated by a vast canopied bed, modelled upon a print of the catafalque prepared for the burial of Nelson.[14] The corner-posts were carved in the form of palm trees and the billowing dark green, almost black silk draperies were trimmed with massive bullion fringing. The walls of the bedroom were hung with shimmering silver net, whilst drapes of mesh, like medieval chain-mail, concealed the radiators, which supplied a touch of modern comfort to this otherwise uncompromisingly funereal room. Next door in James's bathroom the mood lightened: honey-coloured

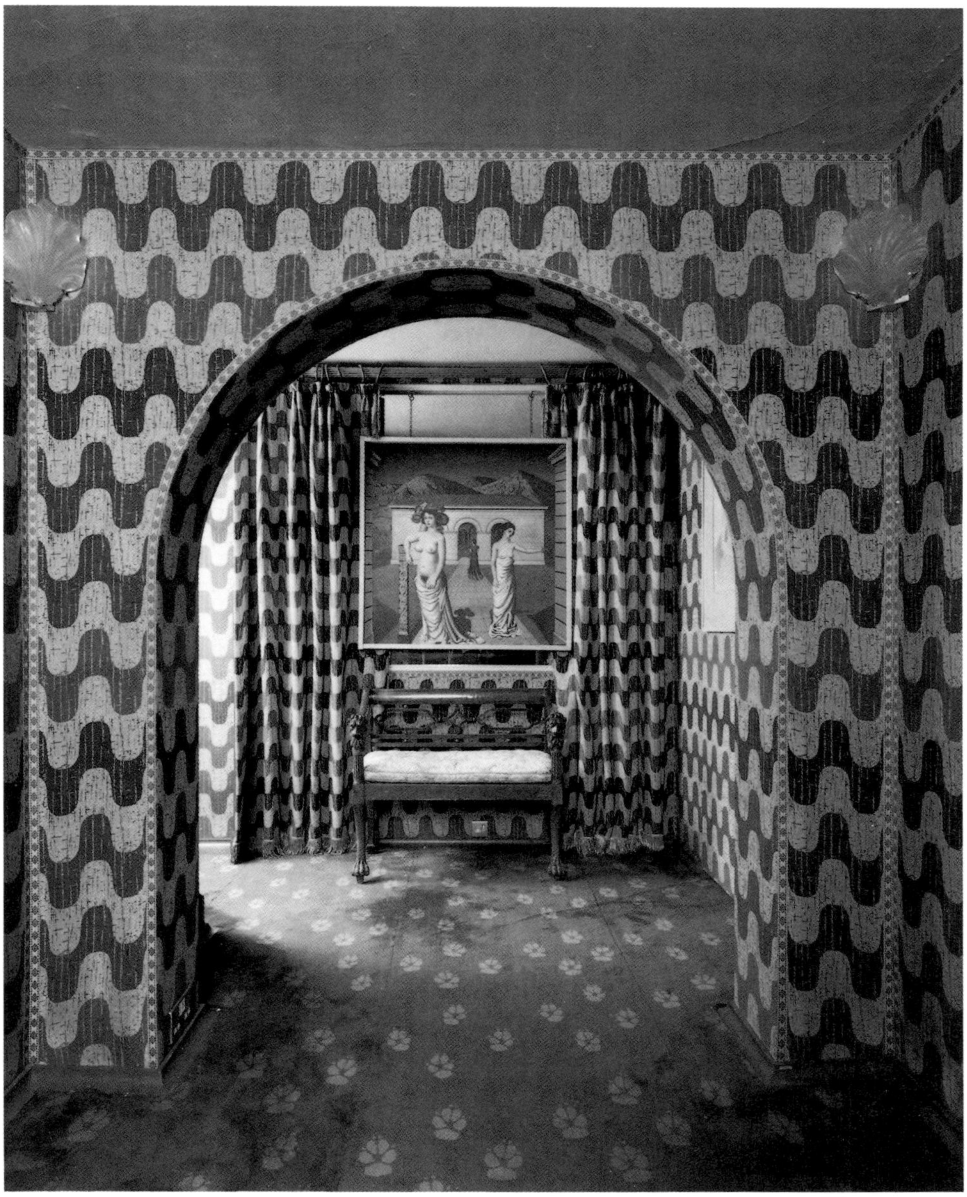

Corridor,
Monkton House.

alabaster walls were crowned by a jade domed ceiling. The circular shaving mirror represented the world, and lights glimmering through the alabaster on either side represented the sun and the moon.

Another famous set-piece in the house, which realised one of James's particular fantasies, was the creation of a ceiling that could be seen from the grand ebony bed in his so-called Map Room, contrived as a representation of the night sky lit up by the planets and stars. As a further sophistication of the original concept, James insisted that the position of the heavenly bodies represented that of the moment of his birth. As a result, Wakefield spent interminable hours 'pushing small pieces of paper representing the Great Bear, the Little Bear and so forth' round and round, whilst James 'lay on the bed directing the operation with great amusement'.[15]

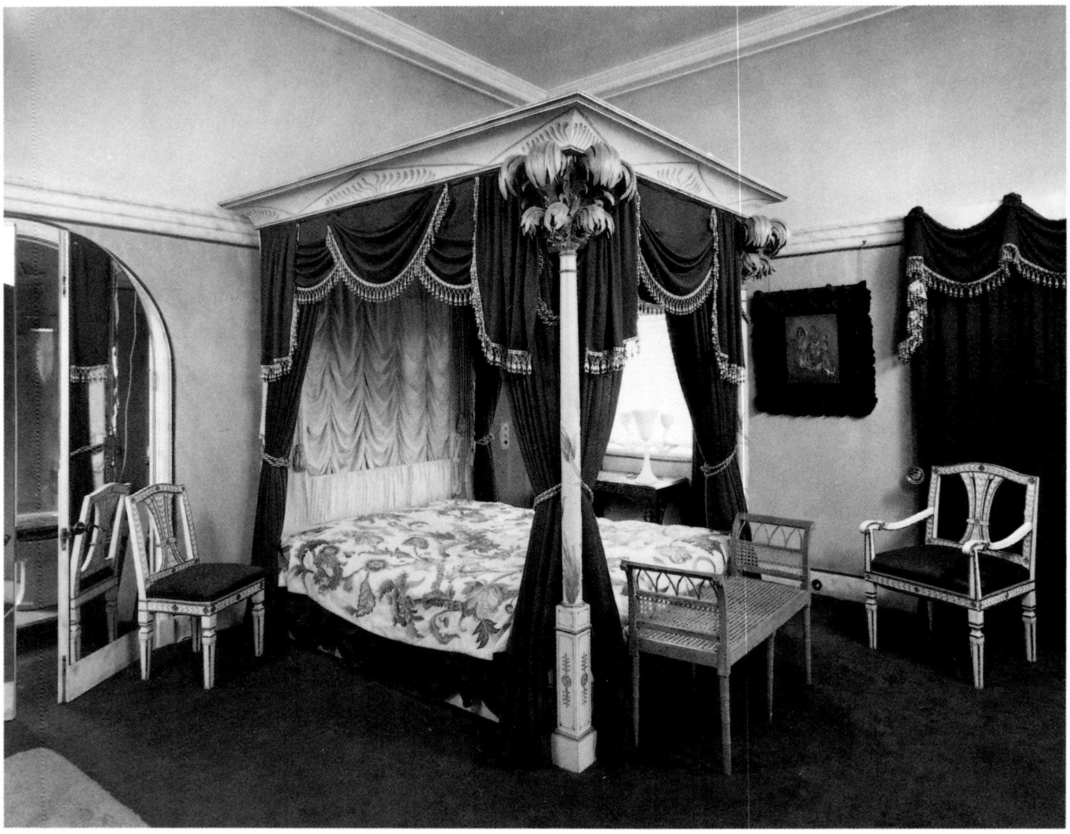

Edward James's bed, Monkton House. Catalogue no. 198.

Finally, in the dining room, where the windows were shaded by black crochet-work pelmets like an old Spanish sacristy, and in which many of the other pieces were black-fringed, stood the most celebrated pieces of furniture in James's collection, Dalí's *Lips* sofas, based on one of his paintings. Two such sofas were made by the Parisian decorator Jean-Michel Frank for the couturière Elsa Schiaparelli; these were covered in 'shocking pink' satin as Dalí originally planned. (One is owned by The Trustees of The Edward James Foundation.) Of those realised for James, carried out by John Hill's decorating firm, Green and Abbott, one was finished in two tones of pink felt (Royal Pavilion, Libraries & Museums, Brighton & Hove), and another pair in red felt (The Trustees of The Edward James Foundation). When the red ones began to show signs of wear on their backs, Dalí and James conceived the delightful notion of having small patches in the form of caterpillars appliquéd over the holes.

Epitomising James's taste, his enthusiasm for the exotic and the extravagant, the *Lips* sofa seems the perfect iconic representation of the achievement of a man whom Dalí characterised as 'a humming bird poet [who] ordered lobster telephones, bought the best Dalís and was naturally the richest [of all his friends]'.[16] Few collectors though, have achieved so much, or so fully realised their dreams in the creation of a collection and its setting. As Julien Levy, the great promoter of the Surrealists and Neo-Romantics, so subtly observed: 'Edward was fabulously rich, generously constructive and annoyingly willful ... he was what certain great patrons of the past must have been, not an employer, but a fortunate man gifted with poetic insight.'[17]

EDWARD JAMES IN XILITLA

XAVIER GUZMÁN URBIOLA
TRANSLATED BY T. G. HUNTINGTON

'Exuberance is Beauty' William Blake[1]

'I understood that what I was looking at, far from being an unfinished house, was originally conceived as a disquieting ruin' Jorge Ibarguengoitia[2]

In 1934, when a scandalous divorce, combined with the bellicose tide in Europe, caused Edward James to flee from England, he turned that great estrangement, his evasion, into his grandest exploit.

James arrived in Cuernavaca, Mexico in 1944, having been invited to the residence of Geoffrey Gilmore, an old companion from Oxford. He came as a tourist on a brief stay that was to determine the rest of his life. Here he met the man who would eventually become one of his closest friends: Plutarco Gastelum Esquer, with whom he toured a treacherous infinity of muddy local roads in a red Lincoln Continental. This Mexico of contrasts, of pyramids and poverty, of great culture and overflowing exuberance, attracted and horrified him at the same time (these conflicting sentiments are typical reactions to this country). Upon his return the following year, he discovered Xilitla, drawn by its orchids.[3]

At the time, Xilitla was a lovely mountain village immersed in thick, semi-tropical jungles in the far south of the Huasteca region of San Luis Potosí. It was here that according to numerous stories,[4] on one particular day, during an excursion to the peak called Huestmolotepl – better known today as La Silleta – he was bathing in a natural pool when the sacred revealed itself to him. Suddenly, the sky was overcast by a thick cloud of butterflies. For a moment, he beheld his companion entirely covered by tiny vibrating wings that transformed him into a butterfly-man. It was The Sign. This was, in his own words, his 'earthly paradise'[5], the place where, to paraphrase Mircea Eliade, he should establish his base, his foundation and orientation within a world of chaos.[6]

James's first condition for the selection of a site had been fulfilled: distance. It could be said that, both geographically and culturally, he found himself at the opposite pole to his origins. However, his choice was also governed by ease of access: Xilitla is located near Tamasunchale on the path of the old, and in those days, the only, highway that ran between Mexico City and Laredo, which continues to be the capital city's nearest border crossing with the United States today. At the same time, unlikely as this may seem, the exuberance of the flora in the Huasteca region is very similar to the prodigious vegetation of West Dean park, different in kind but equally bountiful. A further condition governing James's choice of retreat was of an almost religious, edifying nature: he put his marks on the site with architecture, creating his world and charging it with hierophantic content. It was not the first time he had done so. James's intervention in the foundation, construction and

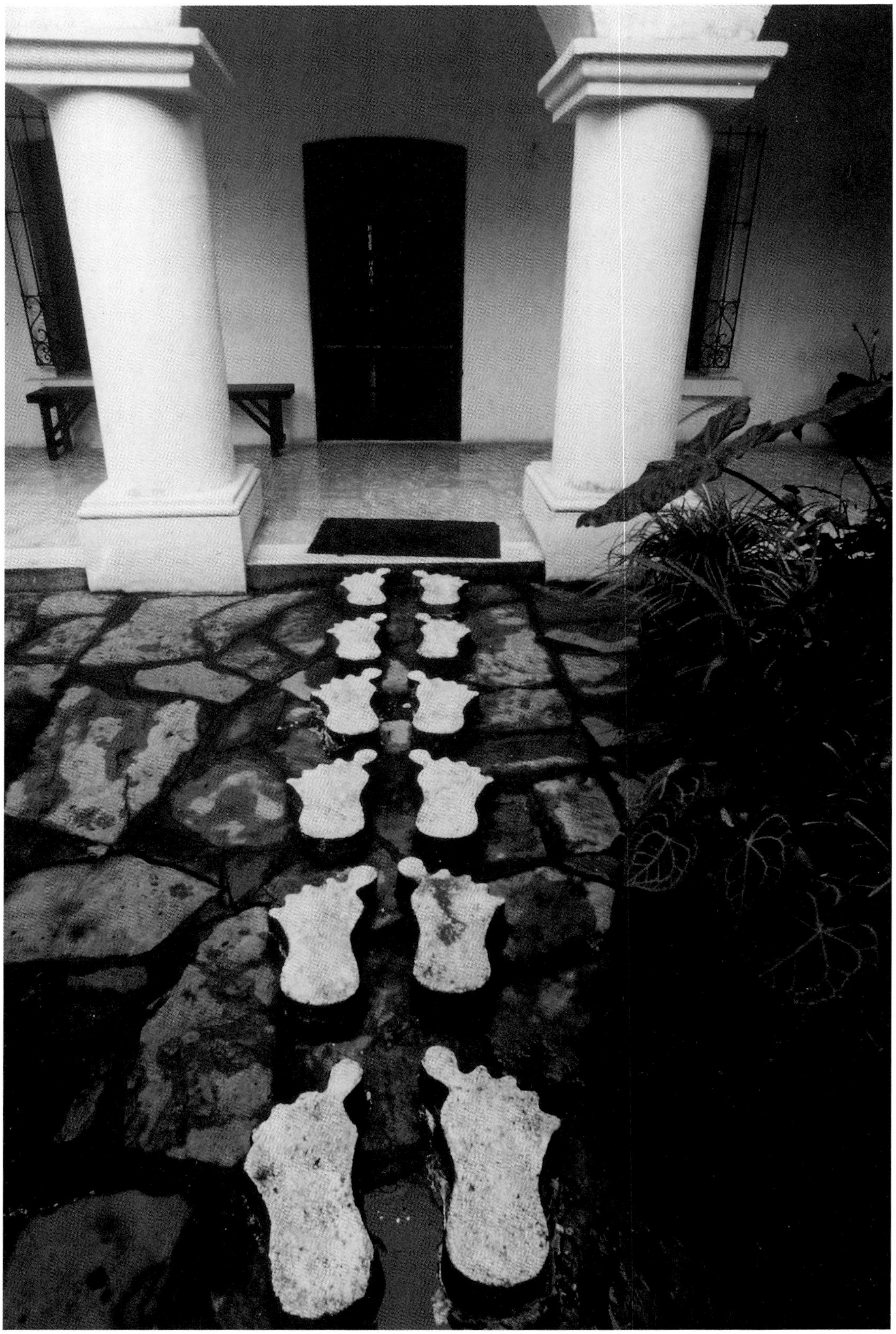

Entrance to Plutarco Gastelum's house, Xilitla, 1993.

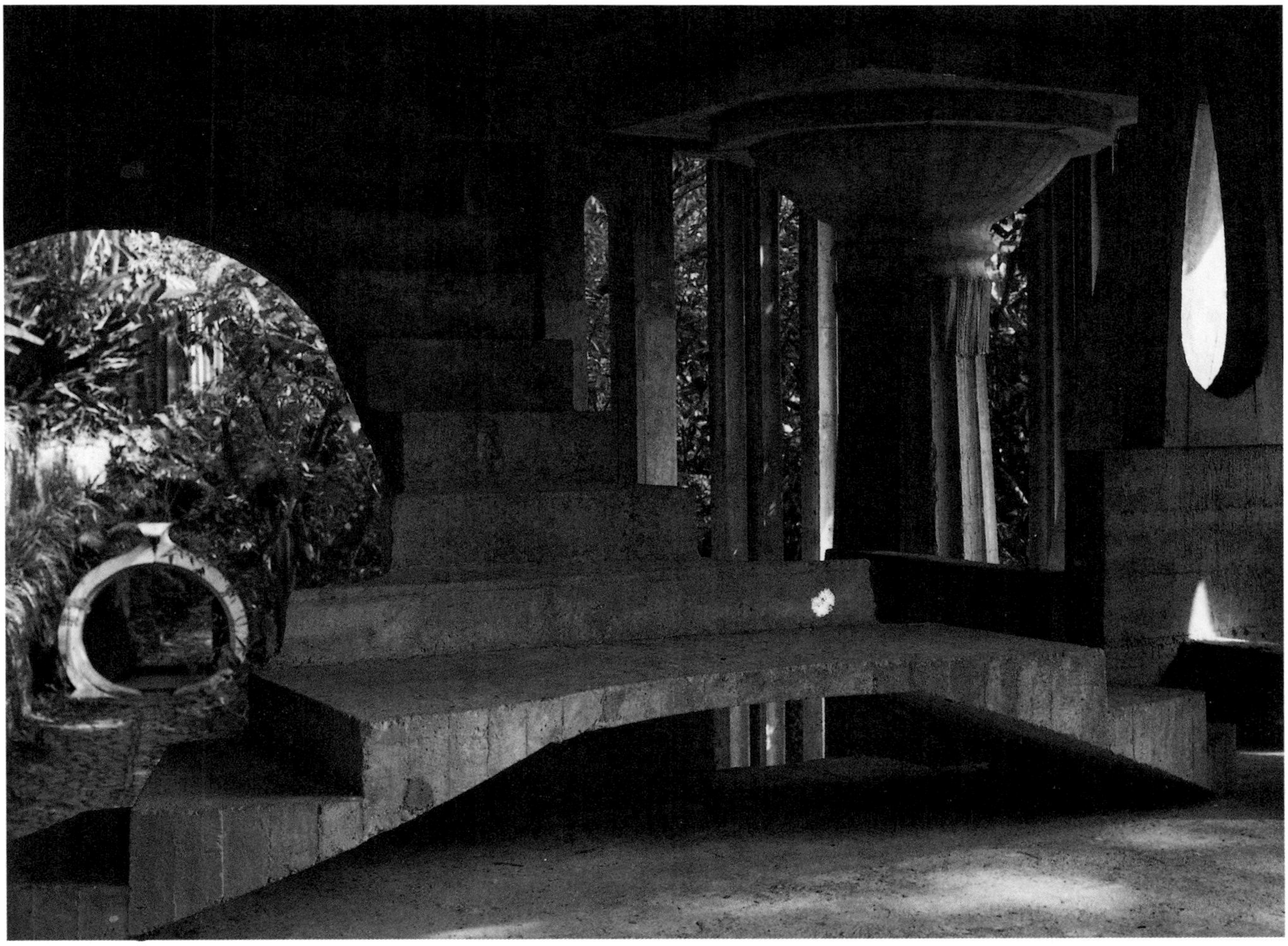

MARIANA YAMPOLSKY
Access to the Cinema Xilitla,
1996. The artist.
Catalogue no. 231.

edification of his homes was a constant theme throughout his life; his incessant search for a home was perhaps never entirely fulfilled, and his arrival in Mexico was plagued by these apprehensions.

The available information suggests that James began, between December 1948 and March 1949, by acquiring a 75-acre ranch in Xilitla called La Conchita, as well as an 'urban estate'.[7] By then, James had commissioned the construction of the first hut – rather more like a tower – as his dwelling. It was both modest and bizarre, located on the slope of a hill bordering the ranch, on the road that led to the neighbouring town.

It is evident that James did not calculate *a priori* the construction of his fantastical, whimsical structures. Any explanation would be provisional; I am inclined to venture the following sequence of events.[8] Gastelum proposed that James construct some sort of attraction at La Conchita, 'some bungalows or swimming pools', but it appears that James was not pleased with the idea. By 1952, Gastelum was referring to the house that James had bought for them in the town of Xilitla as his own property.[9] This was an enormous residence that had once belonged to a general of the Mexican

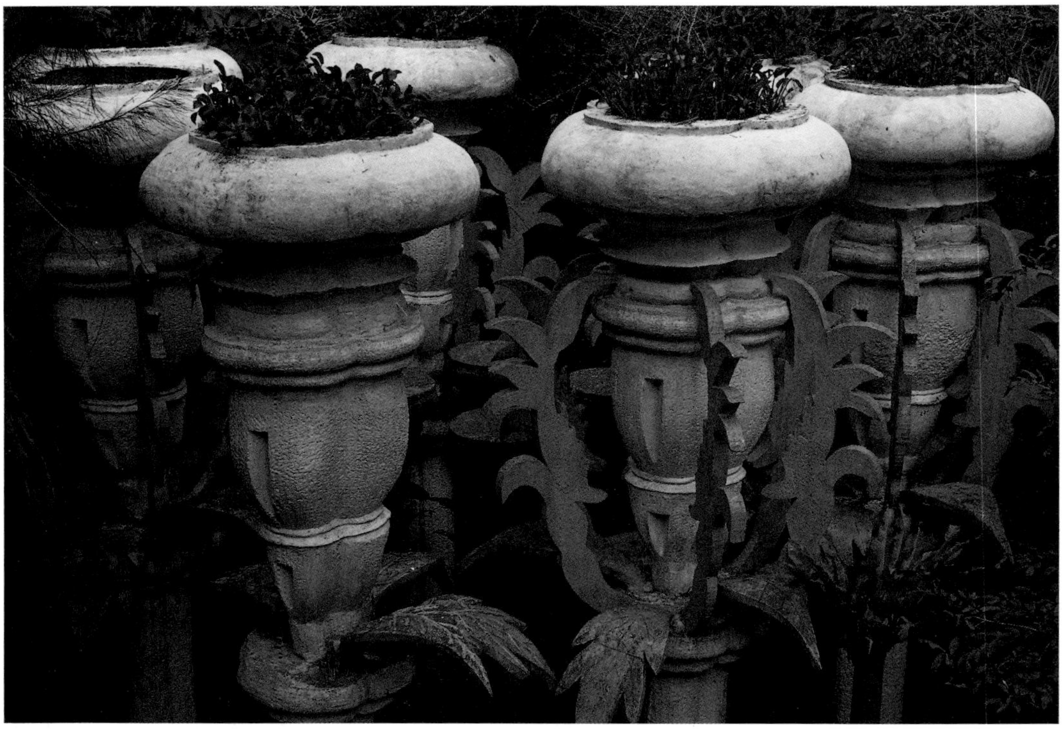

MARIANA YAMPOLSKY
Homage to Max Ernst,
Xilitla, 1996.
The artist.
Catalogue no. 230.

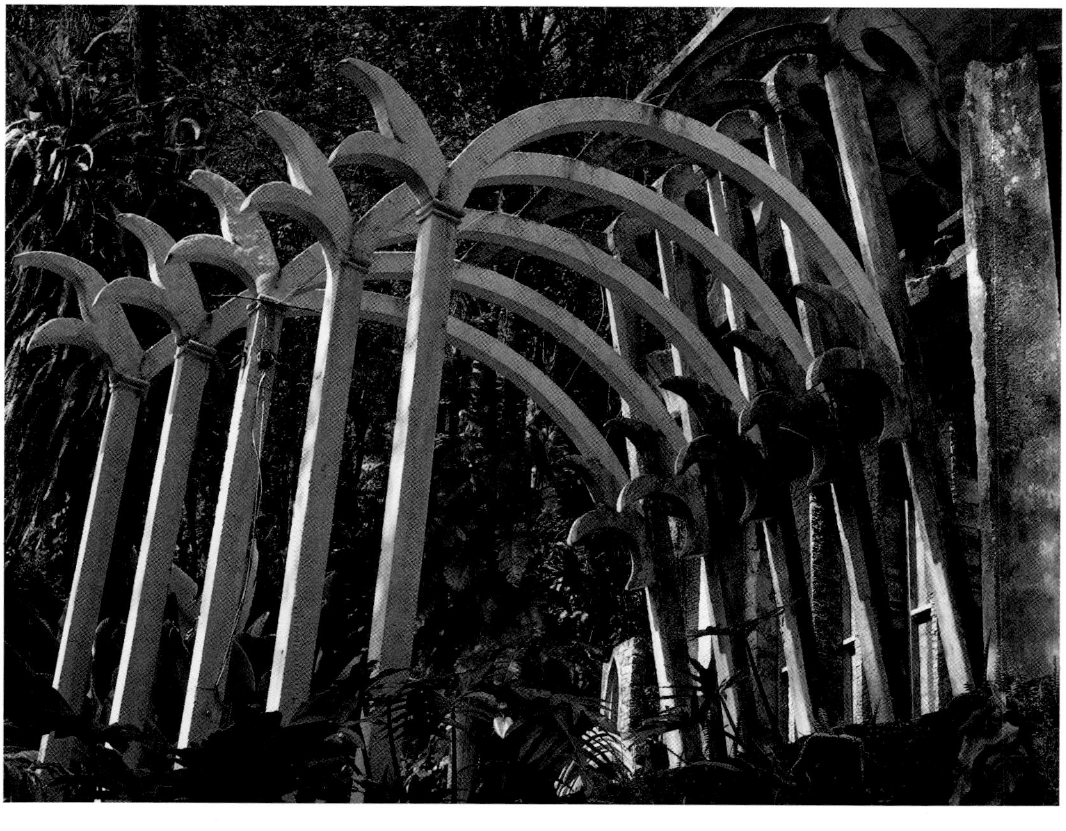

MARIANA YAMPOLSKY
Aviary,
Xilitla, 1996.
The artist.
Catalogue no. 236.

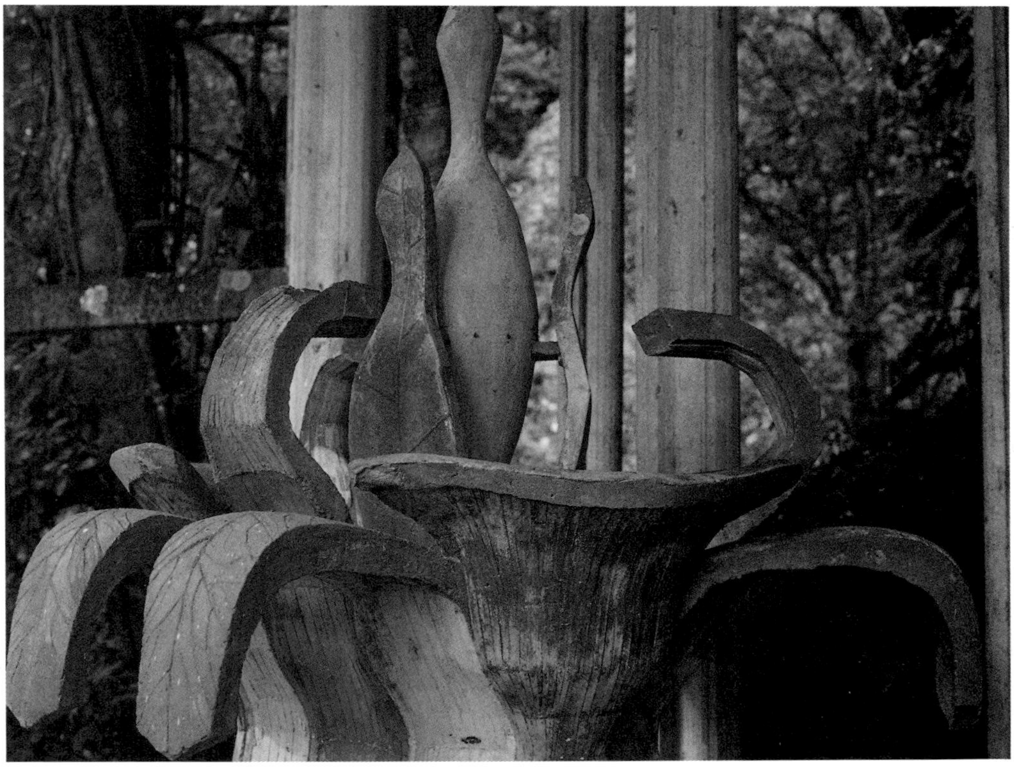

MARIANA YAMPOLSKY
Flowering,
Xilitla, 1996.
The artist.
Catalogue no. 229.

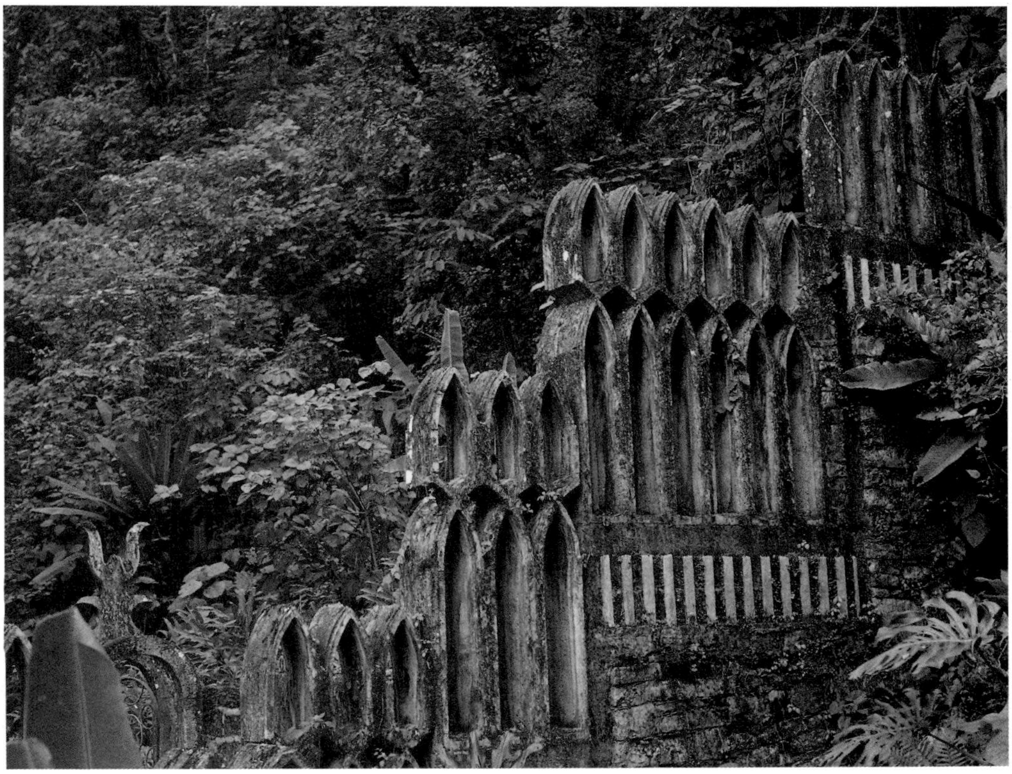

MARIANA YAMPOLSKY
Gothic Wall,
Xilitla,1996.
The artist.
Catalogue no. 232.

Revolution of 1910, and Gastelum intuitively began the construction of a masterpiece of residential architecture. Appropriating a 19th-Century cloister, he added a corridor around the rooms in order to gain maximum natural ventilation. He also built a tower, crowned by prismatic triangles, terraces and a swimming pool. James was fascinated by this house, and Gastelum's family essentially became his own.

On each of his trips to Xilitla, James arrived loaded down with a variety of caged animals: deer, macaws, parrots, ducks, ocelots, doves. He also brought along an overwhelming quantity of plants, giving priority, of course, to the orchids he transported from remote areas. In order to accommodate this Noah's Ark, wooden cages were constructed,[10] which grew increasingly more complex, and, through the intervention of local masons, more and more eye-catching.

By 1960, following a frost that destroyed the huge collection of orchids he had managed to cultivate, James began to talk about creating his unorthodox, Surrealist constructions. He has said that he decided to

MARIANA YAMPOLSKY
Gateway and Snakes,
Xilitla, 1996. The artist.
Catalogue no. 233.

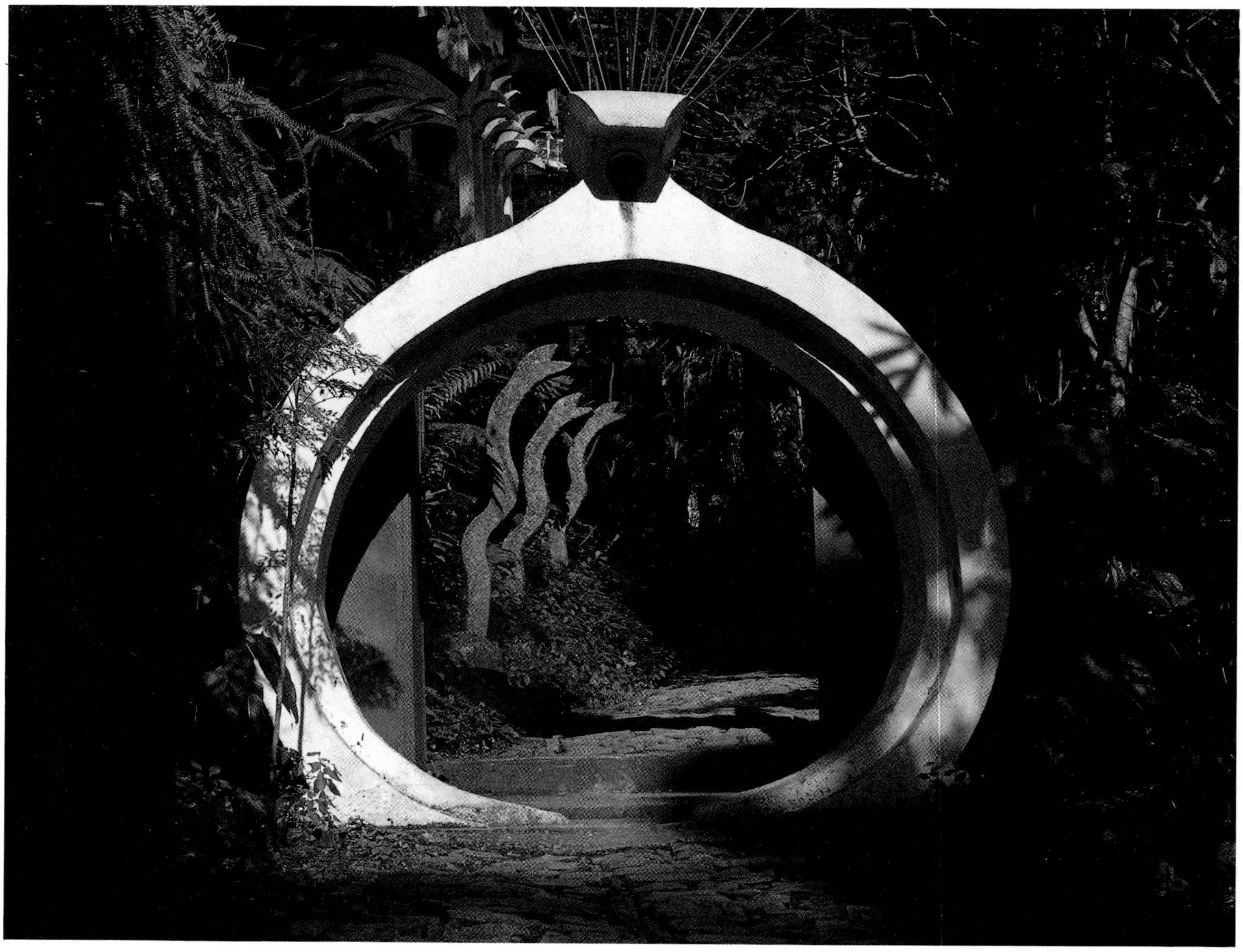

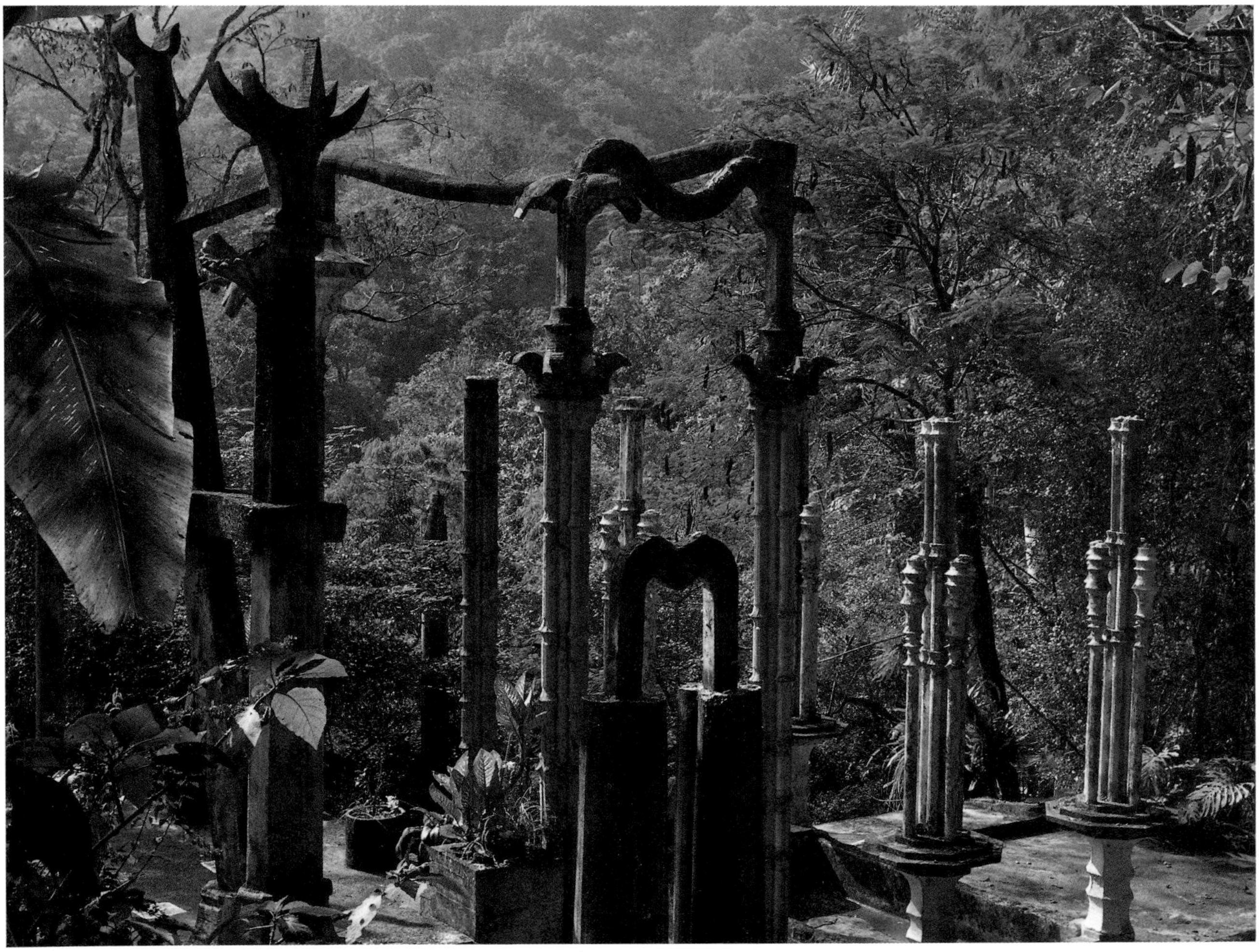

MARIANA YAMPOLSKY
Columns,
Xilitla, 1996. The artist.
Catalogue no. 234.

build them 'simply because I like to see something nice'.[11] Casually at first, and later obsessively, James and Gastelum began to erect James's world. As the Mexican refrain says, 'he who builds his home, builds his life'. This home, James's retreat, would become his main project in life and would leave his mark on the world. Until his death, he patiently dedicated himself to raising a capricious infinity of concrete, an architecture as unbounded as its exuberant surroundings.

The ranch of La Conchita is located on the slope of a craggy hillside. It is graced by rolling hills, and, on one of its borders, by a beautiful waterfall. This was the natural garden where James chose to sow his buildings across the countryside – enormous structures of poured concrete that serve no purpose other than the expression of the soul. This petrified, tactile, architecture-sculpture is at times very lovely, at others, frankly unpleasant. There are doors that cannot be closed, stairs that lead nowhere, buttresses that do not exert pressure, a library without books, an unorthodox 'Cinema' crowned by two gigantic columns, forms that

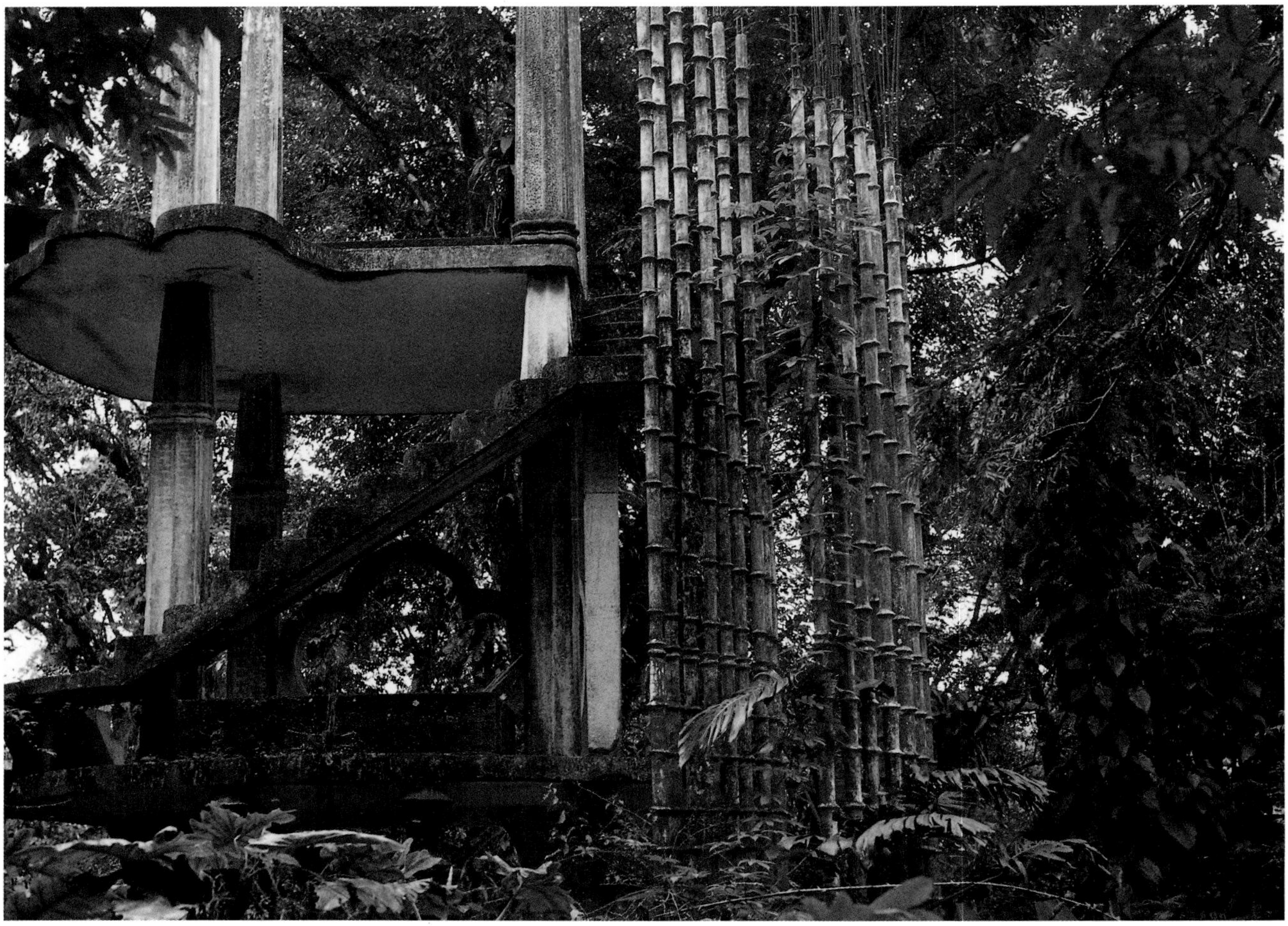

hold no weight, beams chaotically criss-crossed, reclining on a slab, like enormous serpents bearing plants on their backs. Immersed in this singular world, we encounter such structures as the 'House of Three Storeys', which really has five. Nearly all of the sculptures have names: 'Plaza Don Eduardo', 'Homage to Max Ernst' or the 'Aviary', the 'Terrace of the Tigers', the 'Summer Palace'. A total of 68 masons worked on this Surrealist architecture – unthinkably wasteful, expensive, gratuitous, disorderly and irrational – and collected their pay each week, sustaining 68 families in Xilitla by their feat of sheer physical labour. And even today, the site exudes man-hours, the buildings still deeply charged with an activity, a task, potentially capable of humanising and transforming a world resigned to its focus on economy, efficiency and rationality. Thus both the results of the labour and the way in which the work was organised were *sui generis*, while manifesting an argumentative, Surrealist position in contrast to the values on which the Western world is almost entirely founded.

MARIANA YAMPOLSKY
Bamboo Screen,
Xilitla, 1996. The artist.
Catalogue no. 235.

CONCRETE POETRY

JOHN WARREN

TO UNDERSTAND the extraordinary, coloured concrete creations that vie with the jungle plants on a Mexican hillside, you have to go back to the youth of their creator, Edward James, one of the wealthy but profoundly disturbed generation of young British intellectuals who emerged after the First World War.

Edward was an eccentric, even by the standards of his day. Born to immense wealth, he was profoundly sensitive and scorched by the limelight that continually played upon him. He reacted by putting up a shield of eccentricity, which later became a permanent mask. His behaviour was conditioned by what he believed people thought of him.

He is dead now. He lies under a simple stone slab in the arboretum of his estate in Sussex. The slab carries the bald inscription, 'Edward James, Poet'. He published several volumes of poems in which talent is evident, but genius shrouded. Nevertheless, he liked to be thought of as a poet and it is appropriate that this should be the image he wears in death. He may ultimately, however, be more famous as an architect of Surrealism.

His marriage to a ballet dancer was much publicised and the ensuing divorce vastly more so. His relationships and his affections were badly shaken and he settled in America while the Second World War erupted around the globe. Brief relationships and uncertainties characterised this phase of his life, but in 1945, in Mexico, he formed a most unlikely friendship and so began the great creative phase of his life that concerns us here.

His friendship with Plutarco Gastelum Esquer was initially that of gentleman and valet. It took the pair of them inland from the grimy oil town of Tampico to those high, wild, jungle-covered hills that form the rich and exotic core of the Central American landscape. The tiny hilltop town of Xilitla had been subdued by the conquistadores who built a friary church and a monastery there. In the 19th Century they, in turn, were subdued and the town, barely more than a primitive native village, slumbered quietly in the jungle. In 1945 it took Edward and Plutarco two days to reach it. Now, on a hard metalled road, a mere four hours will bring you there from Tampico if you drive fast. There, in the village of Xilitla, where the streets are so steep that they are stepped, Plutarco fell in love with a local Indian lady and married her. Their home became an ultimate retreat for Edward, their family his adopted family and their landscape his, for he bought it and gave it to them.

The house that Plutarco built, wildly eccentric in itself, looks out across a green gulf of valley to face a seemingly vertical hillside. If the light is right, or if the wraith-like fingers of cloud are swirling through the treetops, the hillside takes on more form and you can make out a cleft that cuts its way back into the hill and a lower valley curling away. At floodtime you may even see through the rich canopy of vegetation the silver streak of an immense waterfall that cascades down through the lianas into the valley.

The old mule track has been widened now and a pick-up will jolt down it at walking pace. It takes you into a world of almost unimaginably rich vegetation. Orange trees and coffee bushes rise up through knee-high Busy Lizzies. The forest resounds continually to the rhythmic dripping of water from feathery-topped trees onto the broad, leathery leaves of the plants below. Long tendrils writhe down like snakes to tangle with airborne root systems and soft pads of moss hang on rock and root alike. The sound of water falling is everywhere; the great waterfall plunges into a topmost pool to stream out of concrete openings into secondary pools and then to throw itself from a further precipice into a series of clear, deep and inviting chasms leading it, purling and plashing away down the hillside and into the lower valley.

Edward's obsession with this place began with the remodelling of the bathing pools. Strictly speaking they were not his to remodel since in Mexico a water course is public property and cannot be privately owned, but he was so fascinated with them that they became almost a personal possession.

The place is known as Las Posas – the Pools – and the land that Edward bought for Plutarco and his family rises from both sides of the pools up the mountain side and over the mountain top. It is inhabited by parrots, wide-winged butterflies and huge caterpillars. It is steep and immensely difficult to make your way through. The air is like a Turkish bath and from the vegetation rise the massive concrete forms that, with the aid of dozens of workers, Edward implanted on the hillside.

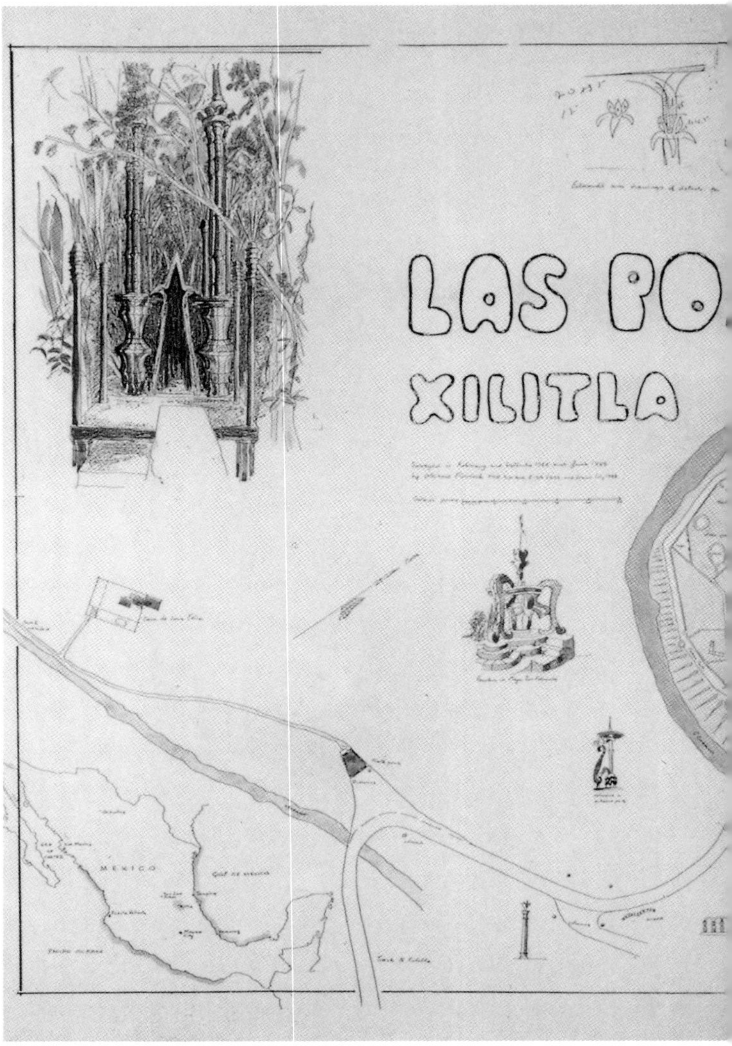

It is a large and irregular area with no obvious boundary. High on the mountain top in the untouched jungle are places where, in the words of Plutarcito, Edward's adopted nephew,' ... you think you are a long way away from him but then you find a concrete sculpture and then you know that Uncle Edward was here ...'. The complex reaches its greatest concentration where the track crosses the stream below the pools. Here rhythmic fencing formed by repetitive concrete casting of slender columns makes winding boundaries interrupted by gates, and there is a sense of entry to a park, the like of which you have never seen

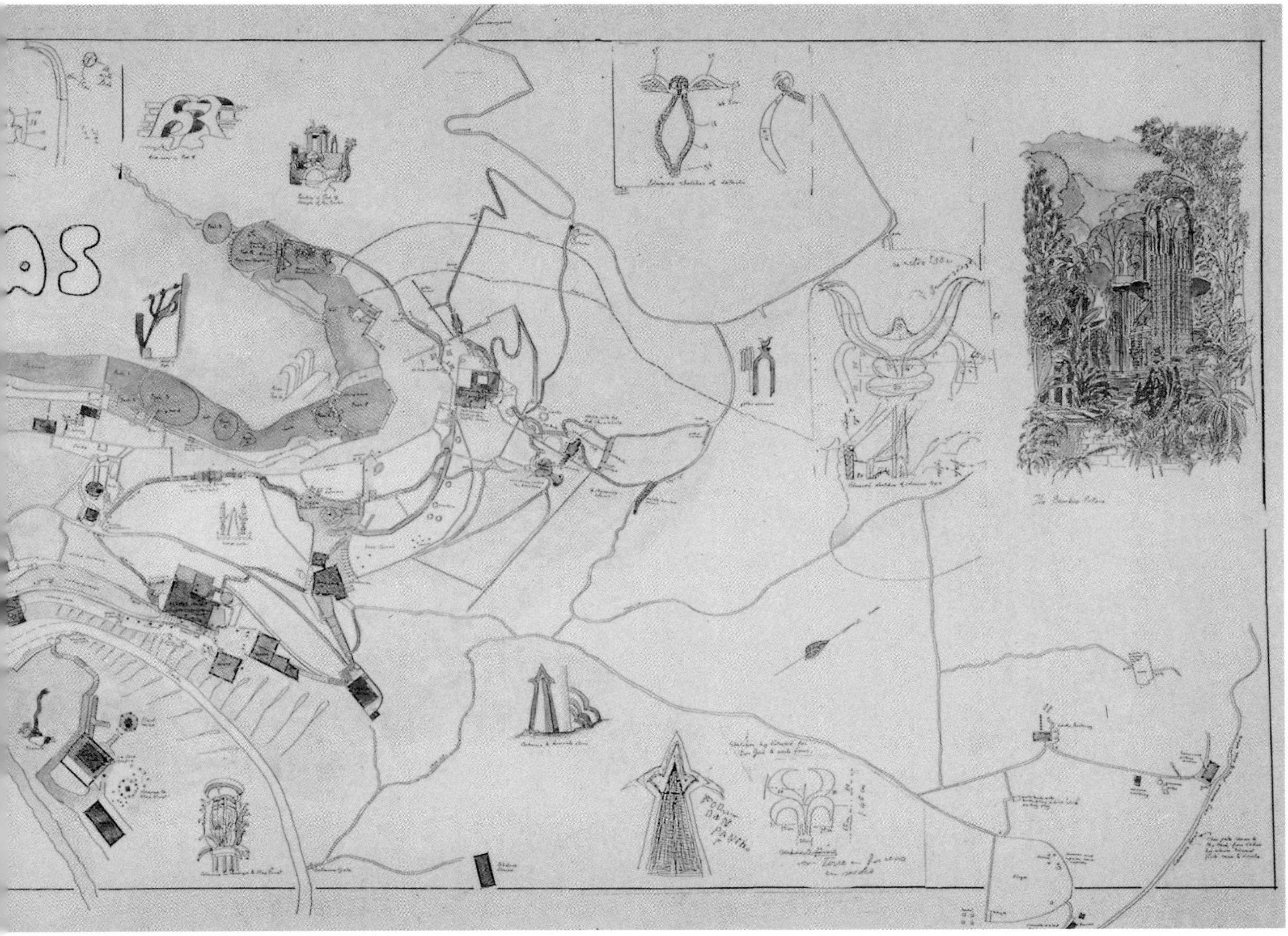

MICHAEL FISHLOCK
Plan of Xilitla
1989
Tinted: John Warren.
EJF. Catalogue no. 228.

before. A canopied entrance built in false perspective commands one vista. Colossal, overblown, pot-bellied Doric columns are the Piranesian entrance to another. Incongruous iron doors bar the way.

A great circular portal filled with thin iron sheet doors prevents your progress up the main path, but is readily circumvented through a slot, which is totally concealed by giant fronds. Paths wreath and writhe across this hill-face between constructions that have no purpose other than sheer delight in form. As you become acquainted with them you perceive the changing mastery of the artist in concrete that was Edward James. In his first essays, conscious symbolism is apparent. Columns have definite Gothic antecedents: the balustrades echo Rapallo. The curvilinear forms beside the path are imitation pythons and the mosaic pavements have a Roman feel.

Edward was building here from the late 1940s until the mid-1980s. His style evolved and his investment

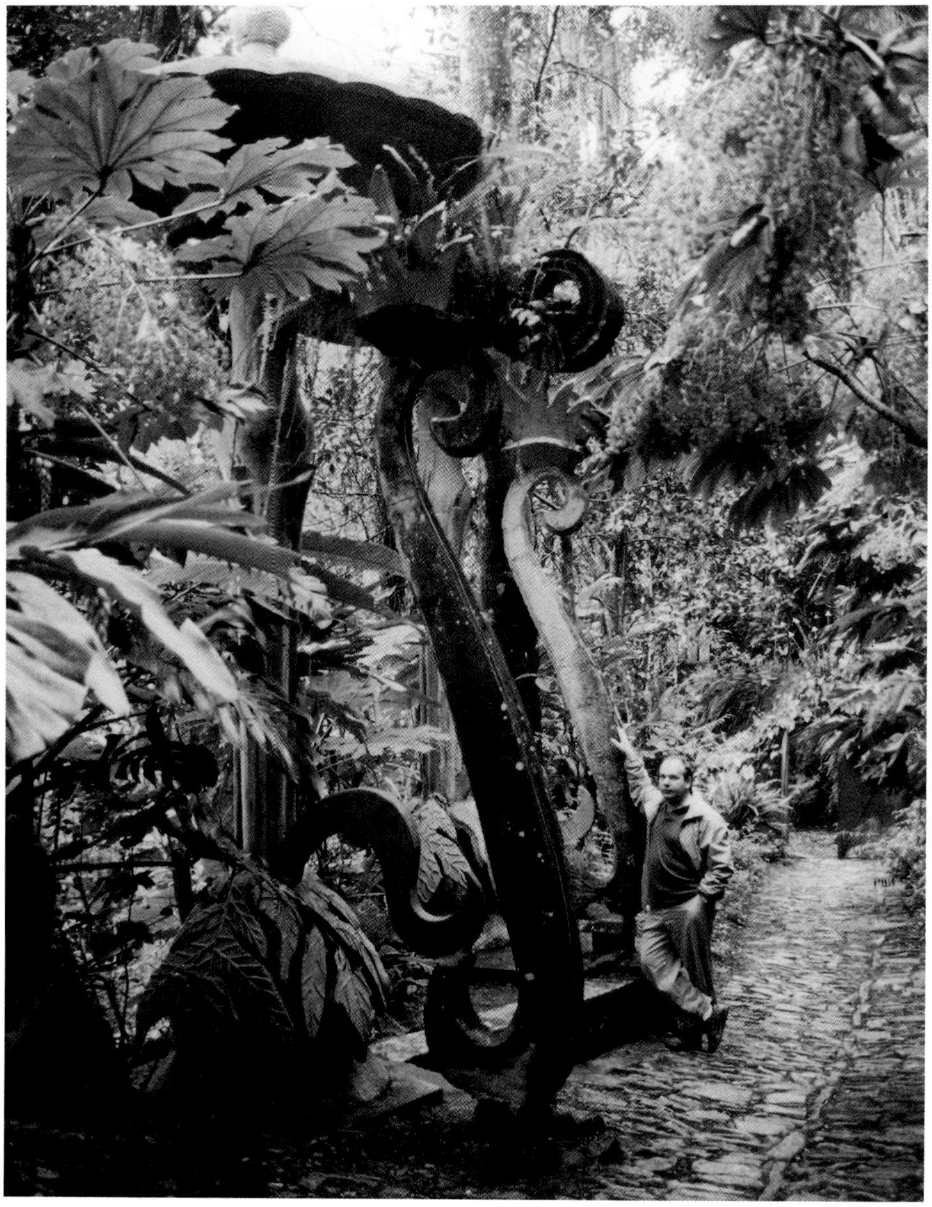

Avenue of the Snakes, Xilitla, 1993.

provided work for much of the community, which repaid him with affection, devotion and skill. His carpenters became masters of curvilinear work. Many of their wooden forms remain, awaiting their next reuse in one of his high pavilions. Plutarco, as the overseer, was a stickler for skill and competence, and the quality of the reinforced concrete work is astonishing. Some of his castings stand nearly 10 metres high, unsupported although they are barely 150mm in cross section and sway gently when a bird lands on them.

Much of the concrete is so lichen-grown that it is easily mistaken for living timber. It rises like roots from the ground to curl against buttresses and rocks. In clefts and caverns squat, fat columns stand like diminutive pit props carrying the world above them.

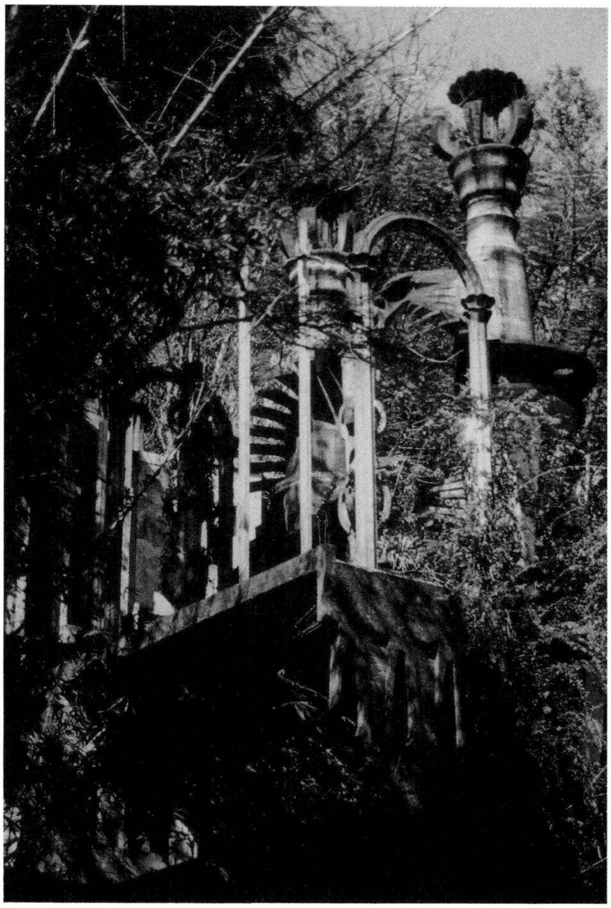

Entrance Tower, Xilitla, 1993.

An Intricate Hillside

A web of paths makes its way improbably around this hillside, diving, for the sheer excitement of it, into little gullies or striding out above chasms on bridges purely for visual effect. Paths turn through archways to face vertical, unscalable cliffs or to end, poised over greenery like a diving board over water. Staircases climb round structures into the sky, ending in apparent nothingness. One, as you climb it, becomes unclimbable because the upper floor forces you to the outer edge of the step and so into space. Other stairs that begin by taking you up end wickedly by delivering you down. Some bifurcate, others coalesce. Some are purposeless and some are so confoundedly natural that you are left looking for the hidden trick.

While the source for the earlier constructions is evident, in the later work artistry has taken over from training and earlier disciplines. Now we see the Surrealist artist at his creative height, using shape and form simply to mould and model space, to delight, disguise, surprise and confound in three-dimensional surreality.

This is the height of Edward's achievement. With his technicians so well-versed that the most improbable shapes were possible, with his conscious artistic background thrown away and with no mentor looking over his shoulder, Edward moved into a state of expensive and unique surreal creativity. His buildings rise exuberantly throughout this jungle, called into being by a highly skilled creative mind and paid for with a purse which, though not bottomless, was equal to the task. His platforms reach out from the hillside like giant fungi. Beneath them concrete curves up in organic forms. Upon them are poised staircases, columns and further platforms, defying gravity and defying the norms of construction in such a way as to send a thrill of terror down the spine and give a building inspector material for a lifetime of nightmares.

The sheer cost of doing what he did, the amazing persistence with which he carried through his vision, the astonishing quality of the work that has allowed it to survive and the powerful success of each of his creations must rank the hillside at Las Posas among the significant creative works of man. That it should have been done in so expensive a medium in so corrosive an environment and with such success, is secondary to the prime artistry but essential to the creation.

Conscious Allusion

It hardly matters what these items are called. 'Homage to Max Ernst' is perhaps the most evocative of all and the ring of coloured, plant-like structures carrying plants themselves is one of Edward's more self-conscious creations. High above it on the hillside rises the 'House of Three Storeys That Might be Five' – a name entirely appropriate to the structure, which seems to grow from the hill and rises incomplete into the tree canopy.

'Plaza Don Eduardo' has a knotted centrepiece of writhing concrete, which is so complex and coloured that it becomes almost vegetal. It grew season by season as, on each return, Edward would be tempted to add yet another tier or layer of clustering curvilinear forms.

The conscious allusions by style or by name are not important. We are better off away from those shapes and titles that hark back to European origins or specific visual precedent. This work is at its finest when its shapes soften and merge with the vegetation, enhancing and adding drama to the natural forms.

Here we catch the true spirit of the man whose clumsy drawing, accompanied by the most elegant gestures, inspired his carpenters to create shapes and contours that would mould concrete, so often brutal, hard and rigid, into a complex multiple-curved, eye-entrancing, mind-surprising piece of reality.

In his later life, Edward put the homes and the life of his thirties behind him and achieved a level of maturity and family contentment that enabled him to produce, uninhibited, his own extraordinary work of art. Plutarco and his family became the focus of his private life. Their birthdays were the ones he remembered, their house was the home where he shared family pleasures, playing with the children, taking them on expeditions, quietening them when he wanted to write his poetry on the kitchen table and refusing to be hustled upstairs to his own suite in what had become the grandest house in Xilitla.

It is hard to know whether he ever anticipated that his efforts would become the focus of the artistic pilgrimage and the film director. I suspect that he hoped so, but my memory of hearing him talk in England of these sculptures in the jungle was of a man who, like Horace Walpole, thought he was building a castle only for his lifetime. But, like Strawberry Hill, Las Posas seems destined to survive.

Despite the very high quality of the concrete work, it cannot last indefinitely without repair. Nature has added to the drama; the land has slipped and carried with it parts of several of the structures. If they are recreated they will have to be locked into the hill by bored piles or something similar. If they are not rebuilt, the world is poorer. If they survive they will be girt about by safety regulations, engineering calculations and appeals for funds. They will be visited by people in their hundreds, if not thousands, daily and then part of the magic will be lost.

To know Las Posas you must be there alone and in the misty rain, with the shrieking parrots darting between the trees, and ripe fruit falling with a heavy plop. There will be the sound of splashing water. You explore paths blocked by cobwebs, go by empty and unused ways to heights of terrifying insecurity. You see the works of man static and the great organic jungle creeping up upon them. There is a sense of apprehension and awe deep in the chest; you turn, and a man with a machete over his shoulder is staring at you, a broad grin on his face. That is Las Posas.

Republished, in this slightly abridged version, by permission of the Editor of *World Architecture*, Issue 9, 1990.

EDWARD JAMES AND HIS STORIES

DESMOND GUINNESS

The Visitor

IN ABOUT 1976, Edward began coming from Mexico to stay with us for long visits at Leixlip Castle in Ireland, as his time in England was 'rationed' for tax reasons. Perhaps he was glad to have a chance to speak his native language after months in Mexico, but his stories would begin in the drawing-room after breakfast, and last all day. After a couple of hours I would find myself making an excuse, such as 'got to go and see about the hay', whereupon he would wander off to the kitchen where he had a willing (and captive) audience in our cook, Eileen Byrne. She adored him, as we all did.

Edward, like his father Willie and his uncle Arthur, was unusually small and his mischievous look, infectious humour and long white beard gave him a puckish appearance. He liked animals best of all, then children; next came plants and trees; last of all, grown-ups. When he was staying, one would come downstairs first thing to find classical music, generally opera, playing very loudly. All the fires would be ablaze and every fire-lighter gone. Our candles and dozens of nightlights bought by Edward would be lit and spread throughout the rooms. Every lamp would be switched on, every bulb smoking with Floris's sandalwood. In the kitchen, Edward would by now have drunk all the cream, straight from the carton. The lids of the Aga would both be up but the large Aga kettles, left to warm up overnight, would be empty because Edward liked to sterilise everything he used in the way of plates, bowls and cutlery, as well as the kitchen sink. Every biscuit would by now have been fed to the dogs; they would also have had first refusal on the sausages he loved to fry.

Our daily helpers were called Mrs Savage and Mrs Cunningham; Edward would write them copious instructions in French, mainly saying 'please do not touch anything', addressing them as 'Mesdames Sauvage et Cunningham'.

The Executive Director of the Irish Georgian Society, run from Leixlip, was called Audrey Emerson; one day a notice appeared in his distinctive writing saying 'Audrey has fused'. What could it have meant? Edward's visit had coincided with a fashion show of clothes designed by Ib Jørgensen, held here to benefit the Irish Georgian Society. Edward had found a lampshade and, as they made their grand finale, he followed the models through the rooms, wearing this huge basketwork horror on his head. He brought the house down.

All his life he got side-tracked. He once complained that he had never found the meaning of the word he

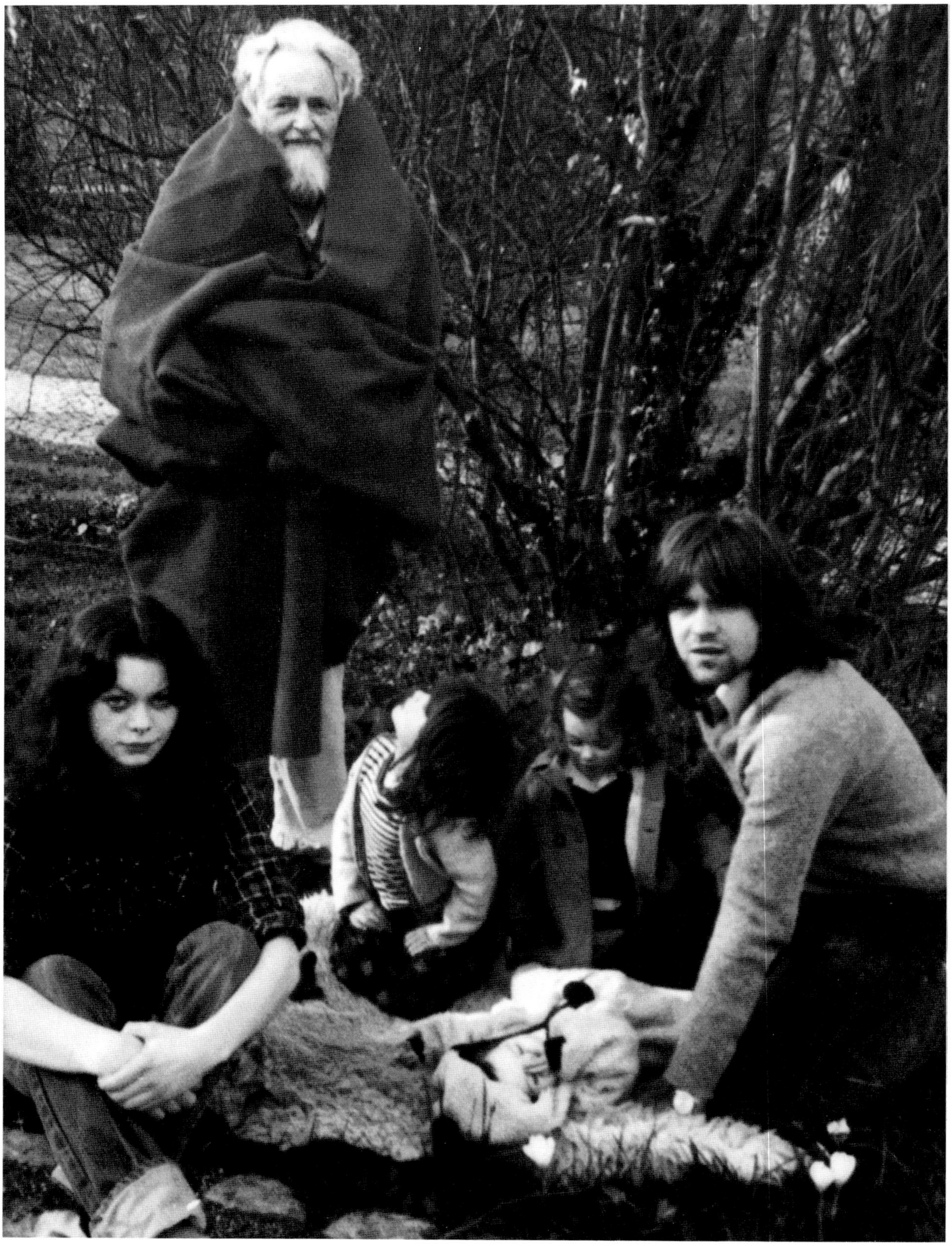

Edward James (standing) at Leixlip with Liz Guinness, Poppy and Zita Lloyd, Jasmine Guinness (baby) and her father Patrick.

was looking up in the dictionary because there were so many other tempting ones to distract him on the way. Once, when he was supposed to come to Ireland, the Chichester travel agent booked him to Iceland by mistake, and, being Edward of course, he went.

His curiosity was boundless, as was his generosity. He bought a Kinsale cape, black and lined in pink silk at Dublin's Shelbourne Hotel gift shop for my wife Penny, the sort of thing she would be far too embarrassed to wear. She returned it in exchange for some useful jerseys for her mother, her aunt and herself, but occasionally Edward would wonder where it was. He also bought her a purple cashmere jumpsuit, in which to feed the chickens, missing a plane in Switzerland to buy it; extremely kind of him, but it was never worn either.

In 1977, when Edward lent 12 pictures by Magritte and 25 by Dalí for exhibition at the Museum Boijmans Van Beuningen in Rotterdam, a series of banquets and visits to art galleries were planned in his honour. However, he sat up late at Leixlip with my cousin Caroline Blackwood, talking all night and of course was unable to find his passport, which was packed, and missed the plane to the Netherlands. Ivan Hicks, the head gardener at West Dean, had flown to Rotterdam to meet him and, 'still in his turtle-neck pullover', was given the red-carpet treatment instead. The trouble was Edward's method of packing, which involved many layers of tissue paper and masses of empty Benson & Hedges cigarette cartons, as he liked their shiny gold appearance; these would be stuffed with Kleenex tissues to keep their shape. He nicknamed my wife 'the penny-pincher' for her supply of tissues never equalled his demand. This led to his posing for a photograph at Monkton, naked behind a veritable mountain of tissues and firelighters.

We stayed with Edward at Xilitla in Mexico, taking my daughter Marina with us. He met us at the airport in Mexico City, his friend Luis Felix driving, with a dead or dying crocodile, about a foot long, on a bath-towel beside him. It seemed to revive in the hotel jacuzzi because the force of the water made its tail wag. When eventually he knew it to be dead, he wrote an *Ode to a Dying Crocodile* and commissioned his old friend, the French composer Henri Sauguet, to set it to music. Few reptiles have been so honoured.

The Stories

Edward's polished stories were so often repeated that I got to know them almost by heart, and could wind him up like a gramophone. I had visions of him as my Elephant Man – of going from one theatre to another shackled to him and of making our fortune out of these sagas, so brilliantly narrated with the various voices and accents and such impeccable timing.

By the time I came to record him over the Christmas of 1983, I found that the stories fell easily into categories or groups concerning various figures from his past or people like Mrs Moore of Neuilly, of whom he must have heard tell but may never have actually known. Edward's memory was phenomenal but he was not above borrowing a good tale from either his friends or from books. He was fascinated by malapropisms and Mrs Moore provided one of his favourites. Apparently she checked into a hotel saying 'J'ai très mal au dos. Il me faut absolument deux matelots et trois cousins dans mon lit.' The concierge took it in his stride and answered simply 'Mais quelle jolie partie que cela fera, madame!'

Mrs Moore of Neuilly always gave a great dinner party when the chestnut trees were at their best. One year it was rather spoilt by Mr Moore's drowning in the Seine on the day of the feast. She put black crêpe around the place cards, but there was a horrible silence when the guests sat down, and to break the ice she explained 'Mon mari s'est noyé'. Deep, embarrassed silence. 'N'est-ce pas extraordinaire, qu'un homme si ordinaire, soit mort d'un mort si extraordinaire?'

When the Paris season was over and the city became a social desert, Mrs Moore would take a house in London, bringing her French servants over with her. Boni de Castellane was lunching with her by himself one day in London, and she was able to catch up on the latest French gossip from him. Noticing that one of her footmen was paying unnatural attention to his revelations, to warn Boni she said 'Faites attention Marquis – mon derrière comprend le français', to which he replied 'Mais qu'est-ce que cela nous fait, madame, pourvu qu'il n'entre pas dans la conversation!'

Fascinated by parsimony on the part of the rich, Edward also told of his Aunt Venetia (Mrs Arthur James) whispering 'D.C.S.C.' to the parlour maid, a secret code, the meaning of which had to be prized out of the reluctant girl. It turned out to be 'Don't cut second chicken'. When Edward's pregnant sister Audrey dropped in on her for a cup of tea, Venetia shouted down to the kitchen 'If the cat has left any of its milk bring it up for Mrs Marshall Field'.

Aunt Venetia and Violet Trefusis went by train to a country wedding in honour of which Venetia had spent an entire pound on a new hat. In order to travel all the way third class, they took a circuitous route, which meant changing trains more than once, and on one remote station it started to rain but the waiting-room was locked. Aunt Venetia was not going to have the new hat ruined and pulled her skirts up over her head, revealing her red flannel petticoats and her bony legs. The station master rushed up to Violet, who pretended that she had 'never met that woman in her life', so he went straight to the dripping statue that was Aunt Venetia and asked her not to disgrace his station by making such a show of herself. Her muffled reply from behind the skirts, imitated by Edward stuffing a handkerchief in his mouth, was 'Young man, what you see may be old, but the hat is new!'

Aunt Venetia was rather jealous of all the fuss that was being made about Alice Keppel's return to England from Italy after war was declared; part of the journey was by submarine. Venetia would have rather liked to have been the much-talked-about heroine of the hour. She said 'The way people talk about Alice Keppel, anyone would think she had swum the Channel with her maid in her teeth.'

Aunt Venetia took part in amateur theatricals with a group called The Windsor Strollers, led by Sir Hugh Rumbold. A modern play was chosen called *Outward Bound*, about people on a ship. All of them were dead but not aware of it, and each had to go before an Examiner to be interrogated about their lives. Venetia was cast as Mrs Kevington Smyth, a tough, bitchy old character. The Examiner said to Venetia 'In your life you were a harlot and you were not even a good harlot'; Venetia quite forgot she was in a play and rounded on him, saying 'I don't know who you think you're talking to, I'm Mrs Arthur James' and they had to bring the curtain down. On the second night a huge crowd came, hoping for a repeat performance, but they were disappointed; she had learnt her lines by then.

Edward had an abiding love of the stage and the company of actors. He attributed this to a childhood memory of a visit to the pantomime in Scotland with his maternal grandmother Helen, Lady Forbes of Newe. Edward described it:

> *A line of chorus girls in white muslin tutus with wands – eight on each side. A very fat dancer with enormous thighs bounded onto the stage in*

the middle of them, in pink muslin, carrying a wand with a pink star on it. As the stage groaned she exclaimed: 'I am the Fairy Bom-Bom!' The white chorus replied: 'Hello Fairy! Your presence, though unexpected, is nonetheless very delightful'. It was that vista of white Scottish chorus girls ending with the vast pink fairy that carried my imagination towards the wonder of a stage dancer and this fixation remained with me all my life. My mother used to say: 'You must never marry an actress – look what happened to ____ , he married a chorus girl and your uncle cut him out of his will.' It somehow got into my subconscious that an actress was the most desirable person to marry precisely because she was taboo.

The lovely young American heiress Gloria Vanderbilt was married for a time to the great conductor Leopold Stokowski and they lived in Manhattan. Gloria was in a play, and used to drive a young actress to the theatre every morning for rehearsals, as she had a car and driver. One day Gloria's part was being radically changed and the director wanted her to come alone, but she had lost the other girl's number and could not prevent her from arriving as usual for her lift. When she turned up at Gloria's house, Stokowski welcomed her with his flowing white hair, in an embroidered dressing-gown, and apologised, explaining that Gloria had already gone. He made a delicious breakfast of scrambled eggs for her. The next morning she arrived as usual for her lift and Gloria was most apologetic over the mix-up, but the girl said it was fine and 'Besides, your grandmother was so kind to me'.

Mrs Patrick Campbell was living in New York, unable to travel to England because of the quarantine laws and her little dog Moonbeam, the love of her life. She was portly and old, and not worshipped in the USA as she was in England, but being hard-up she took the part of Napoleon's young son, le Roi de Rome, in *L'Aiglon*. She barely managed to squeeze into the uniform of a young man, the audience laughed and the play was a disaster. Her great rival Laurette Taylor came backstage afterwards to commiserate but Mrs Campbell, never at a loss said 'Laurette, I thought the play would be a *tour de force*, but clearly I shall be forced to tour!'

Tallulah Bankhead was at '21', a restaurant in New York, lunching with a young actress and at the next table was a married couple, up from Connecticut. The husband was hearing from his wife about how little Jimmy needed a new pair of gymshoes, when it became all too evident that she had lost his attention and that he was listening to the girls at the next table. 'Yes, they are amusing, aren't they?' said the wife, a remark overheard by Tallulah, who retorted 'My good woman, I'll have you know – *we* are no more *they* than *you* are'.

Senator Bankhead was chairman of the Senate, and the exquisite Tallulah was helping her father greet the other senators at a reception. A young senator, who had spent the previous night with Tallulah, fearing his career might suffer if this became known, shook her hand very formally. Tallulah cupped her hands and shouted after him 'Say mister – don't you know me with my clothes on?'

Jimmy Smith, the uncle of Lord Hambledon, was an excellent pianist and would accompany Oggie Lynn and Mrs Stuart Wortley as they sang excerpts from classical opera. Not being up to Wigmore Hall standards, but keen to perform in public, they toured the English prisons, where they literally found a captive audience. One day, visiting the enormous prison on the Isle of Wight, Mrs Stuart Wortley stood on the stage and said 'Prisoners: before we begin, I thought you would enjoy the evening more if I gave you an outline of the story of the opera'. The prisoners yawned and heads dropped. '*Le Coq d'Or*, by Rimsky Korsakoff, is the story of a Hungarian Mujique with the most enormous golden cock. His cock was so huge it became a national sensation and won the prize for the biggest cock at all the fairs in Russia where it was exhibited' – and so on. The prisoners woke up and very soon they were rolling in the aisles, roaring their heads off with mindless laughter. When the evening was over and the prison governor was thanking the performers, he said 'next time though, I would suggest that you leave out the preamble'. Mrs Stuart Wortley replied 'I can't see why – it seemed to go down *awfully* well.'

The butt of many of Edward's stories was Lady Colefax, a relentless social climber who entertained in great splendour at Argyll House on the King's Road, just visible from the rear windows of the Sitwells' house on Carlisle Square. One evening the 'coalbox' (as she was nicknamed) was giving a grand party and the Sitwells took turns with a loud-hailer to shout spurious names and titles as the Maharajas and Ambassadors alighted from their enormous cars.

The Ritz Hotel in London had glass swing doors; one day Edward was waiting by them for a friend when Lord Berners espied him and said, conspiratorially, 'I've just seen Sybil Colefax through glass – do you think it means anything?'

Perhaps the most suitable story to end with in the light of Edward's involvement with Surrealism concerns Salvador Dalí, and is best recounted in Edward's own words:

Salvador Dalí's inventions are curious things, like, for instance, the Pleuvial Taxi. They came out of real occurrences. Dalí and I were waiting one day for a taxi after lunch in Verona. It was pouring, pouring with rain and there was no empty taxi. And Gala was somewhere else in the town, getting impatient; she got very cross if she was kept waiting. Dalí got more and more nervous. Finally it stopped raining, and up came an empty taxi, and Dalí said 'It's almost sure to be raining inside the taxi now that it's stopped outside'. From that he elaborated the idea of a Pleuvial Taxi. He said 'They'll be very elegant. It will cost more money to be in a raining taxi. Everybody will come to lunch a bit wet, wearing a mackintosh, even on sunny days, because they'll have been in one of my Pleuvial Taxis'. He created a Pleuvial Taxi for the first Surrealist show in Paris, with a wax model in it, with snails crawling up her arms. That was the origin of that!

NOTES

Breaking Canons – Sharon-Michi Kusunoki

1. Herbert Read, 'Why the English have no taste', *Minotaure*, No. 7, 1935, pp. 67–68.
2. William James, whose fortune derived from the American railroads, lumber and mining industries, purchased the West Dean Estate in 1891 which then encompassed 12,000 acres of land. At the time of his death in 1912, his estate comprised a large house; a smaller home, Monkton, designed by Lutyens; a church; four villages consisting of 136 houses and cottages; 12 working farms; and 2,000 acres of commercial forestry. In addition, William James enjoyed a home at 38 Bryanston Square in London, a second house, also designed by Lutyens, in Gullane, Scotland (now the hotel, Greywalls), where James was born, and substantial holdings in America.
3. See David Cannadine, *The Decline and Fall of the British Aristocracy*, Yale University Press, New Haven/London, 1990.
4. In one of a series of letters written to his mother when he was a 16-year-old student at Eton in 1924, James writes 'Mr McNiele [James's housemaster] seems extraordinarily narrow-minded in some ways; he actually ... almost objected to my reading Shakespeare, and gives me books like *Life in the Wilds* which doesn't interest me at all. He is trying to crush all my artistic sides and allows me no outlet for them ... '.
5. See David Cannandin, *The Decline and Fall of the British Aristocracy*, op.cit.
6. Evelyn James, letter to Mr. MacKenzie, September 11 1927, EJA (The Edward James Archive).
7. Mr Bridgeman, the 5th Earl of Bradford, was a cousin of Evelyn James, influential in politics and at Court.
8. Edward James, letter to Evelyn James, May 1925, EJA.
9. Edward James, fragment of an undated letter written to his Head Gardener at West Dean, Ivan Hicks, undated, EJA.
10. For an important academic study of Edward James and his poetry, see Didier Girard, *Edward James, poète hypnagogique (1939-1984)*, Paris IV Sorbonne – Montpellier III, 1995, 2 vols.
11. *The New Statesman and Nation*, August 13, 1938.
12. Tom Driberg, *Ruling Passions*, London, 1977, p. 67. Tom Driberg was a friend of James's and along with John Betjeman, Christopher Sykes, Randolph Churchill, Tom Mitford, Freddie Furneaux (later Lord Birkenhead), and Basil, Marquess of Dufferin and Ava, enjoyed champagne breakfasts in James's rooms.
13. Malcolm Gee, *Dealers, Critics and Collectors of Modern Painting – Aspects of the Parisian Art Market between 1910 and 1930*, unpublished PhD thesis, Courtauld Institute of Art, University of London, 1977, pp. 183–184.
14. Shane Maree Dunworth, *The de Noailles as Collectors and Patrons,* unpublished M.Phil thesis, Courtauld Institute of Art, University of London, 1984, p.63.
15. Most books date their meeting to 1933. Although the correspondence between James and the Vicomtesse de Noailles begins in 1933, it is highly likely that they met in 1932, since the Vicomte and Vicomtesse de Noailles were named on a list compiled by James of friends who received three volumes of his poetry: *The Next Volume*, illustrated by Rex Whistler; *Carmina Amico*; and *The Venetian Glass Omnibus*, all of which were published in 1932, the third appearing on a list of First Editions dated 'Christmas 1932'. The first letter in EJA from Marie-Laure de Noailles is dated February 22, 1933, in which they already seem to be on very familiar terms, the Vicomtesse referring to James as 'My angel, my love'. These terms of endearment lend credibility to James's later claims that Marie-Laure was in love with him.
16. From a transcript of an interview conducted by Bevis Hillier with Edward James in 1981, EJA.

17. Wife of Gaston Bergery, later to become the American Ambassador in Moscow.
18. Edward James, letter to Salvador Dalí, September 1 1935, EJA.
19. Edward James, letter to Lady Diane Abdy, October 20 1935, EJA.
20. Rafael Santos Torroella, *Salvador Dalí, Corresponsal de J. V. Foix, 1932–36,* Barcelona, 1986, p.153.
21. Salvador Dalí, letter to Edward James, December 16 1935, EJA.
22. A. Reynolds Morse, *Dalí's surrealist 'Sculptures'*, Dalí – Espace Montmartre, Paris, 1989, p.16.
23. A letter in The Edward James Archives indicates that the idea for the Lobster Telephone came about when James and some friends were sitting on the bed in James's room eating lobster and throwing the shells to the side. One landed on the telephone. James promptly commissioned Dalí to design the lobsters and James supervised the painting and varnishing. Manufacturing receipts date the *Lobster Telephone* and *Mae West Lips Sofas* to 1938, not 1936 as is commonly suggested. The firm hired to execute this project in 1938 was Green & Abbott.
24. Report by Gavin Stamp and Clive Aslet for SAVE Britain's Heritage, February 1986.
25. The room with the pulsating walls for Monkton was never realised. Sir Hugh Casson experimented with fans and different materials to create this effect.
26. See note 23.
27. May 11 1936, EJA.
28. June 2 1936, EJA.
29. Julian Trevelyan relates how Read and Paul Nash visited his studio and made him a Surrealist overnight. Eileen Agar was also surprised to discover she was a Surrealist. Louisa Buck, 'Eileen Agar, Angel of Mercy', *The Surrealist Spirit in England*, catalogue, England, 1988.
30. 'Surrealist in Diving Suit – Helmet Gets Stuck', *The Daily Mail*, July 2 1936, p.9.
31. This fiasco of the diving suit turned out to be of great interest to the press, and the one event everyone remembered. Conroy Maddox, who was a member of the audience, said in a lecture he gave for the Edward James Symposium held at the Institute of Contemporary Arts, London, April 26 1986, that 'Edward James tried to use his walking stick to undo the bolts, getting entangled with the dogs. It was quite a chaotic event, and quite hilarious in many ways'.
32. 'REA£I$M IN SURREALISM – MODERNISTS ARE NOT PRICELESS ASSES', *The Star*, July 2 1936.
33. Undated text, EJA.
34. Edward James, letter to Mae Babitz, August 1981–January 1982, EJA.
35. Edward James, letter to Leonora Carrington, December 21 1962, EJA.
36. Patrick Waldberg, *Surrealism*, London, 1965 (reprinted in 1978), p. 18.
37. Edward James, letter to Ruth Ford, 1941, EJA.
38. Karen A. Siem, *André Breton's Collection of Paintings and Objects in the 1920s and 1930s*, unpublished MA dissertation, Courtauld Institute of Art, University of London, 1985, pp. 1–2.
39. John Lowe, *Edward James. A Surrealist Life* , London, Collins, 1991, p.xiv.
40. From the early 1900s, Roger Fry advocated an individual Aestheticism that resisted the dictates of society. See Christopher Reed, *A Roger Fry Reader*, Chicago & London, The University of Chicago Press, 1996, p. 186.
41. While the author acknowledges Read's ambiguous relationship with Surrealism, his bias towards the causes of Socialism, and his interest in psychoanalysis, Read's view of English society in the 1930s is nevertheless pertinent to understanding the social climate into which James was thrust, and to setting up the context from which British Surrealism was born.
42. The curtains were made for Wimpole Street and have since disappeared. The idea of the sofa was constructed as a chair, and the piano project was abandoned with the advent of war.

Making the Illogical Logical – Sharon-Michi Kusunoki

1. T.R. Schellenberg, *The Management of Archives*, Washington, DC, National Archives and Records Administration, 1988 (first published in 1965), pp. 5 & 90.
2. Edward James, letter to Lord Gerald Berners, January 1949, EJA (The Edward James Archive).
3. In a letter to Lord Gerald Berners from Edward James, March 26 1935, EJA, James explained his compulsion: 'We are taken back to the year 1910 ... to the anticipation, excitement and furore of packing taking place in the old night nursery at West Dean ... The air was magically full of floating tissue-paper and Audrey [his sister] dragged an object out of the cupboard into a drift of tissue-paper which covered the floor like a *gâteau mille feuilles* of dry snow, almost knee-deep ... I have been addicted to tissue-paper ever since that hour.'
4. Edward James, letter to Captain Ronald Button. June 27 1944, EJA.
5. Edward James, fragment of an undated letter to the Hon. Lady Mosley, written on the back of an envelope, EJA.
6. Edward James, letter to Gerald Heard, EJA.
7. A game popular in Mexico in which a papier mâché object, usually an animal, filled with sweets, is suspended from the ceiling. The blindfolded children are given a chance to strike

it with a bat. When it eventually breaks, the sweets drop to the floor, and the children race to collect them.

8. Edward James, letter to Leonora Carrington, EJA.
9. Edward James speaking in *The Secret Life of Edward James*, a television documentary, produced and directed by Patrick Boyle, Central Television, 1978.
10. Patrick Boyle, citing Edward James in 'Eccentric Exile', *Sunday Telegraph* Magazine, 8 May 1977, V. 34, pp. 23–29.

Edward James and Les Ballets 1933 – Stella Beddoe

1. For the most complete coverage of Les Ballets 1933 and the background to the project see Shelley Tobin, Jane Pritchard et al, *Les Ballets 1933* (exhibition catalogue, Royal Pavilion, Art Gallery and Museums, Brighton), 1987, and Jane Pritchard, 'Les Ballets 1933', *Ballet Review* (vol. 16: 3, Fall 1988, pp. 13–35).
2. See Philip Purser, *Where Is He Now? The Extraordinary Worlds of Edward James*, London, Quartet Books, 1978, p. 35.
3. For discussion of the de Noailles as art patrons see Stephen Calloway, *Baroque Baroque*, London, Phaidon, 1994, pp. 72–6.
4. John Lowe: *Edward James, A Surrealist Life*, London, Collins, 1991, pp. 104–5.
5. Diana Menuhin, 'Les Ballets 1933', *Dance Research*, vol. VI, no.2, Autumn 1988, pp. 61–7.
6. See Edward James, *Swans Reflecting Elephants: My Early Years,* edited by George Melly, Weidenfeld and Nicholson, London, 1982, pp. 145–6.
7. Jean Genêt, 'Letter from Paris', *The New Yorker*, 8 July 1933, p. 41.
8. Bayer, Gropius and Gropius, *Bauhaus 1919–1928*, London, George Allen and Unwin, 1939. See illustrations pp. 62–66.
9. Pritchard, 1988, op. cit. pp. 22–23.
10. *The Daily Telegraph*, 29 June 1933, p.6.
11. *The Observer*, 2 July, 1933, p. 5.
12. Donald Windham, 'The Stage and Ballet Designs of Pavel Tchelitchew', *Dance Index*, vol. 3, no.1, 1944, p. 13.
13. Reference from Philip Purser, *Poeted, The Final Quest of Edward James*, 1991, Quartet Books, London, p. 52.
14. Menuhin, op. cit., 1988, p. 68.
15. *The London Evening Standard*, 29 June 1933.
16. *The Star*, 29 June 1933.
17. Signatures and snapshots of the guests, in costume and at leisure can be seen in the West Dean Visitors' Book, in the collection of The Edward James Foundation. They stayed from 19–26 July.

Edward James and Surrealism – Dawn Ades

1. Letter to Leonora Carrington, May 15 1950, EJA (The Edward James Archive).
2. This title may subsequently have been changed; the painting has not been identified.
3. Letter to Julien Levy, June 12 1937, EJA.
4. Edward James, undated letter to Edith Sitwell, EJA.
5. Edward James, letter to Mr Kornfeld, October 12 1938, EJA.
6. Letter to Trustees of The Edward James Foundation, EJA.
7. ibid.
8. Letter to John Betjeman, December 18 1936, EJA.
9. Memorandum by Edward James, April 30 1939, EJA.
10. Letter from Gardner to William Morris, EJA.
11. Salvador Dalí, *Declaration of the Independence of the Imagination and the Rights of Man to His Own Madness*, 1939.
12. Edward James, letter to Dalí, August 22 1939, EJA. James's correspondence with both Dalí and Magritte was conducted in French. Translations here are by the author.
13. Edward James, undated letter to Magritte, EJA.
14. René Magritte, letter to Edward James, July 12 1939, EJA.
15. Edward James, letter to Magritte, April 18 1937, EJA.
16. Comte de Lautréamont: 'Chants de Maldoror', *Oeuvres complètes*, Paris, 1963, p. 327.
17. Edward James, *The Gardener who saw God*, Duckworth, 1937, p. 285.
18. Edith Sitwell, undated letter to Edward James, EJA.
19. Edward James, letter to Dalí and Gala, August 24 1936, EJA.
20. Gala Dalí, letter to Edward James, January 23 1940, EJA.
21. Henry James, *The Wings of the Dove*, 1902, Oxford, 1984, p. 87.
22. Edward James, letter to Dalí and Gala, August 24 1936, EJA. James repeated this account of Breton in letters to other correspondents.
23. Paul Ray, *The Surrealist Movement in England*, Cornell University Press, Ithaca and London, 1971, p. 138.
24. Edward James, letter to Carrington, May 12 1954, EJA.
25. Edward James *'Introduction', Leonora Carrington: A Retrospective Exhibition*, Centre for Inter-American Relations, New York City, 1976, p. 23.
26. ibid p. 14.
27. Leonora Carrington 'Commentary' ibid p. 24.

Edward James Interiors – Stephen Calloway

1. Edward James, *Swans Reflecting Elephants: My Early Years*, edited by George Melly, Weidenfeld & Nicholson, London, 1982, p. 63.
2. ibid.
3. ibid.
4. Quoted in Clive Aslet, *The Last Country Houses*, 1982, pp. 23–24.
5. See Christies, *The Edward James Collection*, West Dean Park, sale catalogue, 5 June 1986, vol. IV, note on 'West Dean Park'.
6. See Philip Purser, *The Extraordinary Worlds of Edward James*, 1978, p. 41.
7. Recalled in conversation with the author, 1986, but see also Madge Garland, *The Indecisive Decade*, 1968, p. 38.
8. Norris Wakefield's recollections of Edward James and of the work carried out at 35 Wimpole Street and Monkton are taken from a conversation with the author, tape recorded in 1986.
9. ibid.
10. Purser, op. cit., p.67.
11. See Clive Aslet, 'Monkton, An Appreciation', in *Monkton, a Vanishing Surrealist Dream, The Thirties Society*, 1986.
12. ibid.
13. See note 9.
14. The print was at West Dean House, and is a hand-coloured mezzotint, *The Funeral Procession of Lord Viscount Nelson*, January 9 1806, engraved by Edward Orme, London, (The Trustees of The Edward James Foundation). The palm trees are Nelson's attribute.
15. See note 9.
16. Salvador Dalí, *The Secret Life of Salvador Dalí,* New York, 1942.
17. From Julien Levy's autobiography, quoted in the Introduction to Christie's sale catalogue, *The Edward James Collection*, op. cit.

Edward James in Xilitla – Xavier Guzmán Urbiola

1. William Blake, *The Complete Poems*, Penguin Classics, 1977, p. 185.
2. Jorge Ibarguengoitia 'En primera persona. Travelogue', from *La casa de Usted y otros viajes*, Joaquín Mortiz, Mexico, 1991, p. 16.
3. James himself described his first visit to Xilitla in great detail in a letter to Geoffrey Gilmore, November 28 1945, EJA (The Edward James Archive).
4. Four examples: John Lowe: *Edward James, A Surrealist Life*, Collins, London, 1991, p. 189; Philip Purser, *Poeted, the final quest of Edward James*, Quartet Books, London, 1991, p. 2; Xavier Guzmán Urbiola, et al, *La habitación interminable,* Universidad Autónoma Metropolitana-Xochimilco, Mexico, 1986, p. 52. Alejandra Islas, 'Edward James', video, Channel 22, Mexico, 1994.
5. Letter from Edward James to Geoffrey Gilmore, November 28 1945, EJA.
6. Mircea Eliade, *Lo sagrado y lo profano*, Madrid, Guadarrama, 1967, p. 25.
7. On the long and difficult process of purchasing the ranch, see the telegrams and letters between Edward James and Plutarco Gastelum, especially those dated from December 16 1948 to February 10 1949. The final writ completing the sale, numbered 25498 and witnessed by licensed public notary Raúl Falomir, is dated March 2 1949, EJA. Today the site is known as Las Posas.
8. This explanation is based on correspondence in Spanish from the EJA, as well as from various conversations held with Plutarco Gastelum Esquer.
9. Letter from Plutarco Gastelum to Edward James, July 30 1952, EJA.
10. On this point I agree with: John Lowe, op.cit. p. 196.
11. Carlos Heinze, 'El templo del surrealismo, enclavado en la selva mexicana', from the Magazine *Dominical* of *Excélsior* newspaper, Mexico City, Year LXV, Book IV, Number 23, 484, August 23, 1981, p. 16.

LIST OF WORKS IN THE EXHIBITION

Dimensions are given in centimetres in the form height x width x depth. Where no artist, photographer or maker is indicated, the work is unattributed. EJF indicates The Trustees of The Edward James Foundation.

1. René Magritte (1898–1967)
La reproduction interdite
1937
oil on canvas
81.5 x 65
Museum Boijmans Van Beuningen, Rotterdam

AN EDWARDIAN CHILDHOOD

1. Circle of Arcimboldo, 17th century
Summer
oil on canvas
98 x 138
EJF

2. Circle of Arcimboldo, 17th century
Winter
oil on canvas
98 x 138
EJF

4. *William James*, c.1905
print after portrait by
R. Brough, 1905
63.5 x 51
EJF

5. *Evelyn James in costume as the Archduchess Elizabeth of Austria for Devonshire House Ball*
1897
black and white copy print from negative by LaFayette
63.5 x 51
National Portrait Gallery, London

6. *Evelyn James and Children*
c.1908
sepia photograph
37 x 30.5
EJF

7. Alice Hughes
Mrs William James with her daughters
black and white photograph
32 x 29.5
Mr Hugo Vickers

8. *Evelyn James and Edward*
c. 1910
black and white photograph
16 x 11.5
EJF

9. *Congratulations on birth of Edward James*
August 27, 1907
telegram from Edward VII
14 x 23
EJF

10. Alice Hughes
Edward and Audrey James
1907
black and white photograph
29 x 21.5
EJF

11. *Edward and Audrey James*
black and white photograph
33 x 33
EJF

12. Rita Martin
Edward James
sepia photograph
31 x 19.5
EJF

13. *Edward James at Eton*
c.1920
black and white photograph
14.5 x 10
EJF

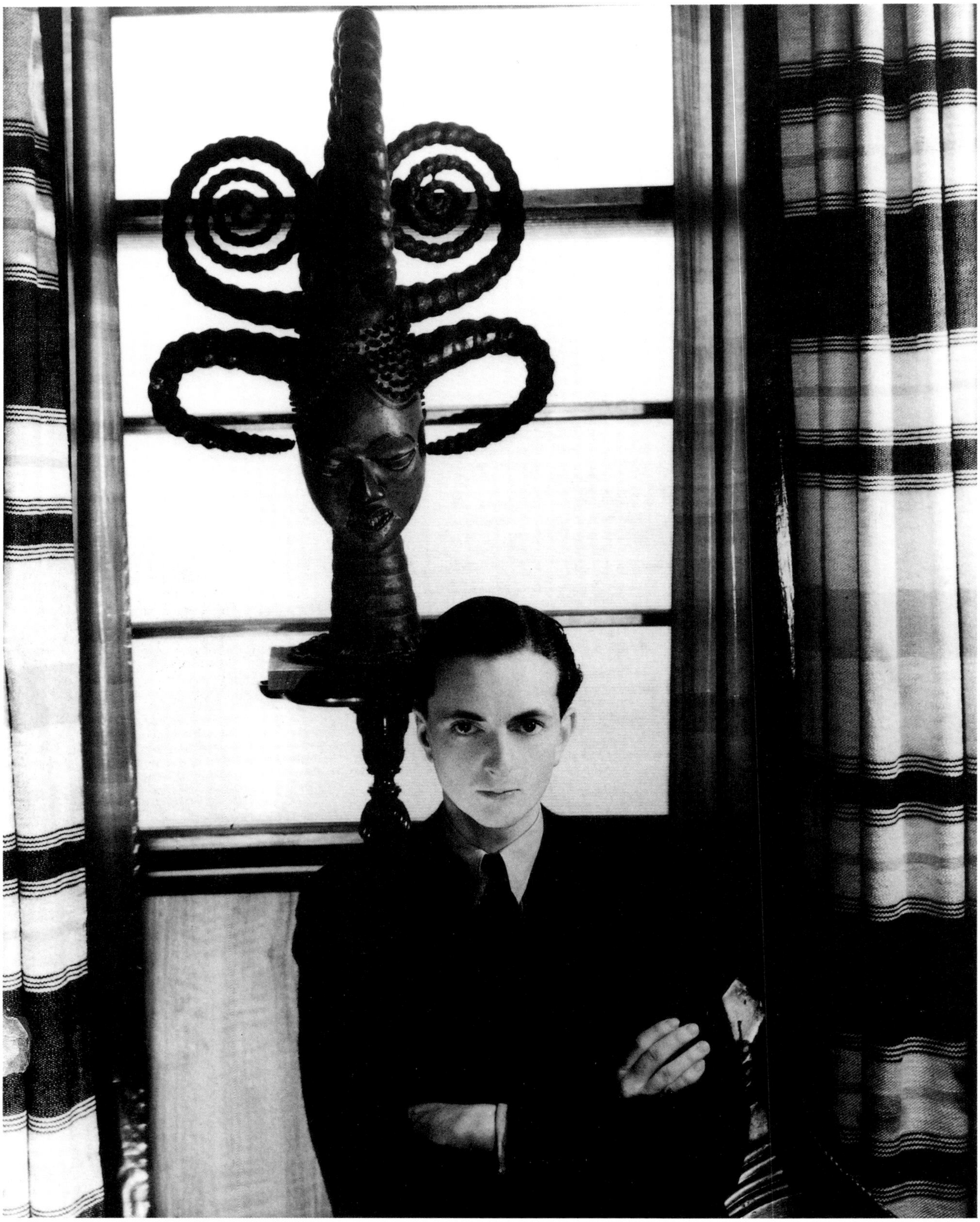

41

14. Jacques Naegeli
Edward James at LeRosey
c.1924–25
black and white photograph
13.5 x 8.5
EJF

15. *Edward James at Oxford*
c.1926–28
black and white photograph
19 x 14.5
EJF

16. *West Dean Shooting Party, November 10–14*
1896
sepia photograph
63 x 78
EJF

17. William Bevis
copy of Louis XV black and gold lacquer bombé commode, before 1737
early 1960s
lacquer with marble top
82 x 134.5 x 61
EJF

18. *Cufflinks belonging to Edward James*
gold and enamel, with monogram of Edward VII
Mr Hugo Vickers

19. *Edward VII and Queen Alexandra*, 1910
black and white photograph
35 x 25
EJF

20. *Evelyn James*
black and white photograph
16 x 17
EJF

21. Alice Hughes
Evelyn James, 1895
black and white photograph
20.5 x 15
EJF

22. *William James*
black and white photograph
16.5 x 13
EJF

23. W.P. Marsh of Bognor
Edward James, Infant heir of West Dean
1907
black and white photograph
9 x 14
EJF

24. *Reception programme for Edward James's homecoming*
1907
8-page pamphlet
20.5 x 25.5
EJF

25. *Edward James*
c.1909
black and white photograph
16 x 11.5
EJF

26. *Evelyn James's scrapbook with clippings of Edward's homecoming*
1907
leather bound scrapbook
30.5 x 44.5
EJF

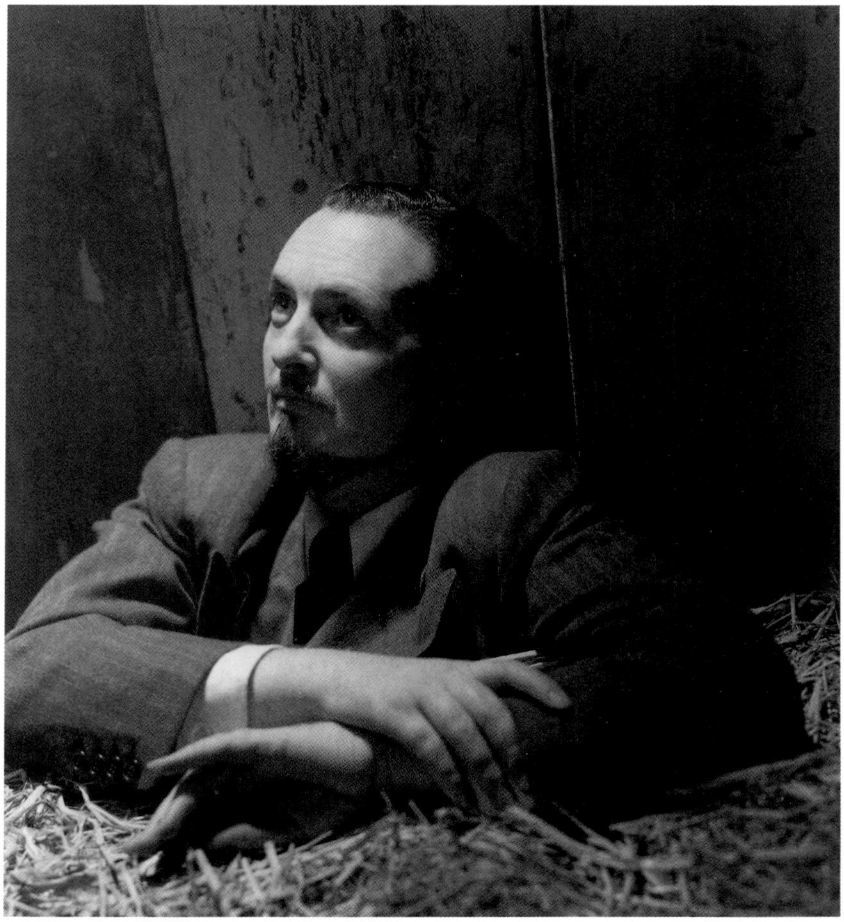

47

27. *Two-handled porringer, cover and spoon*
1907
Inscribed 'To Edward Frank Willis James from his Godfather, Edward R & I, November 2, 1907'
silver, in fitted leather case
12.5 x 20.5 x 15
EJF

28. *West Dean House,*
1800s and 1906
two black and white photographs
51 x 90
EJF

29. Bedford Lemere & Co
West Dean House, Entrance Hall
black and white photograph
26 x 32
EJF

30. *West Dean House, Oak Hall*
black and white photograph
37 x 29.5
EJF

31. London Stereoscopic and Photographic Company
West Dean House, Morning Room
black and white photograph
35 x 44.5
EJF

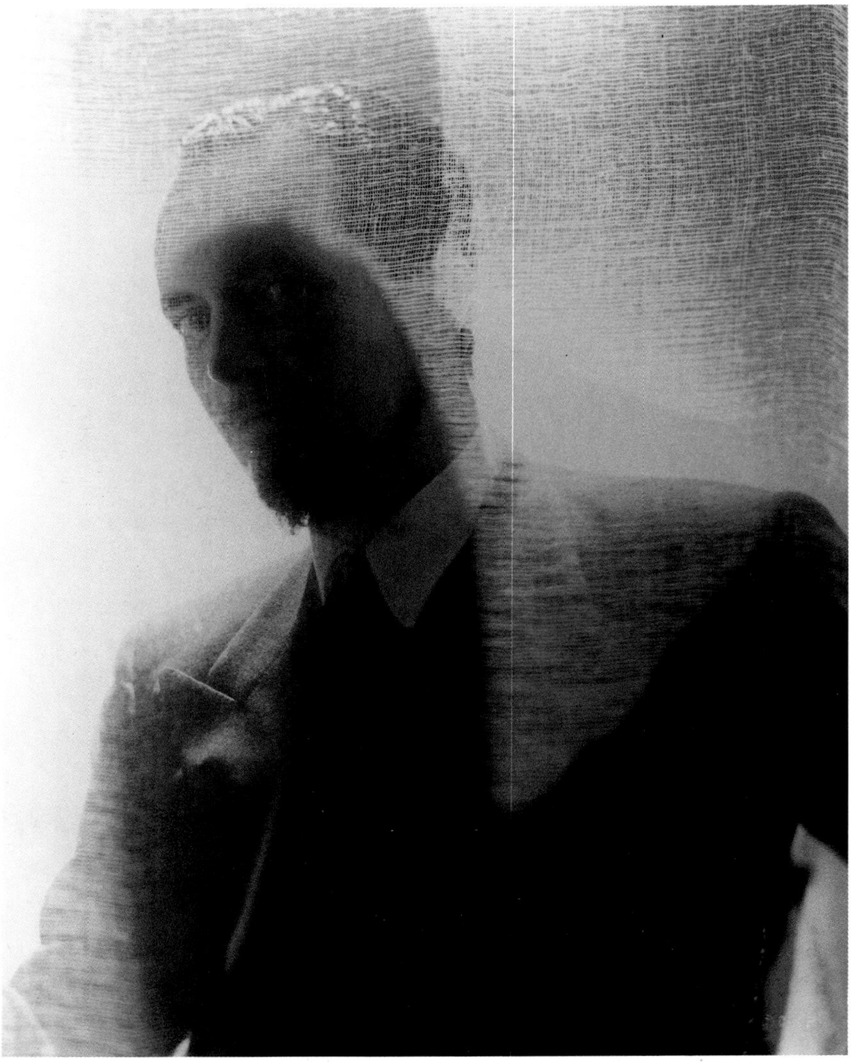

49

32. London Stereoscopic and Photographic Company
West Dean House, Drawing Room
black and white photograph
35 x 44.5
EJF

33. London Stereoscopic and Photographic Company
West Dean House, Library
black and white photograph
35 x 44.5
EJF

34. London Stereoscopic and Photographic Company
West Dean House, Boudoir
black and white photograph
35 x 44.5
EJF

35. London Stereoscopic and Photographic Company
West Dean House, Billiard Room
black and white photograph
35 x 44.5
EJF

36. London Stereoscopic and Photographic Company
West Dean Gardens, Palm House
black and white photograph
44.5 x 35
EJF

37. Russells, Southgate, Chichester
West Dean Gardens, Pergola
black and white photograph
34 x 42
EJF

38. *West Dean Shooting Party, November 19–24,* 1906
black and white photograph
40.5 x 44.5
EJF

THE YOUNG AESTHETE

39. *Edward James in Oak Hall at West Dean House*
black and white photograph
35 x 29
EJF

40. *Ekoi skin-covered headdress with spiralling horns*
Eastern Nigeria, early 20th century
101.5 x 54.5 x 71
EJF

41. Cecil Beaton (1904–1980)
Edward James
late 1930s
black and white photograph
42 x 32.5
EJF

42. *West Dean House Entrance Hall with Salvador Dalí's 'Girl Skipping Rope' (1936)*
after 1936
black and white photograph
23 x 28
EJF

43. Madame Yevonde (1893–1975)
Edward James
black and white photograph
51 x 40
EJF

44. Madame Yevonde (1893–975)
Edward James
c.1937
colour photograph
51.5 x 44.5
EJF

45. *Edward James with Paul Sorrell's portrait of Gerald Heard*
c.1943
black and white photograph
46 x 35.5
EJF

46. Cecil Beaton (1904–1980)
Edward James
January 7, 1948
black and white photograph
56 x 46
EJF

47. Cecil Beaton (1904–1980)
Edward James
January 7, 1948
black and white photograph
51 x 40.5
EJF

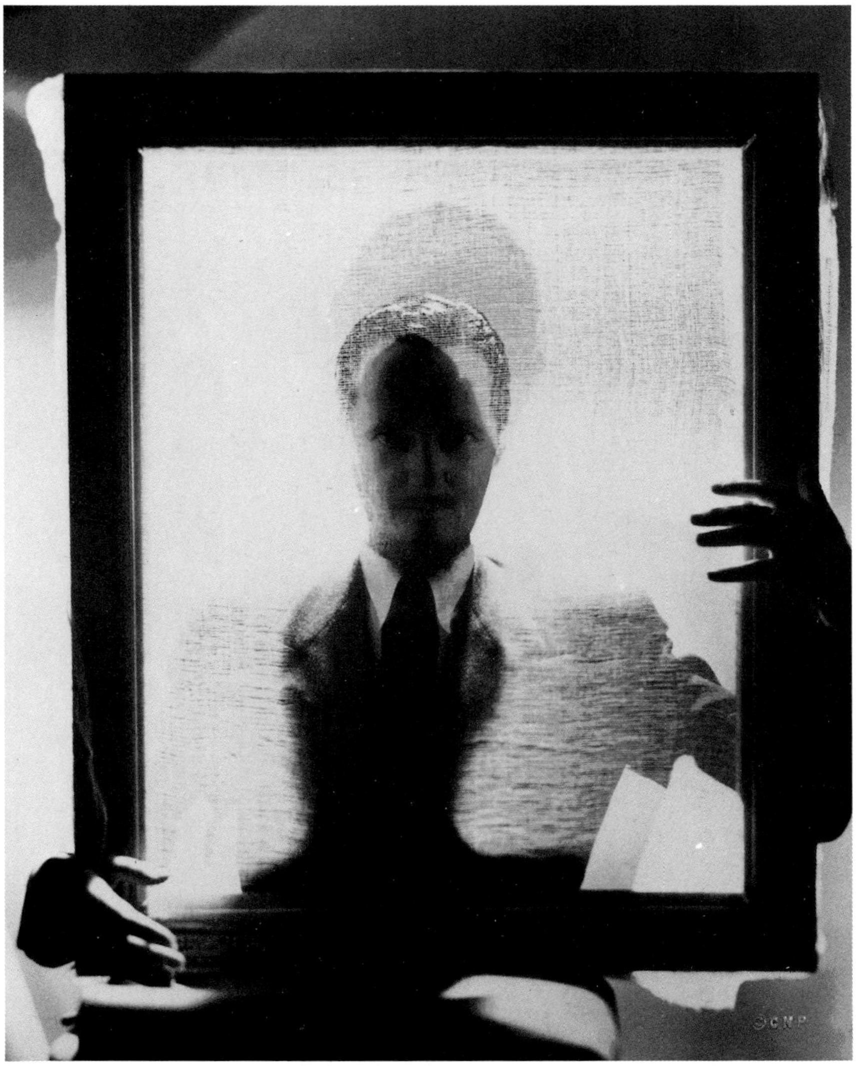

50

48. Cecil Beaton (1904–1980)
Edward James
February 27, 1948
black and white photograph
51 x 40.5
EJF

49. Cecil Beaton (1904–1980)
Edward James
February 27, 1948
black and white photograph
53.5 x 43
EJF

50. Cecil Beaton (1904–1980)
Edward James
January 7, 1948
black and white photograph
53.5 x 43
EJF

51. *Edward James*
black and white photograph
33 x 27
EJF

52. Isamu Noguchi (1904–1988)
Edward James
c.1941–44
marble bust
26 high
EJF

53. *Edward James with bust by Isamu Noguchi*
copy print
53.5 x 43
EJF

54. Pavel Tchelitchew (1898–1957)
Portrait of Igor Markevitch
1930
oil on canvas
89 x 71
EJF

55. Pavel Tchelitchew (1898–1957)
The Concert, Harlequins, 1933
oil on canvas
87.5 x 114.5
EJF

56. Pavel Tchelitchew (1898–1957)
Self-portrait of the artist
1937
dedicated to Edward James
pen, ink, and sepia wash on paper
41 x 32
EJF

57. *Two Hand and Globe lamps from 35 Wimpole Street*
plaster and glass
each 47 x 19.5
EJF

58. *Two Conch Shell Lamps from 35 Wimpole Street*
shell and painted brass
each 29.7 x 18.4
EJF

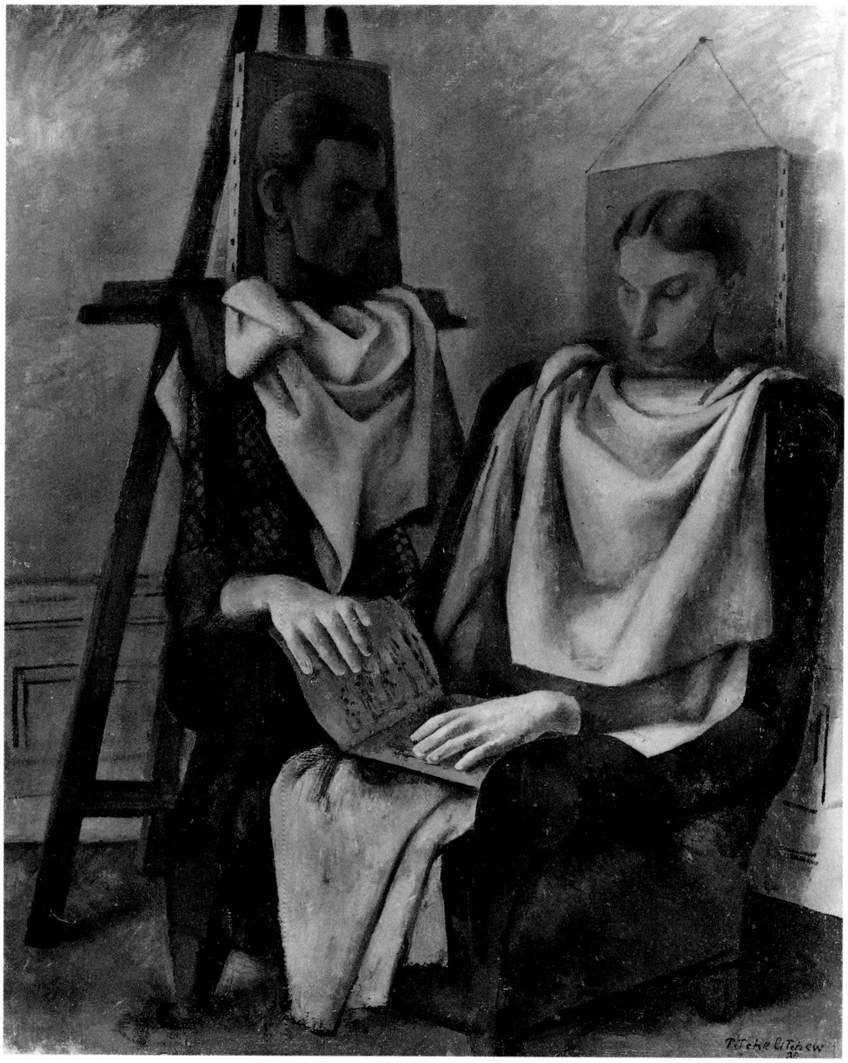

54

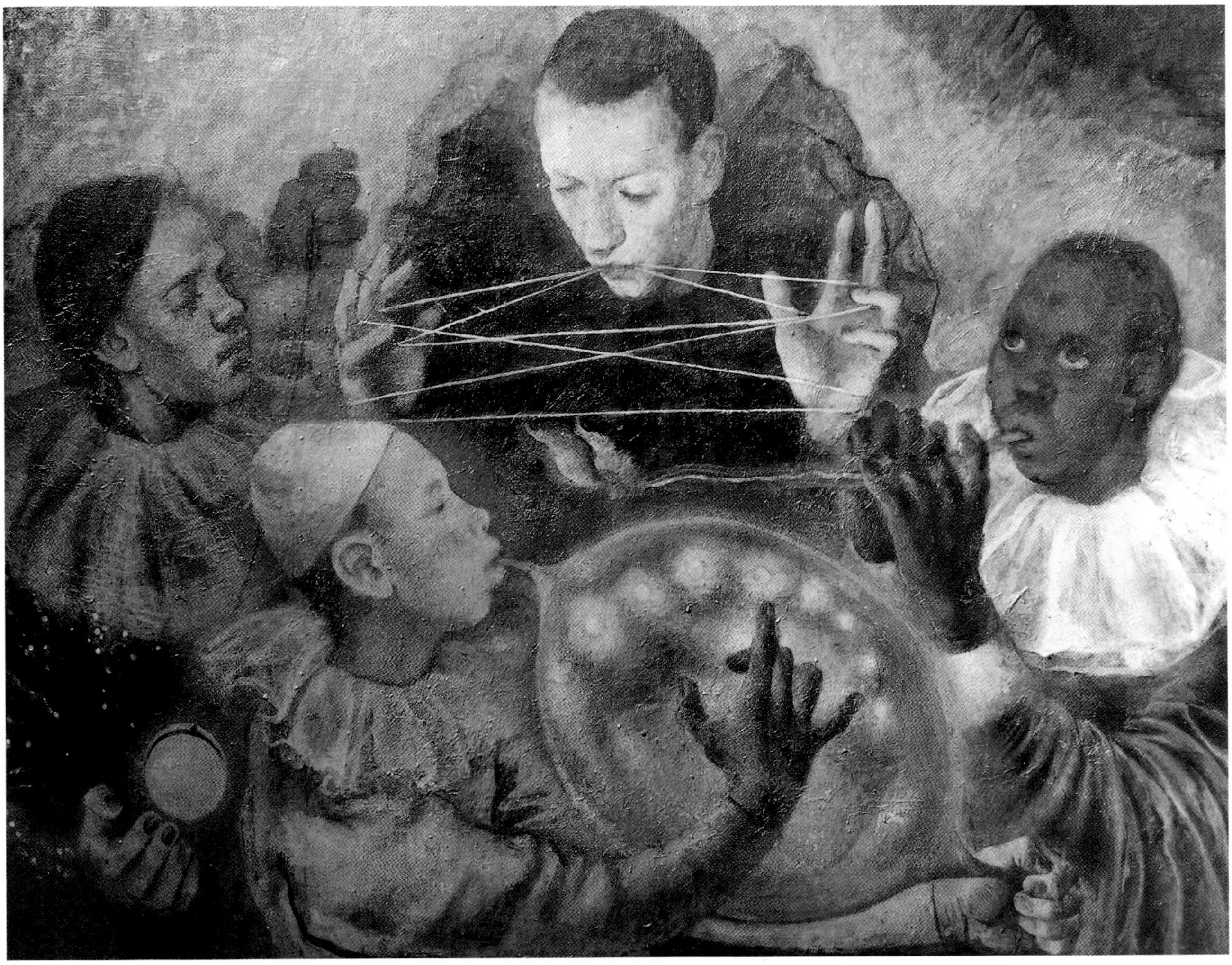

55

59. *Fossilised Fish Skeleton*
fossilised bone
40.5 x 73.5 x 20.5
EJF

60. Pavel Tchelitchew (1898–1957)
The Gardener Who Saw God
1937
pen and sepia ink
35.5 x 27.5
EJF

61. Salvador Dalí (1904–1989)
Drawing on stationery from 35 Wimpole Street
1936
ink and wash
24 x 20
EJF

62. Norman Parkinson (1913–1990)
Edward James with Igor Markevitch and his wife at 35 Wimpole Street
late 1930s
black and white photograph
22 x 29
EJF

63. Norman Parkinson (1913–1990)
Edward James on the Stairway of 35 Wimpole Street
late 1930s
black and white photograph
22 x 29
EJF

64. Norman Parkinson (1913–1990)
Edward James with René Magritte's 'The Future of Statues'
black and white photograph
22 x 29
EJFp

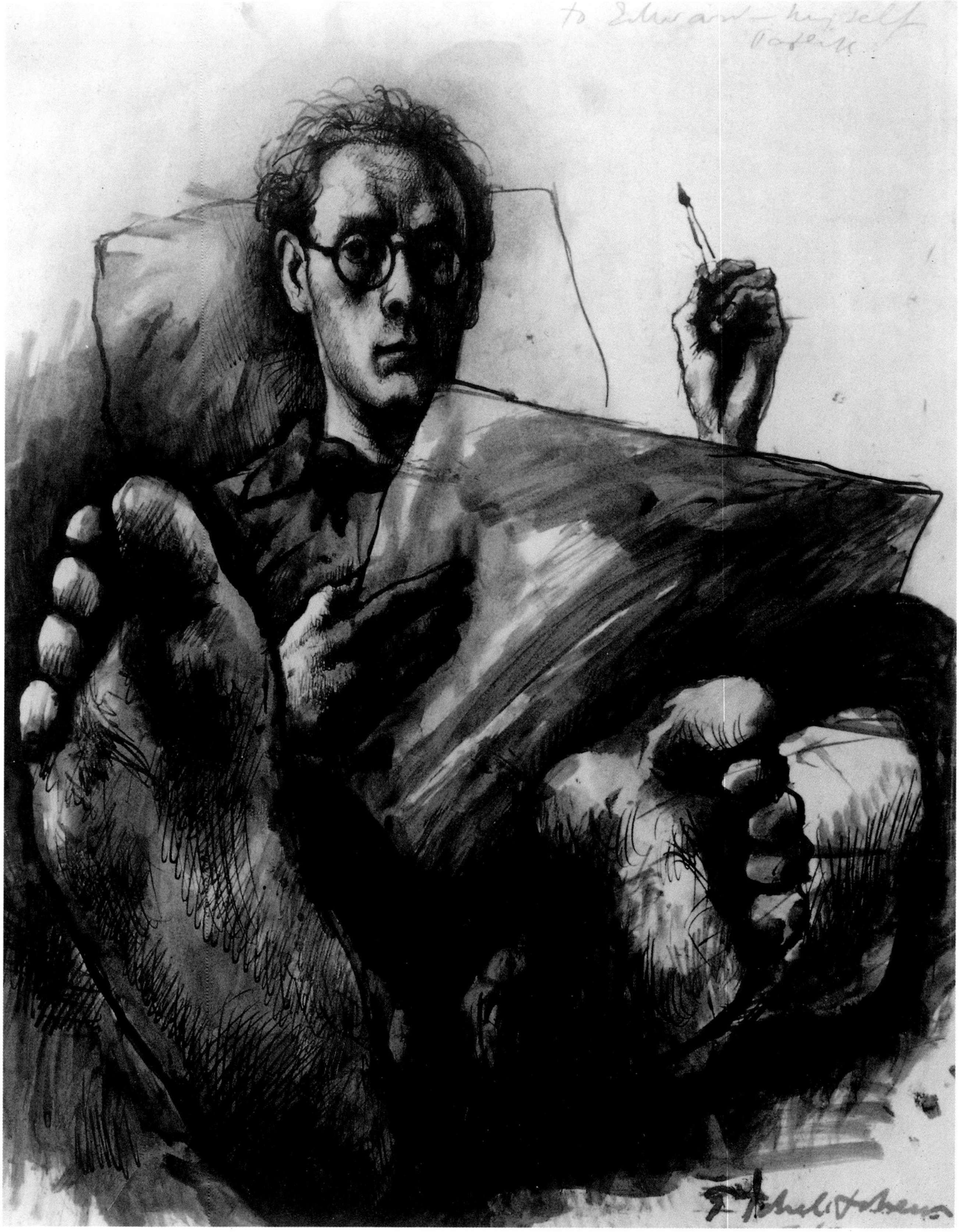

56

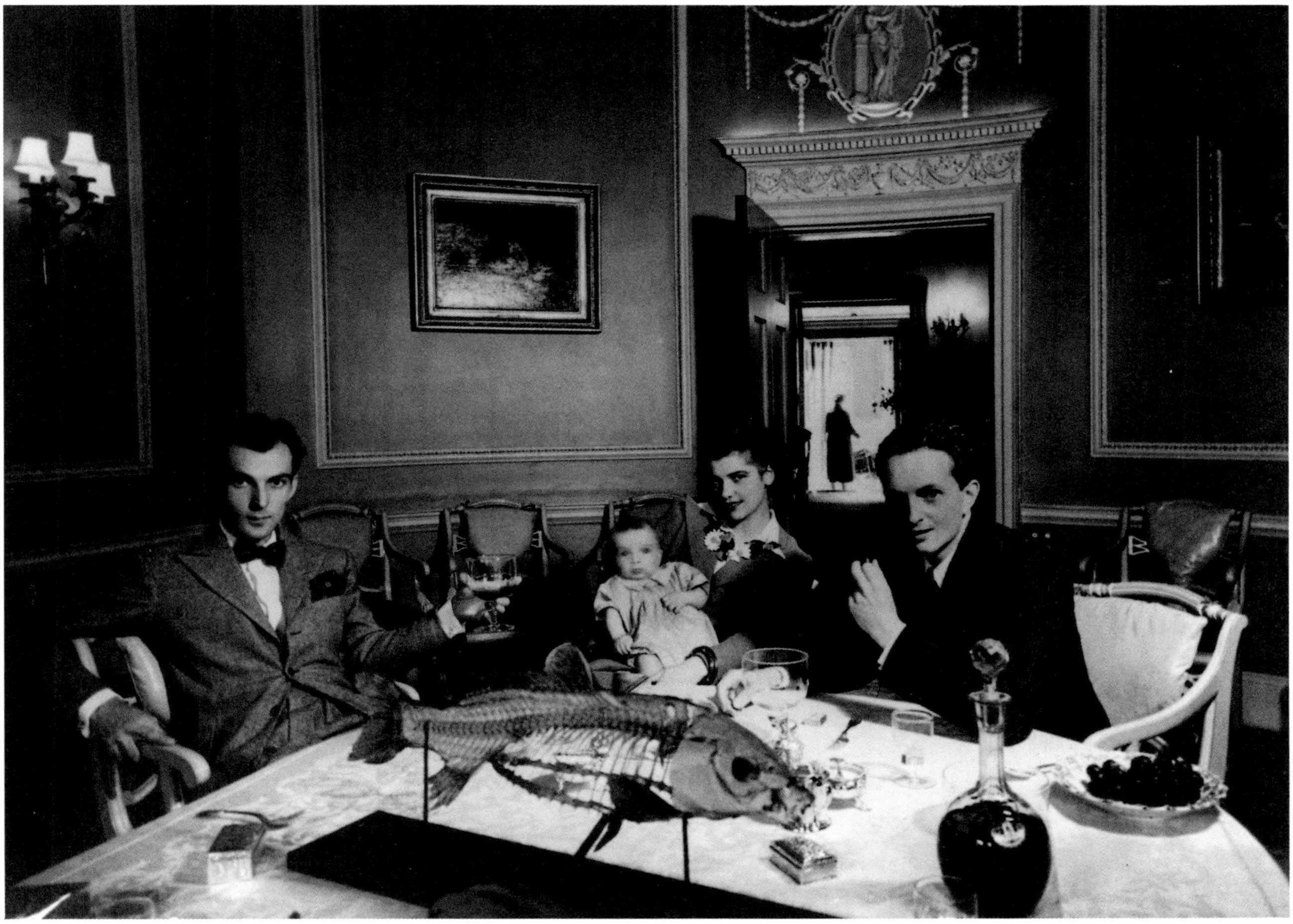

62

65. Norman Parkinson (1913–1990)
Edward James and Igor Markevitch in the 'Tent Room' at 35 Wimpole Street
late 1930s
black and white photograph
24 x 30.5
EJF

66. *Dressing table set owned by Edward James*, 1931–32
9ct gold enamelled with the emblem of the James Press
(i) Two brushes each 15 x 3
(ii) Shaving stick holder 8 x 3
(iii) Glass scent bottle 12 x 5.5 x 4.5
(iv) Glass bottle 14 x 4 (diameter)
(v) Glass jar 4.5 x 10 x 6
EJF

67. *Pocket watch owned by Edward James*
1928–29
Cartier, 18ct gold enamelled with the emblem of the James Press
4 x 46 (diameter)
EJF

68. John Betjeman (1906–84)
Mount Zion
(first edition, proof copy)
1931
book
21 x 14.5
EJF

69. John Betjeman (1906–1984)
Two pages of handwritten manuscript for 'Mount Zion'
ink on paper
25.5 x 20.5 and 21 x 13.5
EJF

70. Edward James (1907–1984)
Juventutis Annorum
published 1931
book and slip-case
23 x 32 open, 24 x 16.5 slip-case
EJF

71. Edward James (1907–1984)
Envelope for letter to Ivan Hicks
ink on paper
12 x 18
EJF

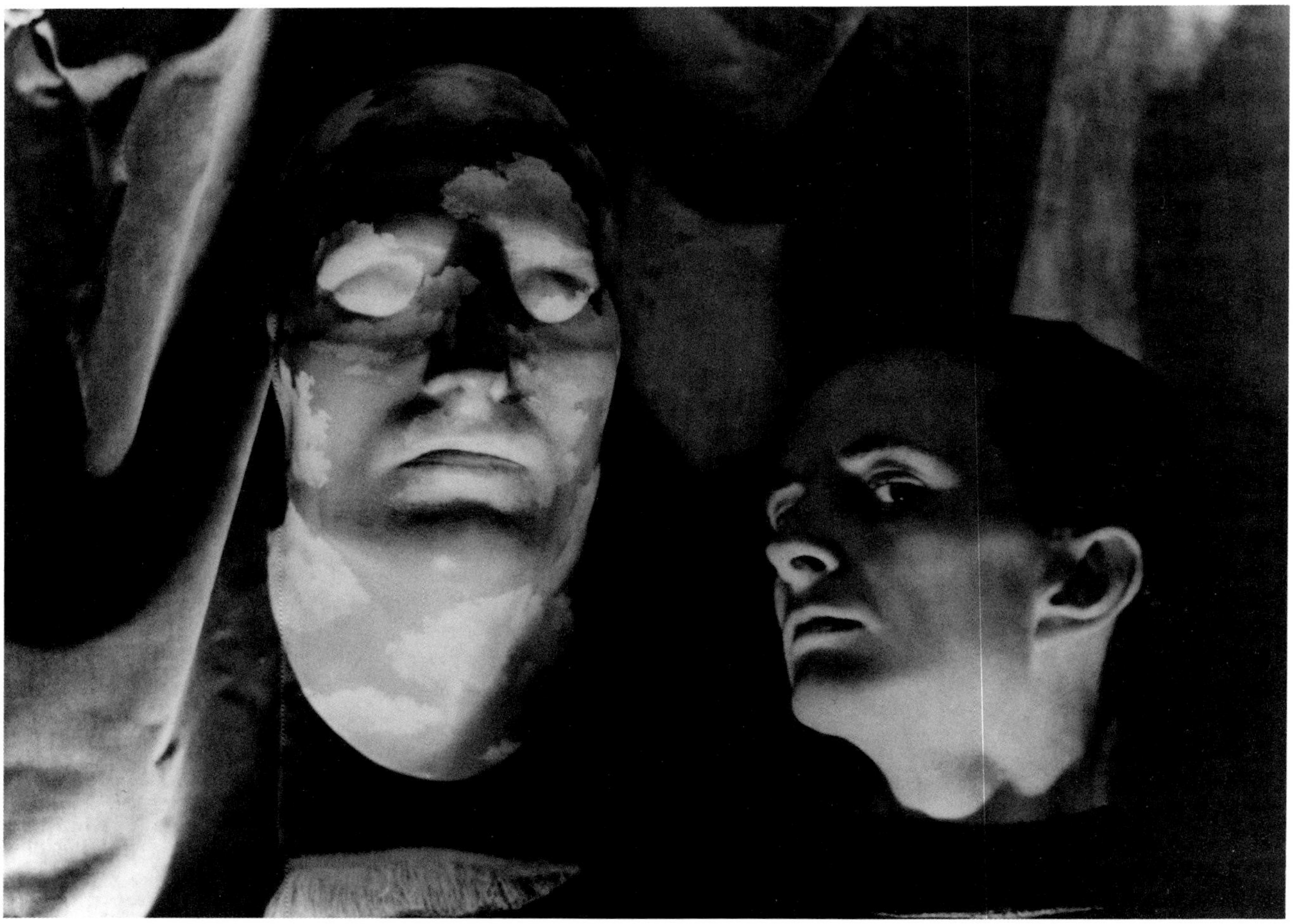

64

72. Edward James (1907–1984)
The Bones of My Hand
published 1938
book and slip-case
29 x 20.5 , 30.5 x 21.5 slip-case
EJF

73. Edward James (1907–1984)
The Next Volume
second edition
1939
book
28.5 x 40.5 open
EJF

74. Edward James (1907–1984)
The Venetian Glass Omnibus
published 1933
book
32.5 x 27
Hugo Vickers

75. Cecil Beaton (1904–1980)
Edward James
February 27, 1948
black and white photograph
53.5 x 43
EJF

76. Hans Fleischer
Fest Musik
1928
musical score
33 x 27
EJF

77. Salvador Dalí (1904–1989)
La Conquête de L'Irrationel
1935
book with pen and ink drawing
16 x 24 open
EJF

78. Salvador Dalí (1904–1989)
Study for portrait of Edward James
1936
pen and ink sketch
21 x 16
EJF

79. *Handmade album dedicated to Edward James*
28 March 1937
Poems by Paul Colinet, Louis Scutenaire and his wife Irène Hamoir and Georgette Berger-Magritte; illustrations by René Magritte
ink, coloured pencil and pastel on paper
28 x 15.5 open
EJF

80. Dylan Thomas (1914–1953) and Edward James (1907–1984)
Letter from Dylan Thomas and Edward James's reply
1948
25.5 x 18 and 21.5 x 28
EJF

81. René Magritte (1898–1967) and Edward James (1907–1984)
Letter from René Magritte
26 July 1938
and Edward James's reply
28 July 1938
28 x 21 and 25.5 x 20.5
EJF

MARRIAGE AND DIVORCE

82. Cecil Beaton (1904–1980)
Portrait of Tilly Losch
pencil and watercolour
58 x 44.5
EJF

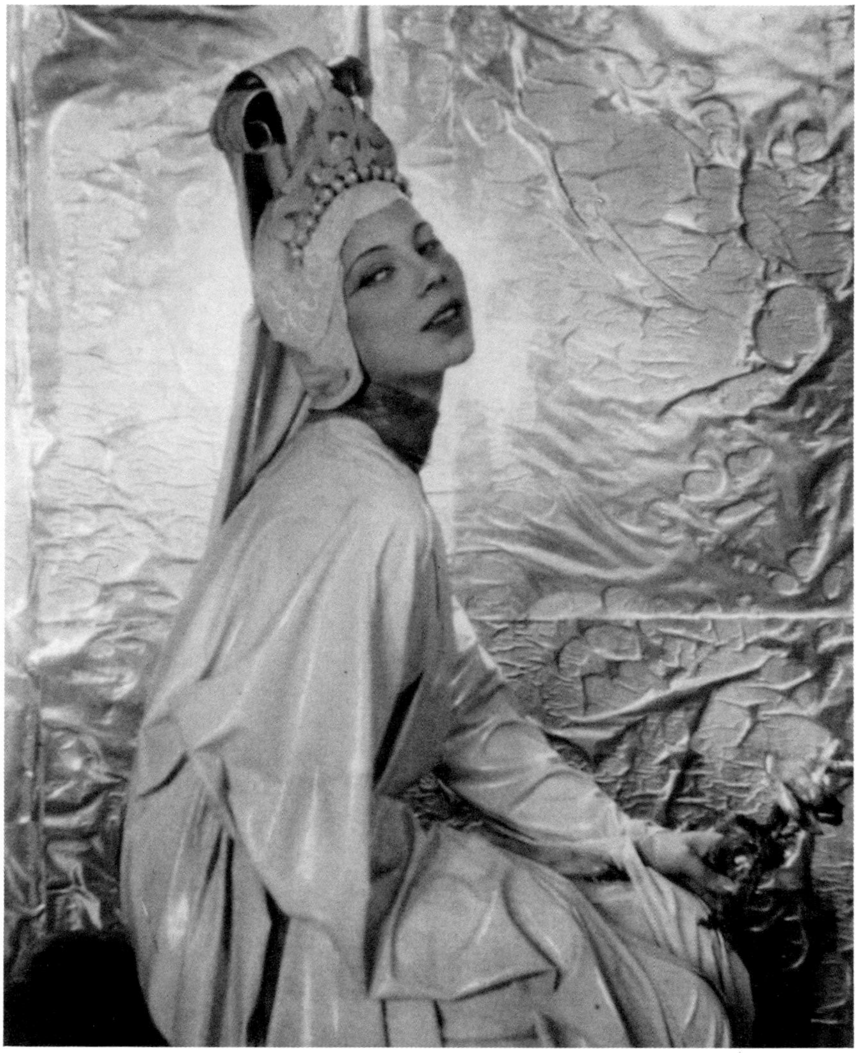

82

83. Cecil Beaton (1904–1980)
Tilly Losch
black and white photograph
46 x 33
EJF

84. *Bathroom designed by Paul Nash (1889–1946) for 35 Wimpole Street*
Photograph published in *Architectural Review*
June 1933
copy print
Architects Journal, London

85. Cecil Beaton (1904–1980)
Edward James in the bathroom designed by Paul Nash for 35 Wimpole Street
black and white photograph
24.5 x 19.5
National Portrait Gallery, London

86. Green & Abbott, London
Design for Tilly Losch footprint carpet
early 1930s
pencil on tracing paper
76 x 91.5
EJF

87. *Piece of Tilly Losch footprint carpet*
early 1930s
wool
92 x 115
EJF

PATRONAGE LES BALLETS 1933

88. *The 'Menuetto' from 'Mozartiana', London*
1933
Ballet designs by Christian Bérard (1902–1949)
copy print
38 x 29
EJF

89. *Pearl Argyle in the 'Preghiera' from 'Mozartiana', London*
1933
Ballet designs by Christian Bérard (1902–1949)
copy print
38 x 29
EJF

90. *Tamara Toumanova and Roman Jasinksi in 'Mozartiana', London*
1933
Ballet designs by Christian Bérard (1902–1949)
copy print
38 x 29
EJF

91. *Tilly Losch and Roman Jasinski in 'L'Errante', London*
1933
Ballet designs by Pavel Tchelitchew (1898–1957)
copy print from original by Sasha (Alexander Stuart)
38 x 29
EJF

92. *Tilly Losch and Roman Jasinski in 'L'Errante', London*
1933
Ballet designs by Pavil Tchelitchew (1898–1957)
copy print from original by Sasha (Alexander Stuart)
38 x 29
EJF

93. *Tilly Losch and Roman Jasinski in 'L'Errante', London*
1933
Ballet designs by Pavel Tchelitchew (1898–1957)
copy print from original by Sasha (Alexander Stuart)
38 x 29
EJF

94. *Les Ballets 1933 at the Théâtre des Champs-Elysées, Paris*
1933
chromolithograph poster
59 x 40
Royal Pavilion, Libraries & Museums, Brighton & Hove

95. *Tilly Losch danse dans les Ballet 1933*
1933
Printed by Bedos & Cie, Paris
photogravure and lithograph poster
58 x 77.5
Royal Pavilion, Libraries & Museums, Brighton & Hove

96. *Les Ballets 1933 at the Théâtre des Champs-Elysées, Paris*
1933
chromolithograph poster
120 x 81
Royal Pavilion, Libraries & Museums, Brighton & Hove

97. *Les Ballets 1933 at the Théâtre des Champs-Elysées, Paris*
1933
Design after Pavel Tchelitchew
Sketch for 'L'Errante'
1933
chromolithograph poster
120 x 81
Royal Pavilion, Libraries & Museums, Brighton & Hove

98. *The Ballets of 1933 at the Savoy Theatre, London*
1933
Printed by John Waddington, London
chromolithograph poster
76 x 51
Royal Pavilion, Libraries & Museums, Brighton & Hove

99. *Backdrop for 'Fastes'*
1933
Designed and possibly partly executed by André Derain (1880–1954)
gouache on canvas
798 x 998 (approx)
Royal Pavilion, Libraries & Museums, Brighton & Hove

100. *Body mask for Bearded Genie (from 'Fastes')*
1933
Designed by André Derain (1880–1954)
papier mâché on wire frame
(repainted in gouache c.1982)
102 x 95 x 30
Royal Pavilion, Libraries & Museums, Brighton & Hove

101. *Three-face mask for Lupercalian Priest (from 'Fastes')*
1933
Designed by André Derain
(1880–1954)
papier mâché on wire frame, painted in gouache
30 x 30 x 22
Royal Pavilion, Libraries & Museums, Brighton & Hove

102. *Mask for bearded Buffoon (from 'Fastes')*
1933
Designed by André Derain
(1880–1954)
papier mâché on wire frame, painted white
30 x 25 x 20
Royal Pavilion, Libraries & Museums, Brighton & Hove

103. *Mask for bald Buffoon (from 'Fastes')*
1933
Designed by André Derain
(1880–1954)
papier mâché on wire frame, painted white
29 x 28 x 20
Royal Pavilion, Libraries & Museums, Brighton & Hove

104. *Ass-head, the 'Donkey of Silenus' (from 'Fastes')*
1933
Designed by André Derain
(1880–1954)
papier mâché on wire frame, painted in gouache
57 high
Christopher Gibbs Ltd

105. *Costume for an Etruscan Matron (from 'Fastes')*
1933
Designed by André Derain
(1880–1954)
Made by Karinska (1886–1983)
green crepe dress decorated with cream satin and black braid, black satin scarf similarly decorated, rayon wig and chenille-covered wire headdress
Length 110
Royal Pavilion, Libraries & Museums, Brighton & Hove

106. *Costume for the Courtesan (from 'Fastes')*
1933
Designed by André Derain
(1880–1954)
Made by Karinska (1886–1983)
peach-coloured rayon body suit, crêpe-de-chine skirt and rayon scarf
length 120
Royal Pavilion, Libraries & Museums, Brighton & Hove

107. *Souvenir programme for Les Ballets 1933*
1933
Théâtre des Champs-Elysées, Paris.
Publisher unknown
printed in sepia with photolithographic plates
31.5 x 24.5
Royal Pavilion, Libraries & Museums, Brighton & Hove

108. *Backdrop for 'Les Valses de Beethoven'*
1933
Designed by Emilio Terry
(1890–1969)
cut cloth of canvas on net
1000 x 1070 approx
Royal Pavilion, Libraries & Museums, Brighton & Hove

109. *Costume for Fire (from 'Les Valses de Beethoven')*
1933
Designed by Emilio Terry
(1890–1969)
cotton leotard fixed to black net skirt; the whole applied with strips of red and orange chiffon
length 141
Royal Pavilion, Libraries & Museums, Brighton & Hove

110. *Costume for Earth (from 'Les Valses de Beethoven')*
1933
Designed by Emilio Terry
(1890–1969)
sleeveless dress in two layers of brown chiffon applied with flock leaves and butterflies
length 130
Royal Pavilion, Libraries & Museums, Brighton & Hove

111. *Costume for one of the 'Train of Apollo' (from 'Les Valses de Beethoven')*
1933
Designed by Emilio Terry
(1890–1969)
short tunic in gold net cross-banded with gold braid
length 80
Royal Pavilion, Libraries & Museums, Brighton & Hove

112. *Chair for Water (from 'Les Valses de Beethoven')*
1933
Designed by Emilio Terry
(1890–1969)
scrim and painted plaster moulded over bamboo chair frame
90 x 70 x 110
Royal Pavilion, Libraries & Museums, Brighton & Hove

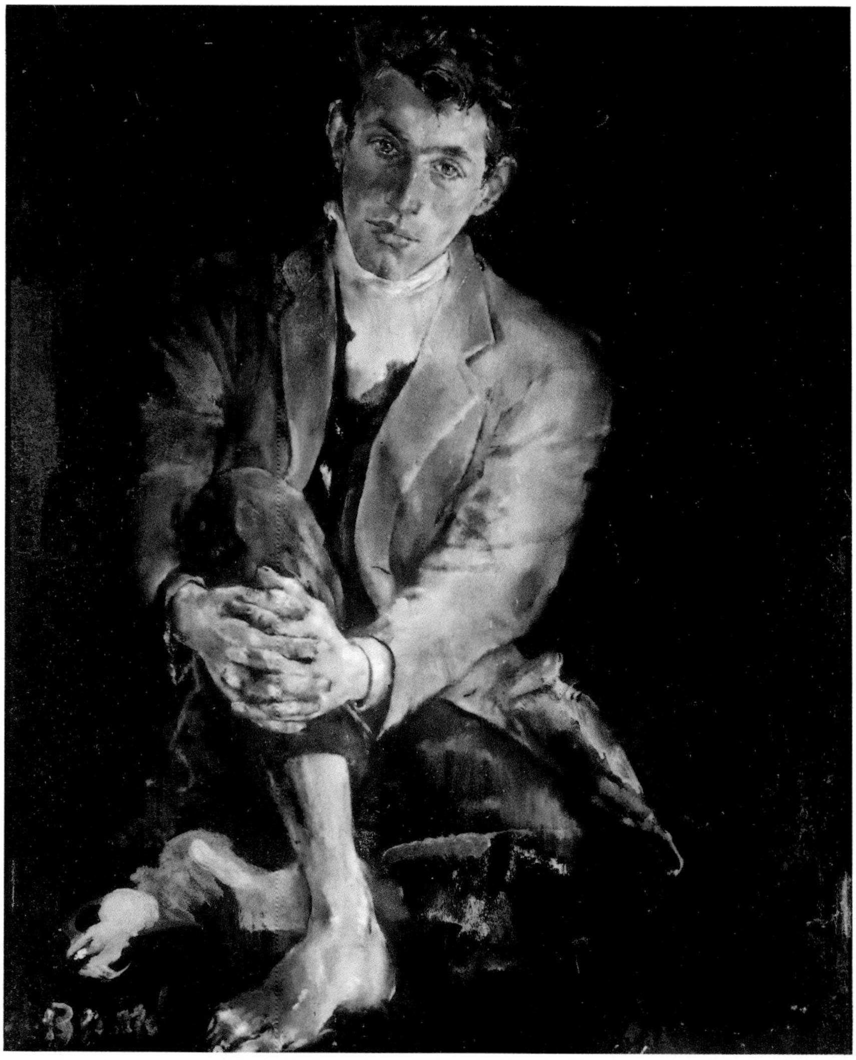

134

113. *Armchair for Air*
(from 'Les Valses de Beethoven')
1933
Designed by Emilio Terry
(1890–1969)
scrim and painted plaster, moulded
over bamboo chair frame
90 x 70 x 100
Royal Pavilion, Libraries &
Museums, Brighton & Hove

114. *Chaise-Longue for Earth*
(from 'Les Valses de Beethoven')
1933
Designed by Emilio Terry
(1890–1969)
scrim and painted plaster, moulded
over bamboo chair frame
120 x 63 x 155
Royal Pavilion, Libraries &
Museums, Brighton & Hove

115. Pavel Tchelitchew (1898–1957)
Study for two Angels
(for 'L'Errante')
1933
ink, wash and gouache on paper
42.5 x 35
EJF

116. Pavel Tchelitchew (1898–1957)
Study for the Funeral scene
(for 'L'Errante')
1933
ink, wash and gouache on paper
35 x 45
EJF

117. Pavel Tchelitchew (1898–1957)
Study for the Lover
(for 'L'Errante')
1933
ink, wash and gouache on paper
20 x 26
EJF

118. Pavel Tchelitchew (1898–1957)
Study for Tilly Losch in 'L'Errante'
1933
ink and wash on paper
29 x 44.5
The Mercury Gallery, London

119. *Costume for the corps de ballet as Revolutionaries in 'L'Errante'*
1933
Designed by Pavel Tchelitchew
(1898–1957)
Made by Karinska (1886–1983)
heavy red crepe robe with hood
overall length 259
Royal Pavilion, Libraries &
Museums, Brighton & Hove

120 *Costume for the corps de ballet as Shadows in 'L'Errante'*
1933
Designed by Pavel Tchelitchew (1898–1957)
Made by Karinska (1886–1983)
chiffon robe, tie-dyed in mottled browns and blues
length 131
Royal Pavilion, Libraries & Museums, Brighton & Hove

121. *Costume for the Demi-Monde in 'Les Songes'*
1933
Designed by André Derain (1880–1954). Made by New Sheridan House, London
leotard foundation clad with white artificial silk and organdie ruffles
length 151
Royal Pavilion, Libraries & Museums, Brighton & Hove

122. *Souvenir programme for Les Ballets 1933*
1933
Théâtre des Champs-Elysées, Paris. Publisher unknown
printed in sepia with photolithographic plates
31.5 x 24.5
Royal Pavilion, Libraries & Museums, Brighton & Hove

123. *Souvenir programme for Les Ballets 1933 at the Savoy Theatre, London*
programme and enclosures
21.5 x 14 and 15 x 12 and 14 x 11.5
EJF

124. Caspar Neher (1897–1962)
Design for banner: LUXURA [sic] (Lust) in 'The Seven Deadly Sins'
ink, wash and gouache on paper
42 x 29.5
EJF

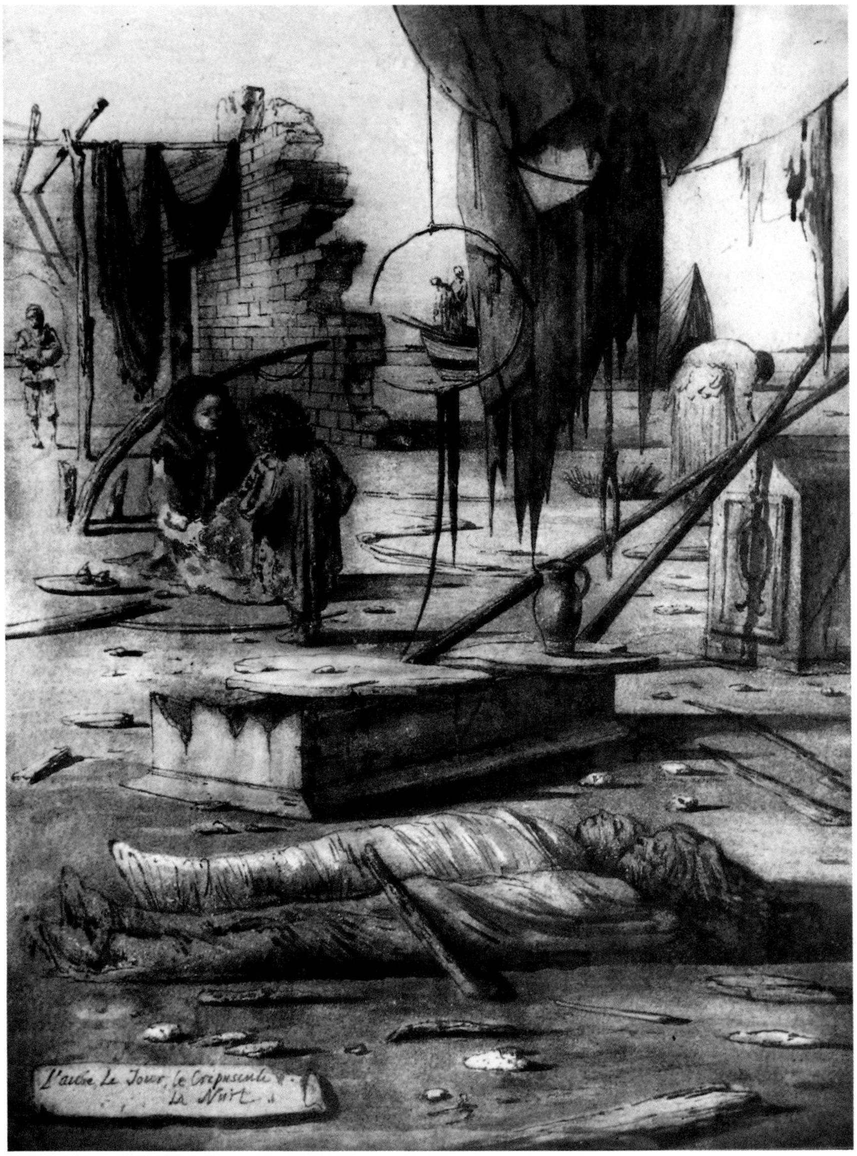

137

125. *Banner for SUPERBIA (Pride) in 'The Seven Deadly Sins'*
Designed by Caspar Neher (1897–1962)
gouache on canvas
600 x 240 approx
Royal Pavilion, Libraries & Museums, Brighton & Hove

126. *Banner for IRA (Anger) in 'The Seven Deadly Sins'*
Designed by Caspar Neher (1897–1962)
gouache on canvas
600 x 240 approx
Royal Pavilion, Libraries & Museums, Brighton & Hove

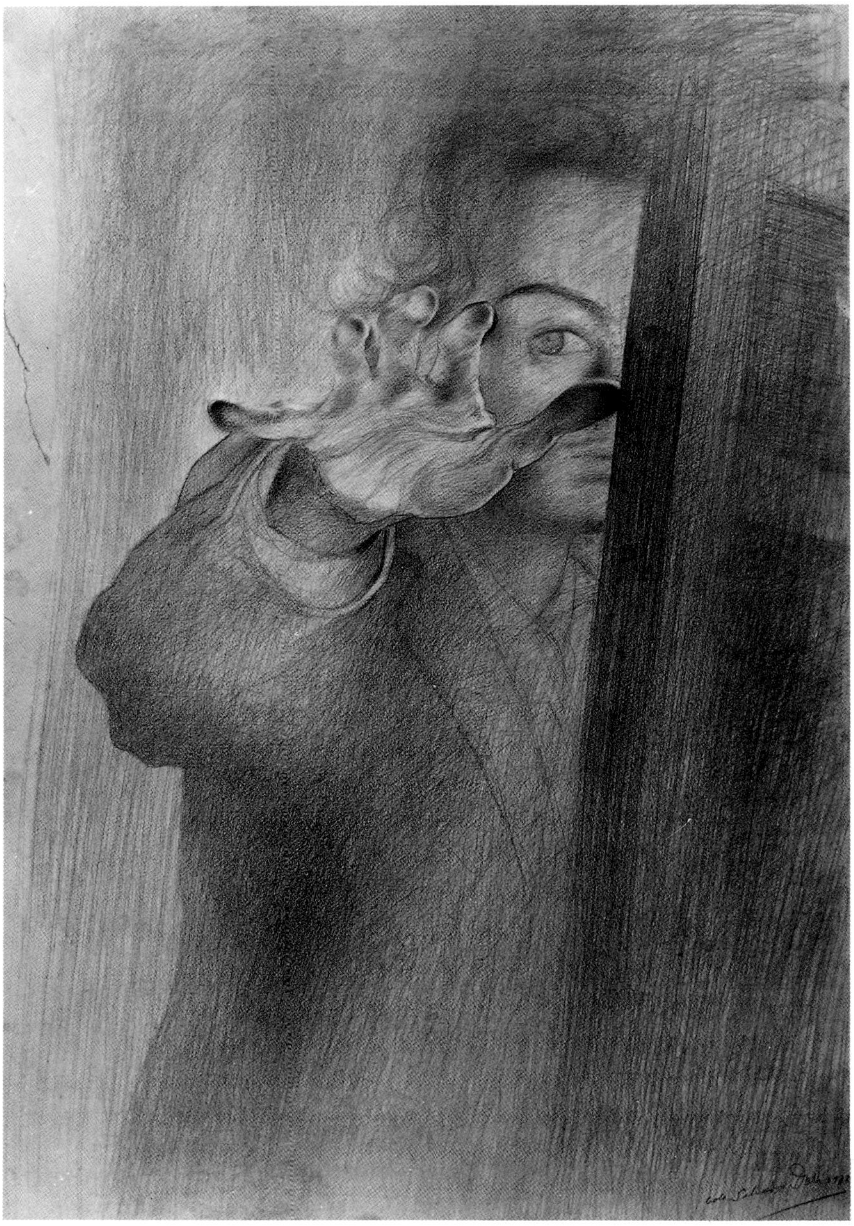

146

127. *Costume for Tilly Losch in Anger scene, in 'The Seven Deadly Sins'*
Designed by Caspar Neher (1897–1962)
leotard covered in grey sequins and tutu in sequinned lilac net and chiffon
length 68
Royal Pavilion, Libraries & Museums, Brighton & Hove

128. *Costume for Pride scene in 'The Seven Deadly Sins'*
Designed by Caspar Neher (1897–1962)
short dress in deep pink silk lined with silk and lace, worn with yellow lace-trimmed knickers, pink belt, gloves and boots
dress length 91
Royal Pavilion, Libraries & Museums, Brighton & Hove

129. *Visitors' Book commemorating visit of dancers from Les Ballets 1933 to West Dean House*
With signatures of dancers who stayed from 19–26 July 1933 and applied snapshots of dancers in costumes from 'Fastes'
34.5 x 53.5 open
EJF

130. *Publicity Flier for Les Ballets 1933 at the Théâtre des Champs-Elysées, Paris*
chromolithography by Rapide, 8 rue Drouot, Paris
1933
36.5 x 14.5
Royal Pavilion, Libraries & Museums, Brighton & Hove

131. *Two fliers advertising additional performance of Les Ballets 1933*
14.5 x 12 each
Royal Pavilion, Libraries & Museums, Brighton & Hove

132. *Unused tickets for special performance of Les Ballets 1933*
Performance of Nabokov's *Job*
16 June 1933
9.5 x 27
Royal Pavilion, Libraries & Museums, Brighton & Hove

133. *Two postcards of Tilly Losch and Roman Jasinski in 'L'Errante'*
Photographed by Sasha (Alexander Stuart), London
1933
each 14 x 9
Royal Pavilion, Libraries & Museums, Brighton & Hove

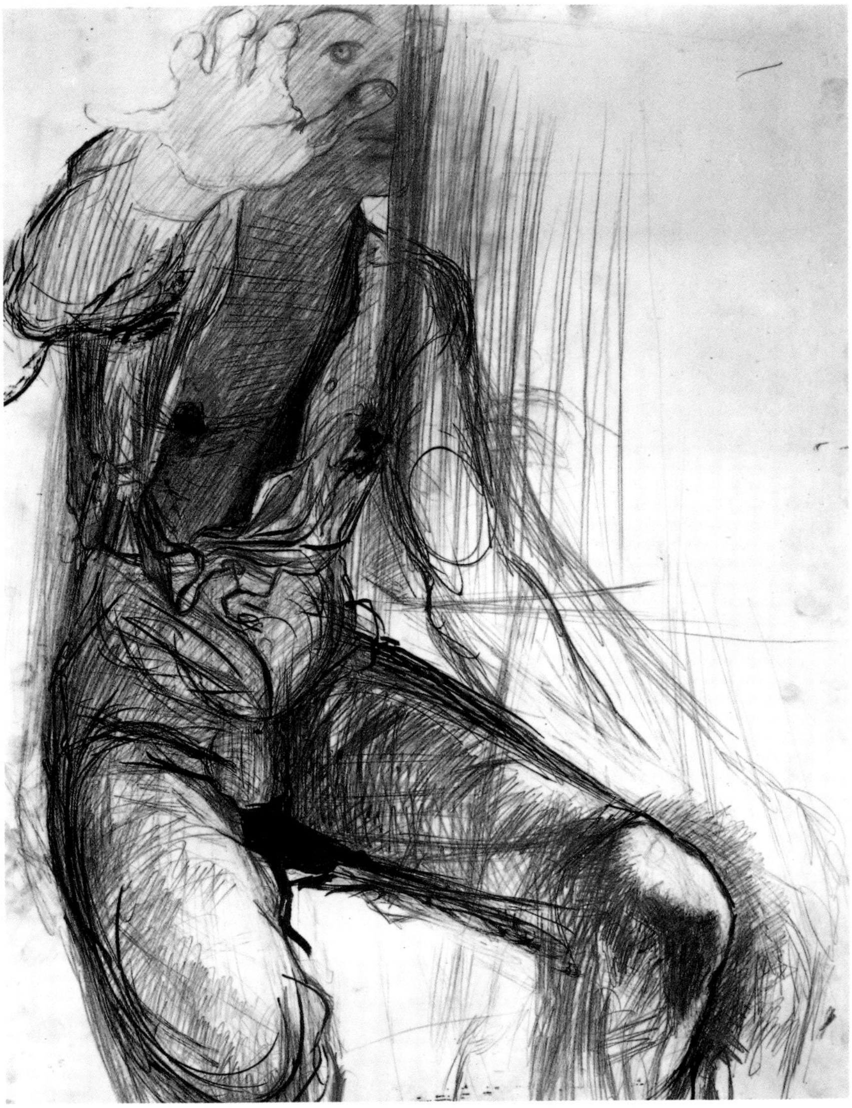

147

THE SURREALIST PATRON

134. Christian Bérard (1902–1949)
Portrait of a Young Boy
oil on canvas
64 x 53.5
EJF

135. Christian Bérard (1902–1949)
Portrait of a Young Boy
oil on board
80 x 63.5
EJF

136. Eugène Berman (1899–1972)
Les Enfants Perdus Sur La Route
1938
oil on canvas
62 x 52
EJF

137. Eugène Berman (1899–1972)
L'Aube, Le Jour, Le Crepuscule, La Nuit
grey wash on paper
100.5 x 74.5
EJF

138. Eugène Berman (1899–1972)
Los Desastros de la Guerra
1938
brush and ink on paper
38 x 28
EJF

139. *Mae West Lips Sofa*, 1938
Designed by Salvador Dalí (1904–1989) with Edward James.
Made by Green & Abbott, London
wood carcass upholstered in pink satin
86.5 x 183 x 81.5
EJF
On loan to The Victoria & Albert Museum, London

140. *Lobster Telephone*
1938
Designed by Salvador Dalí (1904–1989)
Made by Green & Abbott, London
assemblage, plaster and other materials
19 x 31 x 16
EJF

141. Salvador Dalí (1904–1989)
Couple with Their Heads Full of Clouds
1936
oil on panel
2 parts: 92.5 x 69.5 and 82.5 x 62.5
Museum Boijmans Van Beuningen, Rotterdam

142. Salvador Dalí (1904–1989)
The Great Paranoiac
1936
oil on panel
62 x 62
Museum Boijmans Van Beuningen, Rotterdam

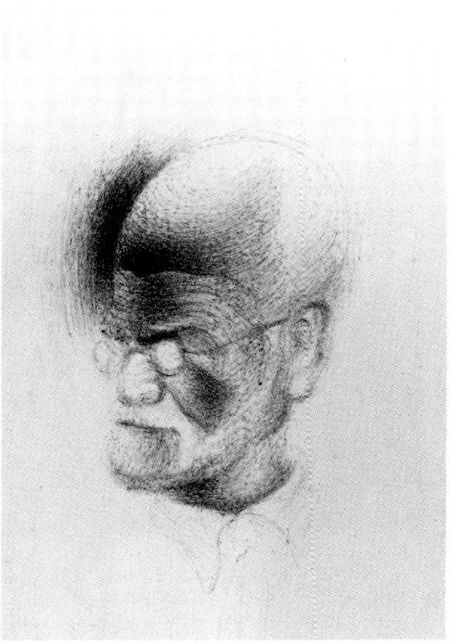

148

143. Salvador Dalí (1904–1989)
Sun Table
1936
oil on panel
60 x 46
Museum Boijmans Van Beuningen, Rotterdam

144. Salvador Dalí (1904–1989)
Metamorphosis of Narcissus
1937
oil on canvas
51 x 78
Tate Gallery, purchased 1979

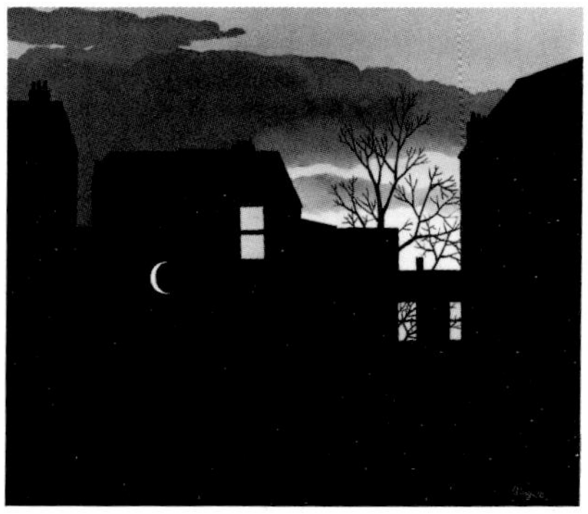

153

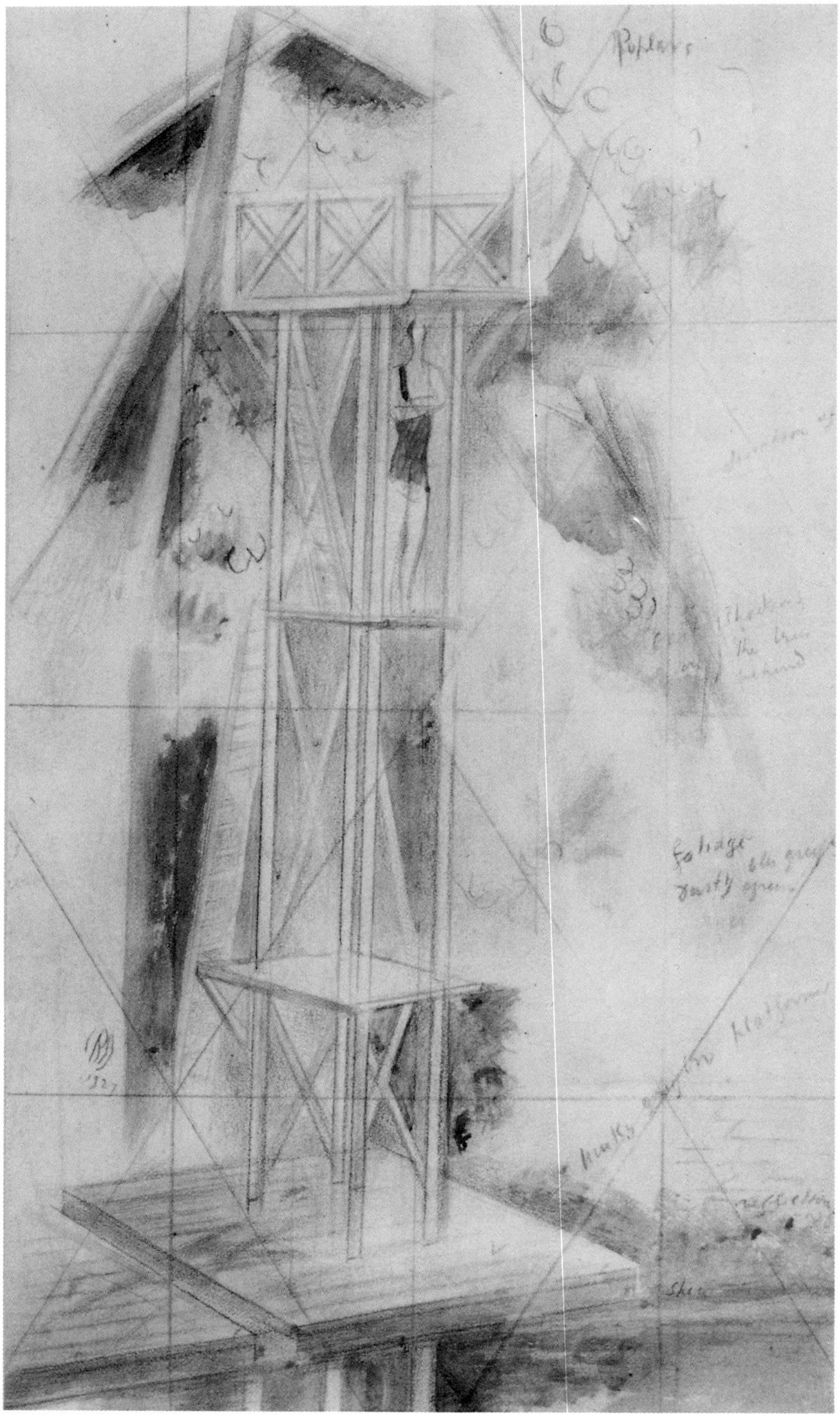

155

145. Salvador Dalí (1904–1989)
Impressions of Africa
1938
oil on canvas
91.5 x 117.5
Museum Boijmans Van Beuningen, Rotterdam

146. Salvador Dalí (1904–1989)
Self-portrait
1938
pencil on paper
53 x 35.5
Museum Boijmans Van Beuningen, Rotterdam

147. Salvador Dalí (1904–1989)
Study for 'Impressions of Africa'
1938–39
pencil and ink on paper
63 x 48
Museum Boijmans Van Beuningen, Rotterdam

148. Salvador Dalí (1904–1989)
Portrait of Sigmund Freud
1938
ink on paper
30 x 27
Freud Museum, London

149. Salvador Dalí (1904–1989)
Spain
1938
oil on canvas
91.8 x 60.2
Museum Boijmans Van Beuningen, Rotterdam

150. Leonor Fini (1908–1996)
Still Life with Eggshells
oil on canvas
25.5 x 29
EJF

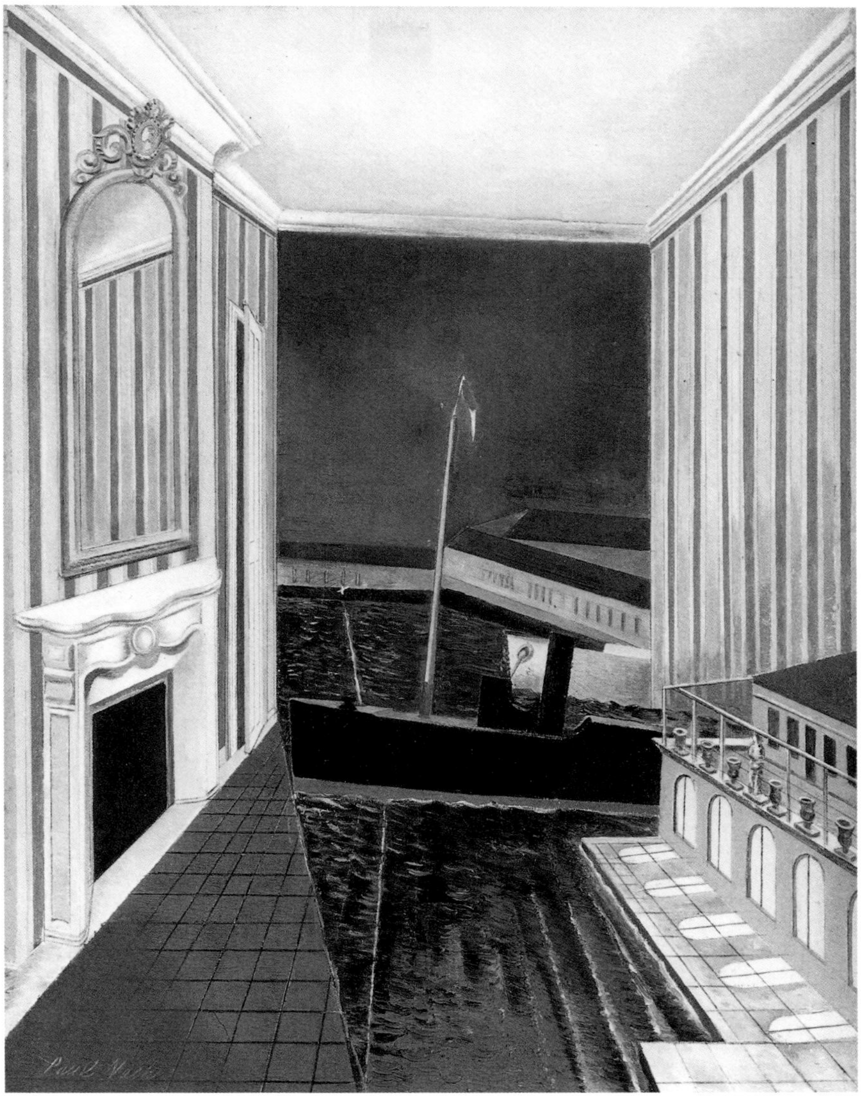

157

151. René Magritte (1898–1967)
La Malédiction
1937
oil on panel
13 x 13
EJF

152. René Magritte (1898–1967)
La Jeunesse Illustrée
1937
oil on canvas
207.5 x 159
Museum Boijmans Van Beuningen, Rotterdam

153. René Magritte (1898–1967)
Le Poison, 1939
gouache on paper
33.5 x 41
Museum Boijmans Van Beuningen, Rotterdam

154. René Magritte (1898–1967)
The Future of Statues
1937
oil painted plaster relief
33 x 16.5 x 20.5
Tate Gallery, purchased 1981

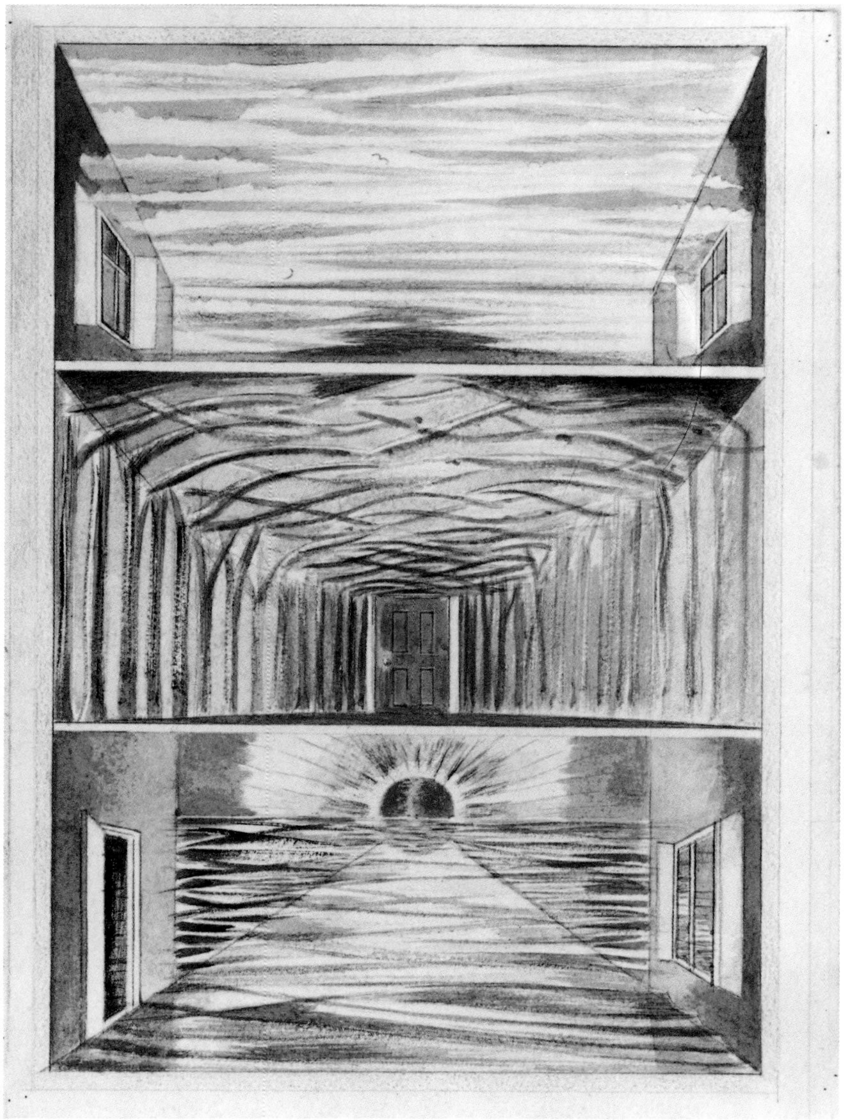

158

155. Paul Nash (1889–1946)
The Diving Board
1927
pencil and watercolour on paper
30 x 17
EJF

156. Paul Nash (1889–1946)
Mansions of the Dead
1932
pencil and watercolour on paper
58 x 39.5
Tate Gallery, purchased 1981

157. Paul Nash (1889–1946)
Harbour and Room
1932-1936
oil on canvas
91.5 x 71
Tate Gallery, purchased 1981

158. Paul Nash (1889–1946)
Three Rooms
1937
watercolour
39.5 x 29.5
Tate Gallery, purchased 1981

159. Pablo Picasso (1881–1973)
Minotaure
pen, Indian ink and collage
21.5 x 25.5
EJF

160. Dorothea Tanning (b.1910)
Crepusculum (Concerning Wishes)
oil on canvas
35.5 x 28
EJF

161. Pavel Tchelitchew (1898–1957)
Edith Sitwell
1937
oil on canvas
163 x 96.5
EJF

162. Eugène Berman (1899–1972)
Head of a Girl
1944
painted shell
18 x 15 x 10
EJF

163. Eugène Berman (1899–1972)
Head of a Girl
(with *Figure of a Man* on verso)
painted stone
13 x 11.5 x 5
EJF

164. Jean Cocteau (1889–1963)
Dessin
February 1933
pen, ink and watercolour on paper
31 x 48
EJF

165. Paul Eluard (1895–1952)
and Pablo Picasso (1881–1973)
'La Barre d'Appui' Poèmes Illustrés de Trois Eaux-fortes par Pablo Picasso
êditions *Cahiers d'Art*
print on Japanese paper
42 x 30.5 open; 21.5 x 16 each print
EJF

166. Salvador Dalí (1904–1989)
Sketch of Mae West Lips Sofa
(with 3 photographs of sofa in the workshop)
c.1938
envelope and black and white photographs
envelope 16 x 21;
photographs 6.5 x 6.5
EJF

167. Man Ray (1890–1976)
and unattributed
Photograph of Edward James (posing as directed by Magritte) and photograph of the painting 'Pleasure Principle' by René Magritte
photograph
30.5 x 44
EJF

168. René Magritte (1898–1967)
Letter with sketch for 'Pleasure Principle', (1937)
18 May 1937
ink on paper
14 x 24
EJF

169. Salvador Dalí (1904–1989)
Letter with sketch of 'Metamorphosis of Narcissus'
15 June 1937
ink on brown paper
25.5 x 20.5
EJF

170. Salvador Dalí (1904–1989)
'Macbeth' by William Shakespeare, illustrated by Salvador Dalí
1946
published by Doubleday & Company Inc, New York
book
24 x 32 open; 24 x 16.5 slip-case
EJF

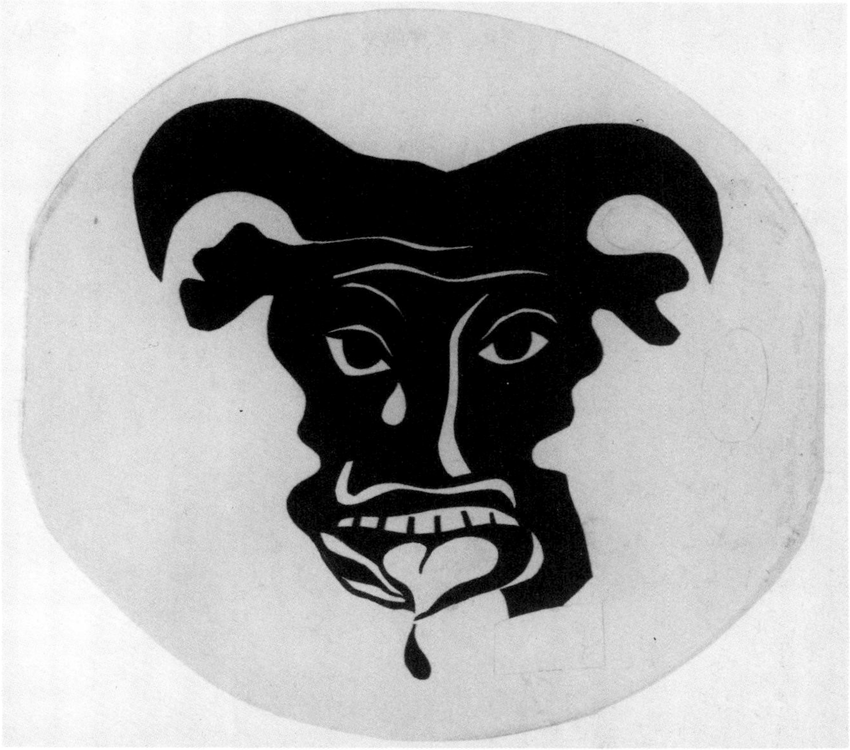

159

171. Leonora Carrington (b. 1917)
Sketchbook
23.2 x 33.5
EJF

172. Jean Cocteau (1889–1963)
Horse Hand
1936
two drawings from a series of eight
pencil and coloured pencil on board
each 28 x 24
EJF

173. Salvador Dalí (1904–1989)
Sketchbook with sketch for 'Girl Skipping Rope'
c.1936
pencil on paper
23 x 37
EJF

174. Jean Cocteau (1889–1963)
and Giorgio de Chirico (1888–1978)
Mythologie
1934
published by Edmond Desjobert, Paris
book with lithographs
text by Jean Cocteau,
illustrations by Giorgio de Chirico
29 x 27
EJF

THE ARCHITECT OF THE SURREAL

175. *Façade of Monkton House (before conversion)*
early 1900s
copy print
EJF

176. *Façade of Monkton House (after conversion)*
c.1985
colour photograph
53.5 x 43
EJF

177. *Exterior view of entrance, Monkton House*, 1986
colour photograph
27 x 20.5
EJF

178. *Interior view of entrance, Monkton House*
1986
colour photograph
53.5 x 43
EJF

179. *Dining Room, Monkton House*
1986
colour photograph
53.5 x 43
EJF

180. *Main Hall, Monkton House*
1986
colour photograph
53.5 x 43
EJF

181. *Study, Monkton House*
1986
colour photograph
53.5 x 43
EJF

182. *Edward James's Bedroom, Monkton House*
1986
colour photograph
53.5 x 43
EJF

183. Leonora Carrington (b. 1917)
Portrait of the late Mrs Partridge
1947
oil on board
100.5 x 70
EJF

184. Leonora Carrington (b. 1917)
The House Opposite
oil on panel
33 x 82
EJF

185. Leonora Carrington (b. 1917)
Bird Pong, 1949
egg tempera on panel
45 x 72.5
Private Collection

186. Leonor Fini (1908–1996)
The Alcove
oil on canvas
91.5 x 71
EJF

187. Leonor Fini (1908–1996)
L'Ombrelle No.1
1948
oil on canvas
53.5 x 44
EJF

188. Leonor Fini (1908–1996)
A Female Nude
watercolour and oil on paper
35 x 23.5
EJF

189. Pablo Picasso (1881–1973)
Femme Au Chignon
1905
etching
29 x 23.5
EJF

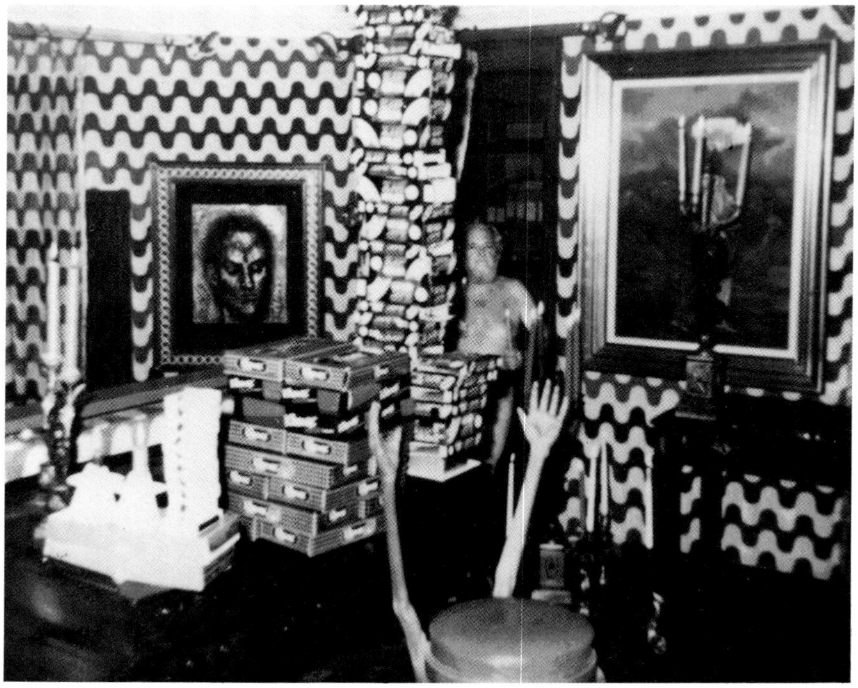

Edward James posing behind a mountain of Kleenex tissue boxes and firelighters at Monkton House.

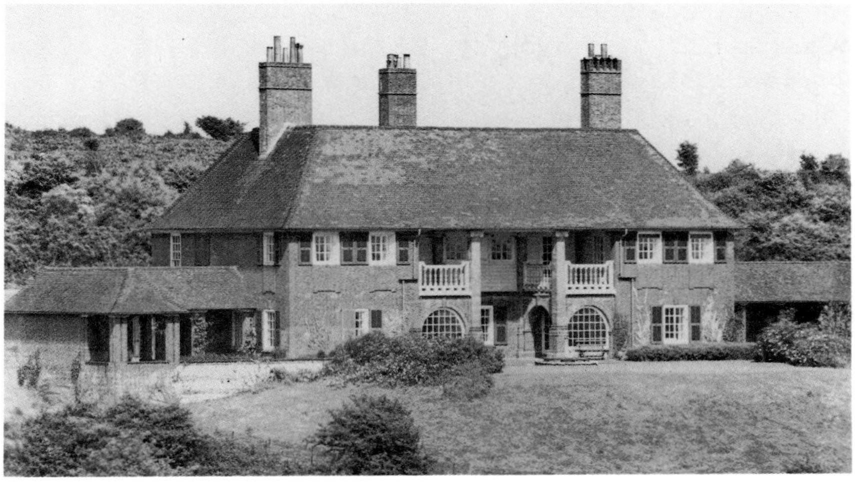

Monkton House c.1902.
EJF.

190. Christian Bérard (1902–1949)
Design for a Programme for ' La Sérénade
c.1934
Indian ink and Chinese white on paper
61 x 47
EJF

191. *Mae West Lips Sofa*
1938
Designed by Salvador Dalí (1904–1989) with Edward James
Made by Green & Abbott, London
wood carcass, upholstered in deep pink and light pink felted woven wool fabric
92 x 213 x 80
Royal Pavilion, Libraries & Museums, Brighton & Hove

192. *Mae West Lips Sofa*
1938
Designed by Salvador Dalí (1904–1989) with Edward James
Made by Green & Abbott, London
wood carcass upholstered in red wool fabric with black fringing
79 x 206 x 91.5
EJF
On loan to The Museum of the Moving Image, London

193. *Two Champagne Lamps*
Designed by Salvador Dalí (1904–1989)
Made by Green & Abbott, London
painted metal and lacquer
each 160 height x 47 diameter
EJF

194. *Chair*
Designed by Salvador Dalí (1904–1989)
Carved by John English
French walnut and purple leather
105.5 x 63
EJF

195. *Firescreen*
Designed by Salvador Dalí (1904–1989)
Made by Green & Abbott, London
blockboard, felt and metal
149 x 68.5 x 2
EJF

196. *Day Suit owned by Edward James*
1930s
Three-piece suit with double-breasted jacket and turn-up trousers grey wool with red and white stripe
The Board of Trustees of The Victoria & Albert Museum

197. *The Funeral Procession of Lord Viscount Nelson, Jan 9th, 1806,*
1806
Engraved by Edward Orme, London
handcoloured mezzotint
34.5 x 43
EJF

198. *Four poster bed,* 1937
Made by D S Mann, London.
Modelled after Nelson's catafalque, with concave cornice, turned posts carved with foliage and palm trees, green fabric hangings with Edward James's monogram, green and gold tassels.
Wood, silk and other materials
241 x 206 x 241
EJF

199. *Lobster Telephone,* 1938
Designed by Salvador Dalí (1904–1989)
Made by Green & Abbott, London
assemblage, plaster and other materials
19 x 31 x 16
EJF

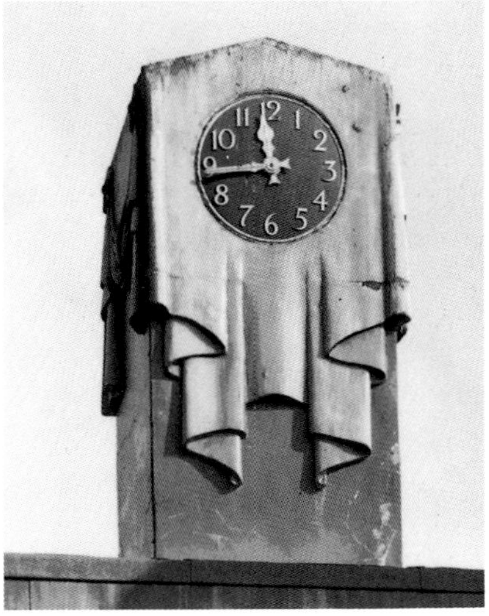

Clock Tower, Monkton House, 1986.

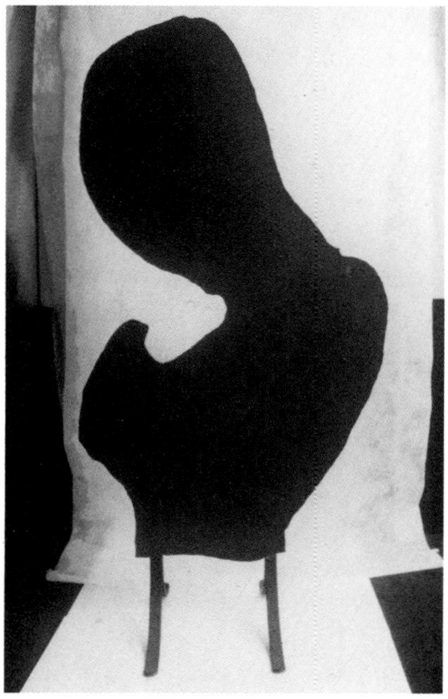

195

200. *Wooden crate containing plaster pieces*
Sent to Edward James by
René Magritte, 1937
Signed in blue crayon by Magritte
wood, plaster and straw
65.5 x 79.5 x 23.5
EJF

201. *Edward James wearing a gas mask at 35 Wimpole Street,* c.1939
black and white photograph
15 x 20.5
EJF

202. *Two Gas Masks from 35 Wimpole Street,*
1937 and 1938
rubber, glass, aluminium, metal and elastic
EJF

203. *Bundles of unused stationery from the Villa Cimbrone, Italy*
(Edward James's summer residence 1934–39)
each sheet 23 x 16.5
EJF

204. *Suitcase belonging to Edward James*
crocodile skin
EJF

205. *Bowler hat belonging to Edward James*
Made by A J White Ltd,
Jermyn Street, St James, London
13 x 24.5 x 30
EJF

206. *Shoes belonging to Edward James*
leather
men's size 8
EJF

207. *Dressing gown owned by Edward James*
patchworked velvet with dark red towelling lining
133 x 136
The Board of Trustees of The Victoria & Albert Museum

THE DREAM OF VENUS

208. Pavel Tchelitchew (1898–1957)
Portrait of Ruth Ford
1936
pen, ink and wash on paper
51 x 40
EJF

209. Salvador Dalí (1904–1989)
Dream of Venus
1939
Poem, handwritten
ink on blue paper
28 x 21.5
EJF

210. *Dream of Venus façade*
1939
colour photograph
36 x 27.5
EJF

211. *Salvador Dalí standing on Dream of Venus façade*
1939
black and white photograph
26.5 x 21.5
EJF

212. *Dream of Venus façade*
1939
black and white photograph
20.5 x 23
EJF

213. *Dream of Venus façade*
1939
black and white photograph
24 x 21
EJF

214. *Dream of Venus taxi with models*
1939
black and white photographs
20.5 x 25.5
EJF

215. *Salvador Dalí painting Dream of Venus interior*
1939
black and white photograph
23 x 20.5
EJF

216. *Salvador Dalí working on Dream of Venus*
1939
black and white photograph
25.5 x 20.5
EJF

217. *Salvador Dalí during the construction of Dream of Venus*
1939
black and white photograph
25.5 x 20.5
EJF

218. *Gala and Salvador Dalí during the construction of Dream of Venus*
1939
black and white photograph
23 x 20.5
EJF

219. *Gala during the construction of Dream of Venus*
1939
black and white photograph
25.5 x 20.5
EJF

220. *Gala during the construction of Dream of Venus*
1939
black and white photograph
25.5 x 20.5
EJF

221. *Dream of Venus interior*
1939
black and white photograph
23.5 x 20.5
EJF

222. *Dream of Venus interior with models*
1939
black and white photograph
20.5 x 23
EJF

223. *Dream of Venus interior with models*
1939
black and white photograph
23.5 x 20.5
EJF

224. *Dream of Venus interior with models*
1939
black and white photograph
21.5 x 20.5
EJF

225. *Edward James with Dream of Venus model*
1939
black and white photograph
20.5 x 12.5
EJF

226. *Edward James with Salvador Dalí during the construction of Dream of Venus*
1939
black and white photograph
9.5 x 11
EJF

227. *Dream of Venus model with Edward James, Gala, Salvador Dalí and unknown person*
1939
black and white photograph
14.5 x 15
EJF

XILITLA, THE MEXICAN GARDEN

228. *Plan of Xilitla*
1989
drawn by Michael Fishlock
photocopy hand-tinted by John Warren
57 x 117.5
EJF

229. Mariana Yampolsky (b. 1925)
Flowering
1996
black and white photograph
40.5 x 51
The artist

230. Mariana Yampolsky (b. 1925)
Homage to Max Ernst
1996
black and white photograph
40.5 x 51
The artist

231 Mariana Yampolsky (b. 1925)
Access to the Cinema
1996
black and white photograph
40.5 x 51
The artist

232. Mariana Yampolsky (b. 1925)
Gothic Wall
1996
black and white photograph
40.5 x 51
The artist

233. Mariana Yampolsky (b. 1925)
Gateway and Snake
1996
black and white photograph
40.5 x 51
The artist

234. Mariana Yampolsky (b. 1925)
Columns
1996
black and white photograph
40.5 x 51
The artist

235. Mariana Yampolsky (b. 1925)
Bamboo screen
1996
black and white photograph
40.5 x 51
The artist

236. Mariana Yampolsky (b. 1925)
Aviary
1996
black and white photograph
40.5 x 51
The artist

237. Lourdes Almeida
Nine Photographs of Xilitla
colour photographs
each 41 x 25.5
EJF

238. *Edward James in Xilitla*
colour photograph by 'Leone'
52 x 43
EJF

239. *Edward James in Xilitla*
colour photograph
43 x 51
EJF

240. *Edward James in Xilitla*
colour photograph
52 x 44
EJF

241. Brenda Herdman
Edward James in Xilitla
1982
bromide print
25 x 19
National Portrait Gallery, London

242. Leonora Carrington
Sketch
1966
sepia ink on paper
62 x 77.5
EJF

243. Leonora Carrington (b. 1917)
Sketch
c. 1966
sepia ink on paper
67.5 x 53.5
EJF

244. Leonora Carrington (b. 1917)
The Foundress of the Sisterhood of the Holy Order of the Little Jumping Virgins
collage, watercolour and gold paint
31 x 24
EJF

WEST DEAN RENEWED

245. *God creating the universe*
1981
Tapestry made by West Dean Tapestry Studio
Design based on William Blake's *The Ancient of Days*, c.1824
wool
EJF

AN ARCHIVAL LEGACY

246. Salvador Dalí (1904–1989)
Letter to Edward James with sketch incorporating the names of Edward James, Dalí and Gala
undated
ink on paper
23 x 15
EJF

247. René Magritte (1898–1967)
Fragment of a letter to Edward James with sketch for 'The White Race' (1937)
August 1937
ink on paper
19 x 21.5
EJF

248. René Magritte (1898–1967)
Letter to Edward James with sketch for 'The Endless Chain' (1938)
c.February 1938
ink on paper
27 x 21.5
EJF

249. René Magritte (1898–1967)
Letter to Edward James with sketch for 'Homesickness' (1941)
30 August 1939
ink on paper
each page 27 x 20.5
EJF

250. George Grosz (1893–1959)
Letter to Edward James
16 January 1941
pen, ink and paper collage
28 x 21.5
EJF

251. George Grosz (1893–1959)
Letter to Edward James
undated
ink on blue paper
20 x 15
EJF

252. René Magritte (1898–1967)
Postcard of 'Mr James's daydream'
c.1942
10 x 14
EJF

253. René Magritte (1898–1967)
Letter to Edward James with sketch showing 'Time Transfixed' (1938), on stairway at 35 Wimpole Street
12 July 1939
ink on paper
28 x 21
EJF

SELECTED WRITINGS BY EDWARD JAMES

COMPILED BY SHARON-MICHI KUSUNOKI

Poems, Shakespeare Head Press, Stratford-upon-Avon, 1926.

Juventutis Annorum, The James Press, London, 1931.

Twenty Sonnets to Mary, The James Press, London, 1931.

Laengselia – A Play by Faustulus (pseudonym for Edward James), The James Press, London, 1931.

Carmina Amico, The James Press, Verona, July 1932.

The Next Volume, with illustrations by Rex Whistler, The James Press, London, 1932, republished January 1933; 2nd edition 1939.

The Venetian Glass Omnibus – peace propaganda for grown-up children and sophisticated tots, illustrated by Oliver Messel, The James Press, London, Christmas 1932; republished 1933.

Your Name is Lamia, The James Press, August 1933 (Also published under the title, *Opus Septimum*).

Reading into the Picture, Parts I and II, with illustrations by Jörg v Reppert-Bismarck, Duckworth, London, December 1934; and republished 1940, with Parts I, II and III.

Minotaure, éditions Albert Skira, Paris
'Trois Sécheresses', June 15, 1936, No.8, pp. 53–56.
'The Marvel of Minuteness', October 1936, No.9, pp. 20–24.
'Le Chapeau du Peuple et les Chapeaux de la Reine', October 1936, No.9, pp. 54–59.

The Gardener Who Saw God, Duckworth, London, 1937; American edition, Charles Scribner's Sons, New York, 1937; Albatross, Leipzig, April 1937–1938.

Rich Man, Poor Man, Beggarman, Wop (pseudonym, Edward Selsey), Vol 1, The James Press, London, 1937–1938, Vol 2, The James Press, London, 1939–1940.

The Bones of My Hand, with Frontispiece by Pavel Tchelitchew, Oxford University Press, London, 1938.

So Far, So Glad (pseudonym, Edward Selsey), with illustrations by Edward Carrick, Duckworth, London, undated (1930s).

Scherzo on a theme from far away, New York, 1940s.

The Heart and the Word. A selection of the poems of Edward James, edited by Noel Simon with an introduction by Peter Levi, Weidenfeld & Nicolson, London, 1987.

BIBLIOGRAPHY

COMPILED BY SHARON-MICHI KUSUNOKI

BOOKS

John Lowe, *Edward James: A Surrealist Life*, Collins, London, 1991.

George Melly, (ed.) *Edward James: My Early Years, Swans Reflecting Elephants*, Weidenfeld & Nicolson, London, 1982.

Philip Purser, *Where Is He Now? The Extraordinary Worlds of Edward James*, Quartet Books, London, 1978.

Philip Purser, *Poeted: The Final Quest of Edward James*, Quartet Books, London, 1991.

The Edward James Collection, Christie's sales catalogue, West Dean Park, Chichester, June 1986.

EXHIBITION CATALOGUES

Thirty Years of Surrealist Painting from The Edward James Collection, Brighton Art Gallery, 1967.

Surrealist Pictures from the Edward James Collection, Manchester City Art Gallery/Arts Council, 1969.

Salvador Dalí bruikleen uit de collectie Edward F. W. James, Museum Boymans-van Beuningen, Rotterdam, 1972.

The Edward James Collection, Scottish National Gallery of Modern Art, Edinburgh, 1976.
Surrealist Paintings from the Edward James Collection, Chichester, 1977.

ARTICLES

Von Monic Amstad, 'Edward James – Poet, Surrealist, Exzentriker', *du*, Zürich, January 1987, pp. 14–55.

Patrick Boyle, 'Eccentric Exile: Edward James and his Garden of Eden', *Sunday Telegraph Magazine*, Number 34, London, May 8 1977, pp. 20–29.

Sharon-Michi Kusunoki, 'Whispering gallery', *Harpers and Queen*, London, March 1991, pp. 88–96 and 232.

Judith Young Mallin, 'The Surrealist World of Edward James', *Quest Magazine*, London, October 1991, starts on pp. 34–38.

George Melly, 'Conversations with Edward James', *Vogue*, London, December 1977, p. 30.

George Melly, 'Under green wings', *Observer Magazine*, London, 13 December 1981, pp. 30–37.

Saber Ver, No.35, July–August 1997, Mexico City. Edition dedicated to Las Posas, Xilitla, by Lourdes Andrade.

CONTRIBUTORS TO THE CATALOGUE

Dawn Ades, Professor of Art History and Theory at the University of Essex, has written a number of books on Surrealism, including *Dada and Surrealism Reviewed* (London, 1978), *Salvador Dalí* (London, 1982) and *Surrealist Art: The Lindy and Edwin Bergman Collection at the Art Institute of Chicago* (1997).

Stella Beddoe is Keeper of Decorative Arts for the Royal Pavilion, Libraries & Museums, Brighton & Hove and has published works on 20th-Century French interior decoration, English ceramics and Fairies.

Stephen Calloway is a curator in the Prints, Drawings and Paintings Department of London's Victoria & Albert Museum. He divides the remainder of his time between research, writing, lecturing and designing. His books include *Twentieth-Century Decoration* (1988), *The Elements of Style* (1991) and *Baroque, Baroque: the Culture of Excess* (1994).

Christopher Gibbs is a Trustee of The Edward James Foundation.

The Hon. Desmond Guinness has written extensively on architecture and the decorative arts in Ireland and has lectured at museums and organisations at home and overseas. In 1958 he founded the Irish Georgian Society for the preservation of Irish architecture.

Xavier Guzmán Urbiola is a historian specialising in themes relating to Mexican architecture. His publications include *La Habitación Interminable* (*The Never Ending Habitat*) (Universidad Autónoma Metropolitana, Xochimilco, Mexico, 1986) about Las Posas, Xilitla.

Sharon-Michi Kusunoki is a post-graduate research student at the Courtauld Institute of Art. In conducting the research for her thesis on Edward James, she has been responsible for compiling and organising The Edward James Archive.

John Warren R.I.B.A., F.R.T.P.I., F.S.A. is an architect, planner, author and conservator.

Mariana Yampolsky, a Mexican photographer, roams the countryside searching for images that celebrate the beauty and creativity of the rich and complex popular culture of her country and its people.

PHOTOGRAPHIC CREDITS

Agence Roger Viollet, Paris p.44

The Architectural Review p.96

© 1997, The Art Institute of Chicago; All Rights Reserved p.79

Museum Boijmans Van Beuningen, Rotterdam pp.68, 71, 75, 76, 80, 84, 85, 86, 144

Christie's Images pp.37, 65, 67, 68, 69, 70, 74–5, 77, 80

Desmond Guiness pp.118, 148

The Trustees of the Edward James Foundation pp.12, 14, 15, 16, 18,19, 20, 25, 29, 32, 35, 36, 38, 39, 42, 47, 48, 65, 66, 67, 73, 74, 75, 76, 77, 79, 81, 82, 83, 84, 85, 86, 87, 88, 89, 90, 93, 95, 99, 112-3, 128, 129, 130, 131, 132, 133, 134, 135, 136, 137, 140, 141, 144, 147, 149, 150

Eric Schall pp.76, 77

Erik Russell pp.34, 38, 40

Freud Museum, London p.144

Mariana Yampolsky pp.82, 83, 105, 106, 107, 108, 109, 110

Mercury Gallery, London p.46

Michael Scultz & Joost Eiffers p.88

National Monuments Record pp.101, 102, 149

Nicholas Sinclair Front cover, p.66

Sharon-Michi Kusunoki p.81, 97, 104, 114,

© Tate Gallery, London pp.70, 78, 87, 146

Terry Pickering p.22

COPYRIGHT CREDITS

© ADAGP, Paris and DACS, London 1998 pp.38, 39, 45, 67, 68, 71, 72, 77, 79, 80, 81, 82, 83, 87, 140, 1 44

© Agence Roger Viollet, Paris p.44

© ARS, NY and DACS, London 1998 pp.23, 74–5, 84, 88, 89, 90

© Cecil Beaton photograph courtesy of Sotheby's, London pp.128, 129, 130, 131, 137

© DACS 1998 pp.29, 32, 34, 35, 36, 40, 65, 66, 67, 69, 70, 71, 75, 76, 78, 79, 81, 84, 85, 86, 87, 142, 143, 144, 150

© The Trustees of The Edward James Foundation pp.12, 14, 15, 16, 18, 19, 20, 22, 93, 112-3, 149

© Foundation P Delvaux – St Idesbald, Belgium/DACS 1998 p.77

© Man Ray Trust/ADAGP Paris and DACs, London 1998 p.38

© Mariana Yampolsky pp.82, 83, 105, 106, 107, 108, 109, 110

© Norman Parkinson/Hamiltons Photographers Limited p. 95, 99, 135, 136

RCHME © Crown Copyright pp.101, 102, 149

© Succession Picasso/DACS 1998 p.12, 68, 147

© Tate Gallery, London pp.87, 144, 146

INDEX

Page numbers in *italics* refer to illustrations; page numbers in **bold** refer to colour plates.